CRY OF THE EARTH,
CRY OF THE POOR

ECOLOGY AND JUSTICE
An Orbis Series on Global Ecology

Advisory Board Members
Mary Evelyn Tucker
John A. Grim
Leonardo Boff
Sean McDonagh

The Orbis Series *Ecology and Justice* publishes books that seek to integrate an understanding of the Earth as an interconnected life system with concerns for just and sustainable systems that benefit the entire Earth. Books in the Series concentrate on ways to:

- reexamine the human-Earth relationship in the light of contemporary cosmological thought
- develop visions of common life marked by ecological integrity and social justice
- expand on the work of those who are developing such fields as ecotheology, ecojustice, environmental ethics, eco-feminism, deep ecology, social ecology, bioregionalism, and animal rights
- promote inclusive participative strategies that enhance the struggle of the Earth's voiceless poor for justice
- deepen appreciation for and expand dialogue among religious traditions on the issue of ecology
- encourage spiritual discipline, social engagement, and the reform of religion and society toward these ends.

Viewing the present moment as a time for responsible creativity, the Series seeks authors who speak to ecojustice concerns and who bring into dialogue perspectives from the Christian community, from the world's other religions, from secular and scientific circles, and from new paradigms of thought and action.

ECOLOGY AND JUSTICE SERIES

LEONARDO BOFF

CRY OF THE EARTH, CRY OF THE POOR

Translated by Phillip Berryman

ORBIS BOOKS

Maryknoll, New York 10545

The Catholic Foreign Mission Society of America (Maryknoll) recruits and trains people for overseas missionary service. Through Orbis Books, Maryknoll aims to foster the international dialogue that is essential to mission. The books published, however, reflect the opinions of their authors and are not meant to represent the official position of the society.

English translation © 1997 by Orbis Books

Published originally in Brazil as *Ecologia: Grito da Terra, Grito dos Pobres* by Editora Ática S.A., Rua Barão de Iguape, 110, São Paulo–SP, Brazil, copyright © 1995 by Leonardo Boff.

This edition published by Orbis Books, Maryknoll, NY 10545-0308.

Manufactured in the United States of America

Manuscript editing and typesetting by Joan Weber Laflamme

Library of Congress Cataloging-in-Publication Data

Boff, Leonardo.
    [Ecologia. English]
    Cry of the earth, cry of the poor / Leonardo Boff : translated by Phillip Berryman.
        p. cm. – (Ecology and justice)
    Includes bibliographical references and index.
    ISBN 1-57075-136-6(alk. paper)
    1. Human ecology–Religious aspects. 2. Human ecology–Moral and ethical aspects. 3. Liberation theology. 4. Environmental ethics.
    I. Title. II. Series.
    GF80.B6313   1997
    179'.1–dc21

                                     97-26788
                                        CIP

Peregrinantibus mecum

CONTENTS

INTRODUCTION

The aim of this book is to connect the cry of the oppressed with the cry of the Earth. The cry of the oppressed has encountered a powerful current of thought drawn from liberating practices of solidarity. It is out of such practices that liberation theology has arisen. Never in the history of Christianity have the poor become so central, in the sense that they should be agents of their own liberation. Liberation theology has served the oppressed and the outcast well, for it has sought to convince them that their cause is connected to that of the God of history and is inscribed in the heart of the message and practice of Jesus; it is no accident that he was persecuted, made a political prisoner, tortured, and crucified. Finally, liberation theology has convinced them that the pursuit of liberation, life, and poetry affects eternity, for the Reign of God, the great utopia of the Hebrew and Christian scriptures, is indeed made up of such things.

The Earth is also crying out. The logic that exploits classes and subjects peoples to the interests of a few rich and powerful countries is the same as the logic that devastates the Earth and plunders its wealth, showing no solidarity with the rest of humankind and future generations.

Such a logic is shattering the fragile balance of the universe, built up with great wisdom by nature throughout fifteen billion years of labor. It has broken humankind's covenant of kinship with the Earth and destroyed its sense of connectedness* with all things. During the past four centuries human beings have felt that they are all alone in a universe seen as an enemy to be subjected and tamed.

Today these issues have gained a seriousness that they have never enjoyed before in human history. The human being—called to be Earth's guardian angel and watchful tiller—may be Earth's Satan. Humans have shown that they can commit not only homicide and ethnocide, but biocide and geocide as well.

---

* Boff frequently uses *re-ligação* and cognates, such as *re-ligar*, which have the sense of "re-binding," partly for the wordplay with "religion"; in this translation they are generally rendered "connectedness" and cognate forms—*translator.*

It is not only the poor and oppressed that must be liberated; today all humans must be liberated. We are hostages to a paradigm that places us–against the thrust of the universe–*over* things instead of being *with* them in the great cosmic community. That is why I am extending the intuitions of liberation theology and demonstrating their validity and applicability for the questions enveloping the Earth, our bountiful mother.

Time is pressing. We nevertheless embrace the hope that, as always happens in the evolutionary process, chaos will give birth to a new and higher order, one that holds promise for all. The aim of this book is to offer hope for the sons and daughters of Earth, heirs of that covenant that God established with Noah and with the whole community of the living after the destruction of the flood. That memory, preserved in the basic passages of the Jewish and Christian spiritual traditions, reads: "As the bow appears in the clouds, I will see it and recall the everlasting covenant that I have established between God and all living beings–all mortal creatures that are on earth. . . . Never again shall all bodily creatures be destroyed by the waters of a flood" (Gn 9:16, 11).

This covenant is eternal. It takes on new meaning particularly in times of crisis like our own. It grounds the hope that our shared future will not be built on the ruins of the planet and humankind. Just as cosmogenesis (the lithosphere, the hydrosphere, the atmosphere, and the anthroposphere) emerged from the original chaos, so also will the noosphere emerge–the communion of minds and hearts–as a center of life, solidarity, and shared growth in love. Everything will point toward the ultimate theosphere where all will be in God and God in all. Such is the truth of panentheism.

The new paradigm that is coming to birth–that of connectedness–will be the basis of a universal religion that will only be truly universal if it seeks convergences in religious diversity. The convergences to be achieved must have to do with restoring the sacredness of all things, reclaiming the dignity of the Earth, rediscovering the mission of the human being–man and woman–called to celebrate the mystery of the cosmos, and finally, encountering God, mystery of communion and life, in the process of cosmogenesis itself. The aim of our observations is to water and fertilize this seminal reality.

In embracing the world, we shall be embracing God.

Fazenda Sossego, Santana do Deserto
Minas Gerais, Brazil, summer 1995

CHAPTER 1

The Ecological Era

The Return to Earth as Our Homeland

Every year since 1984 the Worldwatch Institute in the United States has published a report on the "state of the Earth." Each time this state is more alarming. The Earth is ill and in jeopardy. Of the many signs let us present two.

THE EARTH IS ILL

First, the most threatened of nature's creatures today are the poor: 79% of humankind lives in the immense and poor South; 1 billion people live in the state of absolute poverty; 3 billion (out of 5.3 billion) do not have enough to eat; 60 million die of hunger every year; and 14 million young people under fifteen years of age die each year as a result of hunger-caused diseases. There is practically no solidarity among human beings for dealing with this dramatic situation. Most of the well-off countries do not even devote 0.7% of their Gross National Product (GNP), the amount prescribed by the United Nations for aid to needy countries. The richest country, the United States, devotes barely 0.15% of its GNP.

Second, living species are likewise threatened. It is estimated that between 1500 and 1850 one species may have been wiped out every ten years. Between 1850 and 1950 it was one species every year. Since 1990 a species a day is disappearing. At this rate, by the year 2000 one species per hour will be disappearing. It should be said, however, that estimates by experts of the number of existing species vary between ten million and 100 million, and only 1.4 million have been described. In any case, a death machine is mowing down life in its most varied forms.[1]

1

The awareness of a crisis came to expression in 1972 in the report of the widely known Club of Rome, a worldwide network of industrialists, politicians, high government officials, and scientists from various areas established to study the interdependencies of nations, the complexity of contemporary societies, and nature in order to develop a systematic vision of the problems and new means of political action for solving them. The report was called *The Limits to Growth*.[2]

The crisis means that a way of understanding the world is breaking down. What was once obvious in collective consciousness is now called into question; namely, that everything must revolve around the idea of progress, and that such progress is advancing between two infinites: the infinite of the Earth's resources, and the infinite of the future. Earth was thought to be inexhaustible in its resources and it was assumed that humanity could progress indefinitely toward the future. Both infinites are illusory. The crisis has led to an awareness that resources have limits, because not all of them are renewable; indefinite growth into the future is impossible,[3] because we cannot universalize the model of growth for everyone and forever. If China, for example, wished to provide its families with the number of cars that the United States provides for its citizens, it would turn into a huge polluted parking lot. Nothing would move.

The model of society and of the meaning of life that human beings have projected for themselves—at least during the last four hundred years—is in crisis. In terms of everyday life, the model means that the all-important thing is to accumulate vast amounts of the means of life—material wealth, goods, and services—in order to enjoy our short journey on this planet. In achieving this purpose we are aided by science, which comprehends how the Earth functions, and technology, which acts upon it for human benefit. And this is to be done as speedily as possible. Hence, we strive for maximum profit with minimum investment in the shortest possible period of time. In this type of cultural practice, human beings are regarded as *above things*, making use of them for their own enjoyment, never as *alongside* things, members of a larger planetary and cosmic community. The ultimate result, which is only now becoming strikingly visible, is contained in an expression attributed to Gandhi: The Earth is sufficient for everyone's needs but not for everyone's greed.

The kind of awareness that is becoming more widespread throughout the world, although still insufficiently, can be stated as follows: If we allow ourselves to continue along our present path and give free rein to the logic of our productive machinery we could come to the point of having irreversible impacts on nature and on human life. These include desertification—each year fertile lands equal to the state of Rio de Janeiro become desert; deforestation—42% of tropical forests have already been destroyed, and global warming and acid rain may devastate the rain forest (six billion hectares), which is most important for the Earth-system; overpopulation—in 1990 there were 5.2 billion of us; population is growing at a rate of 3-4% a year, while food production is increasing only 1.3%. Moreover, other disastrous consequences for the Earth-system are beginning to rear their heads, such as possible widespread conflicts as a result of planet-wide social inequities.

This is the dramatic context in which people have been looking to ecology. It has existed and been in the process of being systematized for over a century, but ecologists hardly made themselves heard. Now they are on the scene—ideologically, scientifically, politically, ethically, and spiritually. What do we mean when we talk about ecology?

As understood by its first proponent, Ernst Haeckel (1834-1919), ecology is the study of the interrelationship of all living and nonliving systems among themselves and with their environment.[4] It is not about studying the environment or biotic (living) or abiotic (inert) beings in themselves. What is specific about ecological discourses lies not in the study of one pole or the other but in the interaction and interrelationship between them. That is what makes up "the environment," an expression coined in 1800 by Jens Baggesen, a Dane, and introduced into biological terminology by Jakob von Uexküll (1864-1944).

Hence, what is under consideration is not the immediate but the total environment. A living creature cannot be seen in isolation as a mere representative of its species. It must always be seen and analyzed in relation to the totality of vital conditions that constitute it and in balance with all the other representatives of the community of living beings present (biota and biocenoses). The upshot of such a conception is that science leaves the laboratories and becomes organically a part of nature, where everything lives with everything else and constitutes a vast ecological community.

Ecology is accordingly a knowledge of the relations, interconnections, interdependencies, and exchanges of all with all, at all points, and at all moments. From this standpoint, ecology cannot be defined by itself, in isolation from its implications for other kinds of knowledge. This kind of knowing deals not with objects of knowledge but with relations among objects of knowledge. It is a knowledge of interrelated knowledges.

In short, ecology is defined only within the framework of the relations that it connects in all directions and with every type of knowledge about the way in which all beings are dependent upon one another, constituting the vast fabric of their interdependencies. They make up, as the technical expression goes, a vast homeostatic system, which means a vast balanced and self-regulating system. Ecology does not replace particular bodies of knowledge, such as physics, geology, oceanography, biology, thermodynamics, biogenetics, zoology, anthropology, astronautics, cosmology, and so forth, all with their own specific paradigms, methods, and results. These sciences must continue to be built up but remain ever alert to one another by reason of the interdependence of the objects that they study.

The peculiar feature of ecological knowledge is its transversality; namely, the fact that it relates laterally (ecological community), frontward (future), backward (past), and inwardly (complexity) all experiences and all forms of comprehension as complementary and useful in our knowledge of the universe, our role within it, and in the cosmic solidarity that unites us to all. This approach leads to holism (*hólos* in Greek means totality). It does not mean the sum of knowledges or of a number of analytic standpoints, for that would be a quantity. Rather, it translates the grasp of the organic and open whole of reality and of knowledge of this whole; it therefore represents something new.

Ecology embodies an ethical concern likewise drawn from all knowledges, powers, and institutions: to what extent is each individual collaborating to protect nature, which is in jeopardy? To what extent does each particular knowledge incorporate the ecological dimension not as one more topic for it to discuss, leaving its specific methodology unquestioned, but rather to what extent does each particular knowledge redefine itself on the basis of the findings of ecology, thereby contributing toward homeostasis, that is, toward dynamic and creative ecological balance? Instead of manipulating reality for their own enjoyment or dominating aspects of nature, human beings should learn to manage or deal with nature by obeying the logic of nature itself, or starting from within it, unleashing what is found seminally within it, and always in view of its preservation and further development. The most prominent Brazilian ecologist, José A. Lutzenberger, has offered a fine definition: "Ecology is the science of the symphony of life, and the science of survival."[5] Haeckel himself came to call ecology "the economics of nature."[6] Indeed, because nature is our common dwelling, ecology may also be called domestic economics.

With this ethical concern of responsibility toward creation, ecology has moved beyond its early stage as a green movement or one to protect and save endangered species, and has become a radical critique of the kind of civilization that we are building,[7] which is energy-devouring and tends to demolish all ecosystems. That is why the ecological argument is continually invoked in all matters having to do with quality of life, human life in the world, and the safeguarding of or threat to the totality of the planet or the cosmos.

Invoking ecology in this manner expresses a yearning for a way of redemption. How are we, human beings and environment, with our common origin and common destiny, to survive together? How are we to safeguard creation in justice, participation, wholeness, and peace?

ECOLOGICAL DIAGNOSES AND THERAPIES

In response to such questions, a number of diagnoses have been made and a number of ecological therapies have been proposed aimed at preventing the disease or curing it. Here we are going to be quite brief, because the matter will be discussed in greater detail throughout the various chapters of this book.

Ecotechnology: A Soft Path?

Efforts are being made to develop technologies and procedures intended to preserve the environment or reduce undesired effects harmful to human populations and nature caused by the kind of development that we have created.[8]

We must adopt such a stance. If technology and science have helped destroy the planet, they can also help save and reclaim it. But they have limits; they attack the consequences but do not identify the causes of the pillage and aggression against the creatures of nature as a whole in their balanced relationships.

Ecopolitics: Ecological Justice

Behind technical projects lie policies implemented by governments (industrial development, agricultural, highway, urban, energy, and population policies) or by companies. The latter are in the market and are pressured by competition and the need to assure their profits, often at the cost of pollution, deforestation, and the impoverishment of workers due to low wages.

Ecopolitics seeks to develop strategies of sustained development assuring balanced ecosystems, including the labor system, and at the same time, to maintain a sense of solidarity with future generations. They have a right to a society of fairness, justice, and participation, and to a healthy environment.[9]

There are limits, however. When development and environmental conservation are in tension, development is usually chosen and the cost paid in environmental deterioration. The paradigm of expanding and linear development is not radically questioned. Moreover, ecological justice has to go hand in hand with social justice. What good does it do to provide schooling and school lunches for favela children if they die because they continue living in favelas without basic sanitation? Or to encourage the use of natural gas in public transportation if the bus line does not even run to the outlying poor neighborhoods?

Human Ecology and Social Ecology: Cosmic Community

Human beings and society always establish a relationship with the environment. Human beings are the result of a long biological process. Without the elements of nature of which they are part and parcel, without the viruses, bacteria, microorganisms, the genetic codes, and the basic chemical elements, they would not exist. Societies always organize their relationships with the environment to assure the production and reproduction of life. They define the relationship between countryside and city; they decide how an urban development is to be built so as to include quality of life; how a hospital, a school, or a factory is to be set up ecologically; how traffic is to be routed; how social violence is to be avoided, how the relationship between public and private, labor and leisure, material and cultural production are to be organized. The society establishes a certain kind of social communication and decides what kind of science and technology it desires.[10] Ecology here is displaying what its name declares: domestic science, the science of the human habitat.

All such efforts are important, but are they being made within the existing model of social relationship, economic organization, and creation of meanings—without questioning its very roots? Or are they launching something new, pointing toward a model that is an alternative to the current one? Are they just patching things up? Or is a new vision being created, one that opens more promising hopes, a new style of collective subjectivity and of experimentation with the ways we relate to each other as human beings and together with the universe? Here we run up against the limits of a merely human and social ecology, within the framework of the current paradigm.

Mental Ecology: Nature Is Inside Us

The state of the world is connected to our own state of mind. If the world is ill, that is a sign that our psyche is also ill. Aggressions against nature and the will to dominate exist because visions, archetypes, and emotions that lead to exclusion and violence are at work within the human psyche. There is an internal ecology just as surely as there is an external ecology, and they mutually condition each other.[11] The universe of relationships to things is internalized as reference to father, mother, environment, and so forth; these are transformed into values and anti-values that have a positive or negative impact on ecological relationships. The very world of things made by human hands, the technification of relationships, brings about a collective subjectivity based on power, status, appearance, and a precarious communication with others.

Mental ecology strives to achieve a psychic integration of human persons so as to make them gentler in their relationship with the natural and social environment and to bring them into a more lasting harmony with the universe in reverence and balance.

Here we once more run into limits, however. Does mental ecology simply alleviate the tension or does it create a new horizon for experiencing the world? Does it bring about a new alliance with nature, or does it simply reinforce the truce, giving free rein to the mindset of possession, dominion, and exclusion of other human beings and nature? These are the crucial points for determining whether ecological concern is liberating.

Ecological Ethics: Responsibility for the Planet

The ethic of the dominant society today is utilitarian and anthropocentric. It considers all beings to be at the service of human beings, who may use them as they please in accordance with their desires and preferences. It believes that human beings are the crown of the evolutionary process and the center of the universe. Being ethical would demand developing a sense of the limits of human desires insofar as they easily lead to striving for individual advancement at the cost of class exploitation, subjugation of peoples, and gender oppression. The human being is also, and indeed primarily, a being of communication and responsibility. Thus being ethical would also demand encouraging generational solidarity in the sense of respecting the future of those not yet born. Finally, being ethical would demand acknowledging that other beings have relative autonomy; they also have a right to continue to exist and to coexist with us and with other beings, since they have existed for millions of years before us and without us. In a word, they have a right to the present and the future.[12]

All this must be done and put into practice. There are limits here as well, however. If there is no new mystique, a new spirituality underlying ethics, that is, a new harmony between human beings and all other beings, thereby establishing a new "re-ligation" (derivation of "religion") there is a danger that such an ethics will degenerate into legalism, moralism, and behavioral patterns of restraint instead of a joyous pursuit of life in a reverent and gentle relationship with all other beings.[13]

Radical or Deep Ecology: Crisis of the Spirit

There is yet another way, one that does not intend to rule out the others but seeks to reach down to the roots of the question. Hence, it is called radical or deep ecology.[14] This approach seeks to discern the fundamental question, for the current crisis is a crisis of the dominant civilization. In other words, what is in crisis is our dominant paradigm, our basic model of relationships, our prevailing sense of what life is all about.

What is the basic thrust of societies today around the world? It is, as we have already pointed out, focused on progress, prosperity, and unlimited growth of material goods and services. How is such progress attained? Through the use, exploitation, and unleashing of all the forces and energy of nature and persons. The major instruments are science and technology, which have produced industrialism, computerization, and robotics. These instruments have not been the result of sheer curiosity but of the will to power, conquest, and profit.

The basic objective was well formulated by the founding fathers of our modern paradigm, Galileo Galilei, René Descartes, Francis Bacon, Isaac Newton, and others. Descartes taught that we intervene in nature in order to become "master and owner of nature"[15] Francis Bacon said that we must "subjugate nature, press it into delivering its secrets, tie it to our service and make it our slave."[16] Thus was created the myth of the human being, trail-blazing hero, unconquerable Prometheus, complete with pharaonic projects. In a word, human beings are *above* things in order to turn them into the conditions and instruments of happiness and human progress. They do not understand themselves as standing *alongside* them, jointly belonging as members to a larger whole. Thus we reach the pivotal point into which we intend to probe more deeply.

ECOLOGICAL CRISIS: CRISIS OF THE PARADIGM OF CIVILIZATION?

In this posture of standing *above* things and *above* everything seems to reside the fundamental mechanism of our current crisis of civilization. What is the supreme irony today? That the will to dominate everything is bringing us under domination and holding us in subjection to the imperatives of a degraded Earth. The utopia of improving the human condition has worsened the quality of life. The dream of unlimited growth has brought about the underdevelopment of two-thirds of humankind, and our delight in optimally using the Earth's resources has led to the exhaustion of vital systems and to the breakdown of environmental balance. Both socialism and capitalism have witnessed the undermining of the basis of wealth, which is always the Earth and its resources, and human labor. Today the Earth is in an advanced state of exhaustion; labor and creativity are being bypassed through the technological revolution, the use of computers and robotics; workers are even being excluded from serving as an exploited reserve army of labor. Land and worker both are perilously wounded and bleeding. There has been something reductionistic and profoundly wrong in this process, something we can only now perceive and question with the proper degree of seriousness.

The question raised, accordingly, is as follows: is it possible to maintain the logic of accumulation and unlimited linear growth and yet avoid the

breakdown of ecological systems and the frustration of their future resulting from vanishing species and the plunder of natural resources (to which
future generations also have a right)? Is there not a clash between our
prevailing paradigm of existence and the preservation of the whole of the
earthly and cosmic community? Can we responsibly move forward in this
quest as it has been pursued thus far? With our present consciousness of
these issues would it not be highly irresponsible and hence unethical to
continue in the same direction? Must we change directions?

Some people look to the messianic power of science and technology,
which can do harm, they admit, but can also serve to rescue and liberate.
In response, however, we must consider this: human beings refuse to be
replaced by machines even when we see that we are reaping the rewards
of having our basic needs met. For it is not only our basic needs that must
be satisfied; we are endowed with abilities that must be exercised and
displayed creatively. Humans are made for participation and creation; we
want not only to receive bread but to help produce it, so that we may
emerge as agents of our own history. We hunger for bread but also for
participation and beauty, which are not assured by the resources of technology and science alone.

Some say changing directions is better for us, for the environment, for
all relationships of the environment and human beings, for the common
fate of all, and for assuring life for future generations. To do so will require
profound changes—indeed cultural, social, spiritual, and religious transformations. We ourselves are wagering on this response and proposal,
and it is our intention with these reflections to encourage that approach.

In other words, we have to enter into a process of paradigm change.
Such a change has to be dialectical, that is, it must accept all that is accept-
able and helpful in the paradigm of modernity and place it into another
more all-encompassing and wholesome paradigm.

Will it be new? Strictly speaking, it will not. There has always been
within human cultures and even in the prevailing paradigm of modernity
another kind of relation to nature, one gentler and more holistic, although
it has not always been uppermost. It will be relatively new, however.

We want to clarify what paradigm means, and what is relatively new
about it.

WHAT A PARADIGM IS

In his well-known book on the structure of scientific revolutions Thomas Kuhn gives the word *paradigm* two meanings. The first and broader
meaning has to do with "the entire constellation of beliefs, values, techniques, and so on shared by the members of a given community," which

establishes the basis for a disciplined system by which a given society orients itself and organizes the whole of its relationships. The second and stricter definition flows from the first and denotes "one sort of element in that constellation, the concrete puzzle-solutions which, employed as models or examples, can replace explicit rules as a basis for the solution of the remaining puzzles of normal science."[17]

We may usefully take up the first meaning, that is, paradigm as an organized, systematic, and current way of relating to ourselves and to everything else around us. These are models and patterns of evaluating and explaining the reality around us and acting upon it.

It is at this point that we should epistemologically contextualize our way of approaching nature and society. Every culture organizes its way of evaluating, interpreting, and acting upon nature, on its habitat, and in history. Even though our own way currently prevails around the world, it is simply one among others. Hence it is well to relinquish from the outset any monopolistic pretensions about our self-understanding and the way we have used reason and are using it now. Doing so highlights the fact that science and technology are cultural practices like others and hence limited to a particular culture.

Many today claim—I particularly have in mind two contemporary scientists and sages, Alexander Koyré[18] and Ilya Prigogine[19]—that what defines our relationship to the universe is experimental dialogue. This dialogue involves two constitutive dimensions: understanding and changing. Out of this practice modern science has arisen as being *over* nature in order to know it, and technology as an operation to change it.

Modern science began by denying the legitimacy of other kinds of dialogue with nature, such as common sense, magic, and alchemy. It even went so far as to deny nature by refusing to recognize its complexity and assuming that it would be governed by a small number of simple unchangeable laws (Newton and Einstein as well).

This very dialogue of experimentation, however, has led to crises and further developments. Contact with nature has opened up inquiries and new questions; it has led us to ask who we are and by what right we participate in the overall evolution of the cosmos. Molecular biology in particular has made a marvelous contribution by demonstrating the universality of the genetic code: all living beings, from the most primitive amoeba through the dinosaurs and the primates up to today's *Homo sapiens (demens),* use the same genetic language composed fundamentally of four basic syllables, A (adenine), C (cytosine), G (guanine), and T (thymine), for producing and reproducing themselves.

We dialogue with the universe not only along the experimental path of science and technology but also through other approaches to conversing with and appropriating nature. All accounts that cultures have given of how they came into the world can help us better know and preserve ourselves and our habitat. Thus it emerges that these are complementary approaches, and the monopoly of the modern way of deciphering the world around us is relinquished. Ilya Prigogine, Russian-Belgian physical chemist and Nobel laureate in chemistry (1977), has even raised the question, "How are we to distinguish the modern man or woman of science from a magician or witch doctor, or even from what is much further from human society, a bacterium, for it also questions itself about the world and is constantly testing the decodification of the chemical signals that guide it?"[20] In other words, we are all in a process of dialogue and interaction with the universe; we all produce information and we can all learn from one another, from how viruses are transmitted, from how plankton adapt to changes in the oceans, and from how humans handle in different manners the challenges of extremely varied ecosystems.

Our own way of arriving at what is real is not the only way. We are one moment in a vast process of universal interaction that can be seen to be occurring from the most primitive energies during the first moments after the big bang up to the most sophisticated codes in the human brain.

THE EMERGENCE OF THE NEW PARADIGM: PLANETARY COMMUNITY

Today we are entering a new paradigm; that is, a new way of engaging in dialogue with all beings and their relationships is emerging. Obviously, the classical paradigm of science remains in place with its well-known dualisms, such as the division of the world into the material and the spiritual, the separation between nature and culture, human being and world, reason and emotion, female and male, God and world, and the atomization of scientific knowledge.

Nevertheless, the current crisis is prompting the development of a new sensitivity to the planet as a whole, resulting in new values, new dreams, new behavior patterns, embraced by an ever-growing number of individuals and communities. Out of this growing sensitivity a new paradigm is emerging. It is still emerging, but it is beginning to make its presence felt. A new communication with the universe is now underway.

What is going on? We are returning to the homeland of our birth. We were lost among machines, fascinated by industrial structures, shut up in offices with air-conditioning and dried flowers, surrounded by home appliances and communications devices, and absorbed in myriads of talking pictures. Now we are returning to the vast planetary and cosmic community. We are fascinated by the green forest, we pause before the majesty of the mountains, we are awed by the star-filled sky, and we admire the vitality of the animals. We are filled with admiration at the diversity of cultures, human habits, and ways of signifying the world. We are beginning to accept and value differences. In some places a new compassion for all beings is coming into being, especially for those suffering most in nature and society. Such a feeling has always existed in humankind and some such emotion has always broken its way through, for such feelings are human, deeply human. Now, however, in the context of the crisis they have become stronger and are tending to spread and to create a new way of being, feeling, thinking, appreciating, acting, and praying—in short, a new paradigm.

We are refusing to reduce Earth to an assortment of natural resources or to a physical and chemical reservoir of raw materials. It has its own identity and autonomy as an extremely dynamic and complex organism. At a deep level, it can now be seen as the Great Mother who nourishes and bears us. She is the great and bountiful Pacha Mama (Great Mother) of the Andean cultures, or a living superorganism, the Gaia of Greek mythology and modern cosmology.

We want to experience the Earth firsthand, to feel the wind on our skin, plunge into the mountain waters, enter into virgin forest, and capture the expressions of biodiversity. An attitude of enchantment is resurfacing, a new sense of the sacred is reemerging, and a feeling of intimacy and gratitude is coming into view. We want to taste natural products in their innocence, rather than as treated by industry for profit. Gentleness, which both St. Francis and Blaise Pascal regarded so highly, here finds free expression. A second naivete is emerging, one that is post-critical, the fruit of science, and especially of cosmology, astrophysics, and molecular biology, as the previously unsuspected dimensions of the real are coming to light in the infinitely vast, the infinitely tiny, and the infinitely complex. The universe of beings and of living things fills us with respect, reverence, and dignity.

Instrumental reason is not the only way to use our capacity to understand; there is also symbolic reason and the reason of the heart and the use of all our bodily and spiritual senses. In addition to the *logos* (reason), there is *eros* (life and passion), *pathos* (affectivity and sensitivity), and the *daimon* (nature's inner voice). Reason is neither the primary nor the ultimate moment of existence. We are also affectivity, desire, passion, turbulence, communication, and attention to the voice of nature speaking inside us. This voice speaks within us and asks to be heeded and followed (it is the presence of the *daimon* within us). Knowing means more than a way to tame reality. To know is to enter into communion with things. That is why St. Augustine said, following in Plato's wake, "We know in proportion as we love."[21] This new love for our native land encourages us to a new gentleness and opens to us a gentler direction toward which the world may move. We have a new perception of Earth as a vast community of which we are members. As members, we are responsible for assuring that all other members and factors–from the energy balance of soil and air through microorganisms and up to the races and to each individual person–may live on it in harmony and peace. '

As the basis for this new perception, people feel the need for a new use of science and technology *with* nature, *on behalf* of nature, never *against* nature. It therefore becomes imperative to ecologize all that we do and think, to reject closed ideas, mistrust one-way causality, to strive to be inclusive in the face of all exclusions, to be unifying in the face of all disjunctions, to take a holistic approach in the face of all reductionisms, and to appreciate complexity in the face of all oversimplifications. Thus it is that the new paradigm is beginning to forge its own history.

THE NEW PERSPECTIVE:
THE EARTH SEEN FROM BEYOND THE EARTH

The new paradigm emerges spontaneously from the view of the Earth that astronauts achieved in the 1960s. For the first time in history Earth was seen from beyond Earth. Several astronauts expressed the impact in moving terms.[22]

When astronaut Russell (Rusty) Schweickart returned to Earth he testified to a change in his mental landscape. Seen from above, the Earth

is so small and so fragile and such a precious little spot in that universe that you can block it out with your thumb, and you realize on that small spot, that little blue and white thing, is everything that means anything to you–all of history and music and poetry and art and death and birth and love, tears, joy, games, all of it on that little spot out there that you can cover with your thumb. And you realize from that perspective that you've changed, that there's something new there, that the relationship is no longer what it was.[23]

Indeed, from out there, from the spaceship or the moon, the Earth, a marvelous blue-and-white planet, is seen to be a heavenly body in the vast cosmic chain. It is the third planet from our sun, which is a medium-size star among another two hundred billion suns in our galaxy, a galaxy which is one among a hundred billion other galaxies formed into galaxy clusters. The solar system is twenty-eight million light years from the center of our galaxy, the Milky Way, on the inner side of the spiral arm of Orion. As Isaac Asimov said in 1982, celebrating twenty-five years since the launching of Sputnik, which opened the space age: the legacy of this quarter century of space activity is that, viewed from spaceships, the Earth and humankind make up *a single entity*.[24] Note that he did not say that they make up a unity resulting from a set of relationships. He is saying much more; namely, that we make up a single entity, that is, a single being, complex, diverse, contradictory, and endowed with enormous dynamism—but in the end, a single complex being that many are calling Gaia.

Such a claim assumes that human beings are not just *on* the Earth; we are not wayfarers, passengers from somewhere else who belong to other worlds. Far from it. We are sons and daughters of Earth. We are the Earth itself in its expression of consciousness, of freedom, and of love. Human consciousness will never lose the conviction that we are Earth (*adam-adamá* in the biblical creation story) and that our fate is inseparably connected to the fate of the Earth and the cosmos of which Earth is a part.[25]

Modern Darwinian biology and chaos theory make this perception of mutual belonging and organic unity between Earth and humankind crystal clear.[26] Life has emerged out of the entire evolutionary process, from the energies and particles at the very outset, by way of the primordial gas, the supernovas, galaxies, stars, the geosphere, the hydrosphere, the atmosphere, and finally the biosphere, into which the anthroposphere breaks (Christians can discern the Christosphere and the theosphere). Life, as we will see further on, with all its complexity, self-organization, all-relatedness, and self-transcendence, results from the potentialities of the universe itself. Ilya Prigogine studied how thermodynamics works in living systems, which always appear as open systems and hence as having an ever-fragile equilibrium and ever seeking to adapt.[27] They are continually exchanging energy with the environment. They consume a great deal of energy, and hence they increase entropy (expenditure of usable energy). Prigogine rightly calls them "dissipative structures" (energy spending). They are also "dissipative structures" in a second and paradoxical sense, since they dissipate entropy. Living beings produce entropy and at the same time they escape entropy. They metabolize the disorder and chaos in the environment into orders and complex structures that become self-organized, escaping entropy (they produce negentropy—negative entropy—or, in positive terms, they produce syntropy). Thus, for example, the sun's photons are useless to the sun, simply energy that escapes when the hydrogen from which it lives is dissolved. These photons, which are disorder, serve as food for plants when they perform photosynthesis. Under sunlight plants, through photosynthesis, decompose carbon dioxide, which is food for them, and give off oxygen, which is necessary for animal and human life.

What is disorder for one serves as order for another, and it is through a precarious balance between order and disorder (chaos)[28] that life maintains itself.[29] Order makes it necessary to create higher and more complex kinds of order, with less dissipation of energy. In this fashion the universe moves toward ever more complex forms of life and thus toward lower entropy. On the human and spiritual level, as we shall soon see, forms of relationship and life take shape in which syntropy (economy of energy) prevails over entropy (waste of energy). Thought, communication by word and other means, solidarity, and love are very powerful energies with a very low level of entropy and high level of syntropy. From this stand-point, what we observe is not thermic death but the transfiguration of the cosmogenic process becoming apparent in very highly organized, creative, and vital orders.

EARTH, THE LIVING SUPERORGANISM: GAIA

Life is not merely sitting upon the Earth and occupying parts of the Earth (biosphere). The Earth itself, as a whole, is proclaiming itself as a living macroorganism. What mythologies of the peoples of both East and West witness about the Earth as the Great Mother with two thousand breasts to signify her ineffable fruitfulness is being increasingly confirmed by modern experimental science.[30] We need only refer to the work of the English physician and biologist James Lovelock[31] and the microbiologist Lynn Margulis.[32]

NASA gave Lovelock the job of developing for space travel models capable of detecting life beyond our upper atmosphere. His starting point was the hypothesis that if there was life, it would use the atmosphere and oceans of its respective planets as storehouses and as a means for trans-porting the materials needed for its metabolism. Such a function would certainly change the chemical balance of the atmosphere in such a way that an atmosphere where there was life would be noticeably different from one without it. He then compared the atmosphere of Earth with those of its neighbors, Venus and Mars, by analyzing the radiation com-ing from those planets. The results were surprising. They demonstrated the huge equilibrium of the Earth-system and its astonishing supply of all the elements beneficial for life in contrast to the atmospheres on Venus and Mars, which render life impossible.

On Venus carbon dioxide measures around 96.5% and on Mars 98%, while on Earth it reaches only 0.03%. Oxygen, which is absolutely neces-sary for life, is totally missing from Venus and Mars (0.00%) while on Earth it is around 21%. Nitrogen, which is needed for nourishing living organisms, is 3.5% on Venus and 2.7% on Mars, while on Earth it is around 79%. Methane, associated with oxygen, is crucial for forming carbon di-oxide and water vapor, without which life cannot go on. It is completely missing on our two sibling planets, which are almost the same size as Earth, have a similar origin, and are under the influence of the same rays of the sun, while on Earth it represents 1.7 parts per million.

Thus, there is at work a fine calibration between all the chemical and physical elements—the temperature of the Earth's crust, the atmosphere, rocks, and oceans, all of them under the effect of light from the sun—combining to make the Earth well suited, even excellent, for living organisms. Thus, it comes to be seen as a living superorganism, which Lovelock calls Gaia, in keeping with the classic name of the Earth from our cultural ancestors, the Greeks.

Lovelock states: "We have . . . defined Gaia as a complex entity involving the Earth's biosphere, atmosphere, oceans and soil; the totality constituting a feedback or cybernetic system which seeks an optimal physical and chemical environment for life on this planet."[33]

Lovelock drew attention to how the conditions of all those elements useful for life are maintained under relatively steady conditions. This balance is fashioned by the planet-wide life system itself, by Earth-Gaia. The high level of oxygen (it began to be released billions of years ago by photosynthesizing bacteria in the oceans, since for them oxygen was toxic) and the low level of carbon gas reflect the photosynthesizing activity of bacteria, algae, and plants for millions and millions of years. Other gasses that are biological in origin, forming an oven favorable to life, are present in Earth's atmosphere as a result of life. If there were no life on Earth, methane, for example, would rise by 10^{29}, thereby rendering life impossible.

Thus the concentration of gasses in the atmosphere is apportioned in a way that is optimal for living organisms. Small deviations could mean irreparable catastrophes. The oxygen level in the atmosphere, on which living beings live, has now remained unchanged for millions and millions of years at around 21%. Should it rise to 23% there would be fires around the Earth, ravaging the green layer on the Earth's crust. The level of salt in the oceans is around 3.4%. Should it rise to 6% life in the oceans and lakes would become as impossible as in the Dead Sea. The whole atmospheric system of the planet would be thrown off kilter. During the four billion years of the existence of life on the Earth, solar heat has risen 30% to 50%. In earlier times, when heat from the sun was cooler, how was life on Earth possible? The atmosphere at that time is known to have been calibrated differently than it is now. There were larger amounts of gasses like ammonia, which served as a kind of blanket around the planet, warming the Earth and making possible conditions conducive to life. With the warming of the sun that layer gradually thinned out in close interaction with the requirements of life. The Earth in turn has maintained for millions and millions of years an average temperature of between 15° and 35° centigrade, which represents the optimal temperature for living organisms. "Life and its environment are so intrinsically interconnected that evolution has to do with Gaia rather than with the organisms or the environment taken separately and by themselves."[34] The biota (the totality of living organisms) and their environment are evolving in tandem.

This calibration is not just internal to the Gaia-system, as though it were a closed system. It can be found in the human body, which contains more or less the same proportion of water as the surface of planet Earth (71%) and in which the salt level in the blood is the same as in the ocean (3.4%).[35] This fine tuning is found in the universe itself, for it is an open system that includes the harmony of the Earth. Speaking of the origins and fate of the universe in *A Brief History of Time*, Stephen Hawking says, "If the rate of expansion one second after the big bang had been smaller by even one part in a hundred thousand million million, the universe would have recollapsed before it ever reached its present size."[36] If, on the other hand, the expansion had been a little greater, on the order of one in a million, there would not be enough density for the formation of stars and planets, and hence of life. Everything took place in such a balanced way that it created conditions suitable for the emergence of the biosphere, and out of the biosphere, the anthrosphere as we have it today.

Likewise, if the weak nuclear force (which causes decay of radioactivity) had not held the level that it has, all hydrogen would have turned into helium. The stars would dissolve, and, without hydrogen, water, which is essential to life, would be impossible. If the strong nuclear force (which balances atomic nuclei) had risen by 1%, carbon would never have been formed in the stars. Without carbon, DNA, which stores the basic information for the appearance of life, would not have appeared.

Likewise, if the electromagnetic force (responsible for charged particles and photons of light) were a little higher, the stars would turn cold. They would not be able to explode as supernovas, and such explosions would not thereby give rise to the formation of planets; neither would the formation of other heavier elements such as nitrogen and phosphorus, which are crucial for the production and reproduction of life, be possible.

Finally, if the force of gravity had not held the level that it has, there would be no reason for the universe to be so broadly uniform, nor would the Earth revolve around our sun, the main source of energy for all the living organisms on the planet.[37]

The harmonious interconnection of these four basic interactions of the universe, which are indeed the internal logic of the evolutionary process (the organizing mind, as it were, of the cosmos itself) continues to act synergetically to keep the cosmological arrow of time heading toward ever more relational and complex kinds of beings.

Just as the cell is part of an organ, and each organ part of the body, so each living being is part of an ecosystem, and each ecosystem is part of the overall Earth-system, which is part of the sun-system, which is part of the Milky Way-system, which is part of the cosmos-system. The Gaia-system can thus be seen to be extremely complex and profoundly farsighted. Only an organizing intelligence would be able to calibrate all these factors. We are accordingly pushed back to an intelligence far exceeding our own. To recognize this fact is an act of reason; it does not mean relinquishing our reason but humbly surrendering to an intelligence much wiser and more exalted than our own.

The Gaia hypothesis enables us to see how robust the Earth as a macroorganism is in standing up to attacks on its immune system. Over the long course of its billions of years of life, it has withstood a number of terrifying assaults. Five hundred and seventy million years ago a great extinction occurred in the Cambrian period, in which 80-90% of the then-existing species disappeared. In the Permotriassic period, 245 million years ago, what was probably the breakup of the single continent Pangéia or Pangaia into two continents is said to have led to the destruction of 75-95% of the then-existing species. Sixty-seven million years ago, in the Cretacean period, Gaia probably collided with a large meteor, believed to be twice the size of Mount Everest, at a speed of 65 times the speed of sound. The result: 65% of the then-existing species disappeared, notably the dinosaurs, which had ruled the Earth for 166 million years, marine plankton, and countless species of life. Again, 730,000 years ago during the Pleistocene era, there was another cosmic impact that led to yet another huge species extinction. More recently, during the last ice age (between 15,000 and 10,000 B.C.E.), species were mysteriously devastated on all continents except Africa. It is estimated that 50% of genera weighing more than about 10 pounds, 75% of those weighing 165-220 pounds, and all those weighing more (such as, for example, mammoths) disappeared, possibly under the combined effects of bad climate and the heedless hunting activity of human beings.

On each occasion, whole libraries of genetic information that had been built up over millions and millions of years disappeared forever.[38] Taking into account the several mass extinctions, scientists suggest that such ecological cataclysms have occurred every 26 million years. Such cataclysms could be caused by a hypothetical twin star of the sun, two or three light years away from us. It would cyclically draw comets out of their orbits in the Oort cloud (a band of comets and cosmic districts identified by the Dutch astronomer Jan Oort) and would cause them to head toward the sun, some of them colliding with the Earth and devastating large portions of the biosphere.[39]

Gaia has had to adapt to being assaulted and decimated, has regenerated the genetic inheritance from among the survivors, has created other durable forms, and remains alive, continuing the evolutionary process.[40]

Currently around 1.4 million species have been catalogued, but biologists claim that there must be from 10 to 13 million uncatalogued; others propose that the number might be as high as 100 million. These represent a mere 1% of the species that have existed on Earth since the emergence of life four billion years ago and that have been exterminated in the various catastrophes.

These extinctions raise the issue of violence in nature. Violence is fundamental. It flared out with inconceivable force in the big bang, and in the explosion of large stars into supernovas, and it continues on all levels. This is mysterious for linear reasoning, but just as the human being is both *sapiens* and *demens*, so likewise is the universe both violent and cooperative. The overall tendency of all beings and of the entire universe, as quantum physicists like Heisenberg have observed, is to pursue their tendency toward their own fulfillment and perfection. Violence is subject to this positive thrust, its overwhelming mysteriousness notwithstanding.[41]

Today, as a result of excess chlorofluorocarbons (CFC) and other polluting ingredients, the Earth-superorganism may be about to devise new adaptations, which will not necessarily be easy on the human species. Chronic famines might break out and prolonged droughts might occur, even large-scale death of species. Some analysts say that the possibility of the species *Homo* disappearing should not be ruled out. Gaia may eliminate it, very painfully, in order to allow the overall balance to remain and so that other species might live and continue the cosmic thrust of evolution. If Gaia has had to rid itself of myriad species over its life history, who can assure us that it will not be forced to rid itself of our own? Our species is a threat to all other species; it is terribly aggressive and is proving to be a geocide, an ecocide, and a true Satan of the Earth.

The well-known economist and ecologist Nicolas Georgescu-Roegen suspects that

> perhaps it is the fate of humankind to have a short but feverish, exciting, and extravagant life rather than one that is long, vegetative, and monotonous. In that case, other species, with no spiritual pretensions, such as amoebas would inherit an Earth that would continue to be bathed in sunlight for a long time.[42]

Earth would be impoverished, but who is to say that after millions and millions of years the principle of intelligibility that is present in the universe might not break forth out of another complex being? Such new "humans" would perhaps emerge with a greater awareness of, and devotion to, their cosmic and evolutionary mission regarding the universe and its Creator. Earth would have recovered an evolutionary advance that it had lost due to the excessive arrogance of the species *Homo*.

The Gaia hypothesis seems very plausible, and it is gaining greater acceptance in both the scientific community and the wider cultural realm. It embodies one of the most fascinating discoveries of the twentieth century, the deep unity and harmony of the universe. Quantum physics speaks of a unified field in which the four basic forces interact: gravity, strong and weak nuclear forces, and electromagnetic force. Biology speaks of the unified phylogenetic field, since the genetic code is common to all living things. The Gaia hypothesis translates into a splendid metaphor a philosophical and religious vision that underlies ecological discourse. This vision holds that the universe is made up of a vast network of relationships in such a way that each one lives through the other, for the other, and with the other; that the human being is a node of relationships going in all directions; and that the Divinity itself is revealed to be an all-relational Reality. If all is relation, and nothing but relation exists, then the most universal law is universal synergy, syntropy, interrelationship, collaboration, cosmic solidarity, and communion in kinship. Darwin and his law of the natural selection of the fittest must be complemented with this all-ecological and synergetic vision.[43] The key for understanding survival and the multiplication of species is to be found in the *inter(retro)relationships*–a gestalt of relationships both current and reaching back through the whole of history–of the beings most suited for interacting with others and not simply in the power of the individual who rises above others by reason of its own strength.

THE UNIVERSE UNDER THE ARC OF TIME AND OF EVOLUTION

This vision of Gaia and its eras makes it possible to understand the historicity of the universe and nature.[44] Historicity is not a property solely of conscious beings such as humans. Nature is not a clock set ticking once and for all. Nature comes from a very long cosmic process; it is cosmogenesis. The "clock" has been set up slowly; beings appeared on the scene starting with the simplest and moving toward the increasingly complex. All the factors comprising each ecosystem with its beings and its organisms have first been in a latent state, and then their ancestral state, before finally emerging themselves. They are historic. All these natural processes presuppose a fundamental irreversibility proper to historic time.

Ilya Prigogine has shown that open systems–and nature and the universe are open systems–challenge the classical notion of linear time postulated by physics. Time is not a mere parameter of movement but the measure of the internal developments of a world permanently undergoing changes, passing from disequilibrium to higher levels of equilibrium.[45]

Nature comes to be seen as a process of self-transcendence. It contains an ever active cosmogenic principle by which beings continually arise, and in proportion to their complexity, they overcome the inexorability of entropy proper to closed systems. The possibility of a new dialogue between the eco-cosmological vision and theology thereby opens up, for such self-transcendence can point toward that which religions and spiritual traditions have always called God, absolute transcendence, or that future that is more than "thermal death," namely, the supreme realization of order, harmony, and life.[46]

It accordingly becomes clear how unreal it is to establish a tight separation between nature and history, and between world and human being, the separation that has legitimized and grounded so many other dualisms. Like all beings, humans beings, with their intelligence and their capability for love and communication, are also the product of this cosmic process. The cosmic energies and factors that are part of their makeup share their ancestry with the universe. The human being cannot be regarded as outside the cosmogenic principle, like some errant being sent to Earth by some deity. *All* are sent by the Deity, not just the human being.

This inclusion of the human being within the totality of beings and as the result of cosmogenic process stands counter to anthropocentrism (which in reality is an androcentrism, centered on the male, excluding the female). Anthropocentrism reveals a narrow, atomized view of the human being, torn away from other beings. It claims that the sole meaning of evolution and the reason for the existence of other beings is to produce the human being, man and woman. Of course, the entire universe is involved in making the human being; but it is not only the human being that it makes but all other beings as well. We all depend on the stars, for they transform hydrogen into helium, and it is from that combination that carbon, nitrogen, phosphorus, and potassium emerge, without which there would be no amino acids and none of the proteins needed for life. Without the stellar radiation emitted in this cosmic process, millions of stars would grow cold and the sun might not exist, and without the sun there would be no life on our Earth. Without the preexistence of the whole set of factors favorable to life, factors prepared over billions of years, and the beginning of life itself, which allowed for the emergence of human life, there would be no such thing as the individual person that each of us is. Hence, we must say in a thoroughly circular fashion that the universe is intended for human beings just as human beings are turned toward the universe from which we came. We belong to one another: the basic elements of the universe, the energies that are active from the expansionary process of the big bang, the other factors making up the universe, and we ourselves as a species that has come onto the evolutionary scene very recently. Unless all are involved in evolution there is no evolution of the universe. That is the starting point from which we must think cosmo-centrically and act ecocentrically. That means thinking about the involvement of the entire universe in this construction of each being and action with the awareness of the inter(retro)relationship that all have among themselves in terms of ecosystems, and of the species on the basis of which the individual is situated. We must leave behind any sort of anthropocentrism and androcentrism as illusory and arrogant; they are capital ecological sins.

However, we must not confuse anthropocentrism with the anthropic principle.[47] The latter means that we can only perform the kind of thinking in which we are engaged if we take into account the singular place of the human being within the totality of species and beings. It is not the amoebas or hummingbirds or horses that are engaging in reflexive discourse on the cosmos; it is human beings who are doing so. It is only for humans (and hence the word *anthropic* from the place [*topos*] of the human being [*anér, andrós*]) that this discourse on the universe, on our connection to the whole, has meaning. Human beings accordingly establish a basis, a reference point, whose function is cognitive, which merely reveals their singularity as a thinking and reflexive species. That uniqueness does not entail a break from other creatures but strengthens our relationship to them, because the principle of understanding, reflection, and communication first exists within the universe. Only because it is in the universe can it emerge on Earth, gradually in various complex beings, and finally in the highly complex beings of the sons and daughters of Earth, human beings. If it is in the universe, it is also found in other beings, in a manner appropriate to them. The point is not that the principle is different, but simply that the degrees of its presence and embodiment in the cosmos are different.

COMPLEXITY: CHARACTERISTIC OF THE
NEW PARADIGM AND OF NONLINEAR LOGIC

These observations bring up a topic that is extremely important from the standpoint of the new paradigm, namely complexity.[48] Reality, by reason of its web of relationships, is by its very nature complex. Myriad factors, elements, energies, and irreversible temporal conjunctures enter into synergy and harmony in the actual constituting of each ecosystem and its individual interfaces. The complexity of living organisms is especially intense.[49] They constitute open systems. They exhibit the phenomena of self-production and of self-organization based on a dynamic nonequilibrium seeking new adaptations. The closer a living organism comes to complete equilibrium the closer it is to death. But distance from equilibrium—that is, the situation of chaos—creates the possibility of a new order. Hence chaos is generative, and it is the principle for the creation of singularities and novelties. Through internal self-organization, living beings create structures that dissipate entropy, as we have seen above, thereby making possible negentropy and syntropy.

The complexity of living organisms is shown by the presence of the holographic principle[50] at work in them. This principle states that the whole is in the parts and the parts are in the whole. Thus, in every cell, as simple as it might be, on the epidermis, for example, is present all the genetic information in the universe. The human being is singularly complex. There are a billion nerve cells in the cerebral cortex and around a trillion others throughout the body. In just one cell of a human muscle a trillion atoms are interacting. More impressive than these numbers is the operational relevance of all this information in a logic of inclusion and inter(retro)-relationship moving from order to disorder, to interaction, in order to create a new order, this process constituting an organic whole. As if that were not enough, we should also note that from an ecological standpoint, human beings are a genetic, a bio-sociocultural, a temporal, and a transcendent genetic component.

Approaches to understanding complexity have led to the development of open and closed cybernetic and systems theories. They are used to attempt to grasp the interdependence of all elements and their overall functionality, the upshot being that the whole is more than the sum of the parts and that the whole is realized in the parts (hologram). As astonishing as it may seem, there is room in the open system not only for order but for disorder, antagonism, contradiction, and competition. They are all aspects of organization.

Such is the reality of the complex. There are so many interactions of all kinds taking place in it that Niels Bohr once commented, "The interactions that a dog has during its life are of such a magnitude that it would be impossible to study it *in vivo*. To study it properly, it would have to be killed."[51]

Here we see the limits of the classic paradigm of science based on the physics of inert bodies and mathematics: it only manages to study living beings by reducing them to inert beings, in short, by destroying them. But what kind of science is it that in order to study living beings needs to eliminate them? Other methods must be found that are suited to the complexity that keeps living organisms alive. There is a need for another logic that will do justice to the complexity of the real. We are familiar with five expressions of logic (how the realities of the universe are connected and related among themselves).

There is the logic of *identity*. It studies the thing in itself without considering the interplay of relationships around it. It is linear and simple, and it underlies all authoritarian systems or systems of dominance, for its tendency is to enclose within its framework or its sphere of influence whatever is other than it.

There is the logic of *difference*. It recognizes nonidentity, that is, otherness and its right to exist, its autonomy and individuality. It is the presupposition for any personal and intercultural dialogue, for any political system that tends toward participation and inclusion of what is different.

There is *dialectical* logic, which seeks to contrast identity and difference, enclosing them in a dynamic process in which identity is seen to be like a thesis (proposition), difference is like an antithesis (counter-position), and the result is a synthesis which includes both in a higher level that is more open to new encounters and inclusions. Any creative thought, any system of communication, and any shared human community or political life presuppose a dialectical logic. Opposites have their rights assured and their place in the building up of the dynamic and organic whole. Contradiction is part of reality, and hence thought must do it justice.

There is the logic of *complementarity and reciprocity*, which extends dialectical logic. Leaving cultural anthropology aside, this logic was elaborated in modern times by the quantum physicists of the Copenhagen school (Bohr, Heisenberg) when they realized the extreme complexity of the subatomic world. In this logic, matter and antimatter, particle and wave, matter and energy, positive and negative charges of the elementary particles, and so forth, are related and make up a force field. Rather than seeing oppositions, as in dialectical logic, the emphasis is on seeing the complementarities or reciprocities in the sense of the formation of ever more dynamic, complex, and unified fields of relationships. It is in this context that Niels Bohr issued his famous statement: "A superficial truth is a statement whose opposite is false; a profound truth is a statement whose opposite is also a profound truth."[52] The logic of complementarity and reciprocity is at work in all groups that value differences, dialectical opposition, listening carefully to various positions, and accepting contributions no matter where they come from. And it is by the logic of complementarity and reciprocity that creative relationships are established between genders, races, ideologies, and religions, and the different ecosystems in a single ecological niche are appreciated.

Finally there is *dialogical* or *perichoretic* logic, which strives for dialogue in all directions and at all times. It accordingly takes the most inclusive stance possible and the one that is least inclined to produce victims. The logic of the universe is dialogical; everything interacts with everything at all points and under all circumstances. This circularity was expressed by the Greeks in the expression *perichoresis*, which etymologically means circularity and inclusion of all relationships and of all related beings.[53] In Christian trinitarian language, *perichoresis* captures the relationship of mutual presence and interpenetration between God and the universe or between the three Divine Persons among themselves and with all creation.

Dialogical logic can accordingly be called perichoretic logic. It is the most complex, and hence the most complete logic.

Complexity demands another kind of rationality and science. Classical science was guided by the paradigm of reduction and simplification. Its basic approach was to tear the phenomenon out of its ecosystem in order to analyze it in isolation. It excluded anything that was merely of the moment, temporary, or connected to passing contingencies. Science, so it was said, has to do with the universal, that is, with that phenomenon's structure of intelligibility and not its uniqueness. Hence, the effort was to reduce the complex to the simple, since the simple forms the constants, which can always be reproduced. Everything must obey the principle of order, which alone is rational and functional. Imponderables and situations of dynamic nonequilibrium are disregarded.

Moreover, in order to assure that knowledge is objective, the subject must not become involved with the object being analyzed. The subject may not bring his or her own problematic presuppositions or prior options into the process of knowing. Linear and causal logic are accorded absolute confidence in deciphering the truth of theories and reality. Any contradiction in this process is said to indicate that there was a mistake from the beginning.

The ideal realization of this paradigm was found in physics and mathematics. It proved fruitful in the mechanics of Newton and in Einstein's relativity physics. Applied to biology, it revealed the physical and chemical composition of living organisms. The reductionism of the complex to the simple is lived by the dream—Einstein's obsession to the end of his life—that there is at work at the foundation of the universe a single simple formula that explains everything and by means of which everything is created.

Ecological thought, based on the Earth sciences, does not reject the positive features of the method of reduction and simplification, but it realizes that it has major limits. Beings, organisms, and phenomena cannot be isolated from the totality of the inter(retro)relationships that actually constitute them. Hence, we must distinguish without separating; getting to know a being means comprehending its ecosystem and its web of relationships. It is important to grasp the part in the whole and the whole present in the parts. All phenomena are under the arc of temporality, that is, of irreversibility. Everything is in evolution: it comes from the past, is embodied in the present, and opens to the future. The past is the space of what is done (the future that has been realized); the present is the field of the real (the future that is now being realized and made evident); and the future is the horizon of the potential (the possibility that may yet be realized).[54]

Because of evolution we must pay attention to the universality of movement but also to the uniqueness of the individual event and to local developments, for they may be the condensation point for the entire meaning of the universe and the bearers of the forward leap. There is a logic in phenomena that very specifically underlies the logic of complexity, which refuses to be reduced to simplification. The movement of such logic is as follows: order-disorder, interaction, organization, creation. These connections must be considered from forward to backward and from backward to forward. Such a procedure always leads to organic wholes, whether in the domain of microphysics (atoms) or macrophysics (stars, galaxy clusters); or in the domain of biology (morphogenetic fields); or in the human realm (ecological, biological, sociological, or anthropological entities; cultures; types of social organization).

The subject doing the analysis is not outside this omni-relational reality but is part of the process of reality and of its reflex awareness. Beings have their relative autonomy, but always within a context of imbrication and interconnection. That is why the ideal of strict objectivity, which leaves out the history and the concerns of the subject, is a fiction. The subject is part of the object and the object is a dimension of the subject. This inclusive logic of complexity makes necessary a certain style of thinking and acting: it forces us to connect the various bodies of knowledge related to the various dimensions of the real; representations must never become hardened, but rather we must comprehend the multidimensionality of the whole; and the local is connected to the global, the ecosystem with history, the contrary and even contradictory with the more all-encompassing whole.

Dialogical (perichoretic) logic is necessary inasmuch as it is the type most suited to this kind of experience of ecological reality. Through it we learn from all human experiences and the way they handle nature, whether from those experiences mistakenly called primitive or magical, those using alchemy, shamans, those that are archaic and religious, or from contemporary experiences linked to empirical, analytic, and epistemological discourse. They all reveal the communication of human beings with our surroundings. They all attest to a truth, and we humans have a wonderful landscape to admire and a marvelous message to ponder.

THE CONTRIBUTION OF ECOFEMINISM

The topics of complexity, the interconnectedness of all things, and the centrality of life prompt us to consider women and ecofeminist thinking.[55] By instinct and by the unique way that they are constituted, women grasp and live out the complexity and interconnection of the real. By nature women are connected directly to what is most complex in the universe, namely, life. They are the most immediate generators of life. For nine months they carry the mystery of human life in their womb, and they caress and comfort that life throughout its existence, even when the fruit of their womb has gone away, followed the most adverse paths, or even died. Their son or daughter will never leave their heart.

Women are related to life more by care than by labor. Care presupposes an ethic of respect, a basic stance required when facing the sacred. Moreover, it requires attention to every detail and an appreciation for every sign that speaks of life—its birth, its joy, its crises, its maturation, its full expansion, and its death. The ethic of care is especially crucial in managing the complex everyday life of a family. It is here that the logic of the complex comes into play, for a common life must be fashioned out of opposites, even the most contradictory things, such as the diversity of genders, desires, mindsets, behaviors, life ambitions, and so forth, with as little wear and tear as possible. It is primarily (though not exclusively) women who, with their presence as wives, mothers, companions, and counselors, handle this art and technique of the complex, who in their wisdom constitute the technique and art of the very cosmogenic evolutionary process.

If we seek to work out a new covenant with nature, one of integration and harmony, we find sources of inspiration in women and the feminine (in both man and woman). Women do not allow themselves to be ruled by reason alone; they more holistically incorporate intuition, heart, emotion, and the archetypal universe of the personal, group, and cosmic unconscious. Through their bodies, by which they enjoy a relationship of intimacy and wholeness quite different from that of men, they help overcome the dualisms introduced by patriarchal and androcentric culture between world and human being, spirit and body, and interiority and efficiency. They have developed better than men a consciousness that is open and receptive, able to see the sacramental character of the world, and hence to hear the message of things, the beckonings of values and meanings that go beyond merely decoding intelligibility structures. They are privileged bearers of the meaning of the sacrality of all things, especially as related to the mystery of life, love, and death. They possess a special openness to religion, for they are particularly capable of connecting all things in a dynamic whole, which is a function that every religion sets for itself.

The wholeness of female experience points us toward that stance that we must build and develop together, if we intend to live in an ecological era in harmony and in a loving relationship with the entire universe. It is the merit of ecofeminism to have developed critically (against rationalism, authoritarianism, compartmentalization, and the will to power, which are historic expressions of androcentrism and patriarchalism) and constructively the new pattern for relating to nature within a perspective of kinship and a planetary and cosmic sacredness.[56]

THE SPIRITUAL DEPTH OF THE UNIVERSE

In the classic paradigm the universe was said to have a phenomenological side (that which appears and can be described), which the so-called natural sciences analyzed marvelously. It was also said to have another side, its interiority and spirituality, which other sciences called human sciences (or sciences of the spirit) investigated keenly. At first these two approaches ran along separate tracks, human sciences on one side and natural sciences on the other. However, philosophical reflection and even scientific reflection after quantum physics have shown persuasively that what we have are not two worlds but two sides of the same world. Hence it came to be seen that there is no basis for the separation into natural sciences and human sciences, matter and spirit, body and soul, since the spirit belongs to nature and nature is permeated with spirit.

In the new paradigm the unification of perspectives becomes more obvious.[57] Indeed, considered in quantum terms, each process is indivisible; it encompasses the whole universe, which becomes a participant helping it to emerge. The universe and every phenomenon are regarded as the result of a cosmogenesis. One of the features of cosmogenesis is autopoiesis, as some cosmologists call it.[58] *Autopoiesis* means the power of self-organization present in the universe and in each being, starting with the most basic elements of creation. An atom, with all that pertains to it, is a system of autopoiesis or self-organization; so is a star that organizes hydrogen, helium, and other heavy elements, and the light that it emits from an internal dynamism centered within it. Hence it is not enough to simply look at the physical and chemical elements that make up the composition of beings, but we must also consider how they become organized and relate to others and manifest themselves. They possess an interiority, a basis of their organization and self-manifestation. Even a simple atom has a *quantum* of spontaneity in its self-manifestation. Such spontaneity increases in proportion to complexity to the point of becoming dominant in the more complex beings called organic.

The category of self-organization is fundamental for understanding life.[59] As we noted earlier, life is an interplay of self-organizing relationships and interactions allowing syntropy (economy of energy) to prevail over entropy (dispersal of energy). However, these principles of relationship and interaction were already present at the origin of the universe when the primordial energies begin to interact among themselves and to form force fields and the very first complex unities. This point in relationship and the resulting complexity is where we find the cradle of life and of the spirit, which is self-conscious life among humans.

Biochemists and biophysicists like Prigogine, Stengers, and others have recognized and have demonstrated what Teilhard de Chardin intuited back in the 1930s: the more the evolutionary process advances, the more complex it becomes; the more complex it becomes, the more it is internalized; the more it is internalized, the more consciousness it has; and the more consciousness it possesses, the more self-conscious it becomes. Everything interacts, therefore, and everything has a certain level of life and spirit. The most ancient rocks, whether examined in microphysics or macrophysics, obey the logic of interaction and complexity. They are more than their physical and chemical composition. They are in contact with the atmosphere and influence the hydrosphere. They interact with the climate and thus they relate to the biosphere. An almost infinite number of atoms, subatomic elements, and force fields make up their mass. A poet swept away by the grandeur of the mountains produces an inspired poem. The mountains share in this creation. In their own fashion they are alive, because they interact and connect with the entire universe, and even with the poet's imagination. They are accordingly bearers of spirit and life. That is why we can grasp the grandeur, solemnity, might, and majesty that they continually impart to alert spirits, who are so well represented by the indigenous peoples, poets, and mystics who understand the language of things and decipher the vast discourse of the universe.[60] To represent the vast number of witnesses we need only recall the mystic line of William Blake:

> To see a World in a grain of sand,
> And a Heaven in a wild flower,
> Hold Infinity in the palm of your hand,
> And Eternity in an hour.

Division into the biotic and the abiotic, living and nonliving beings, reflects another way of understanding reality, which is valid only for a closed system of beings who are seemingly substantial and permanent, like stars, mountains, and physical bodies, as opposed to beings that are complex, dynamic, and alive. In such a system the distinction is valid. When we break this barrier, however, and unveil the web of underlying relationships and interactions in them all, we realize that such substantiality and permanence vanish. We are in a system that is open, not closed. All beings are at the mercy of inter(retro)relationships, of energies and fields. As the quantum physicists—and Einstein himself—say in the understandable language of everyday life: large concentrations of energy are perceived as matter while the small ones as mere energy and force fields. Hence, everything is energy in different degrees of concentration and stabilization in extremely complex systems of relationships, where everything is interconnected with everything, giving rise to universal harmony, mountains, microorganisms, animals, and human beings. Everything has its interiority, and hence everything is spiritual.

Life and spirit accordingly give rise to things that are ever more complex and richer. At the current level of the cosmic evolutionary process with which we are familiar, it appears most intensely in the human being, man and woman. At this point interiority and complexity have reached self-conscious expression. They accordingly take on their own history, the history of the contents of that consciousness (phenomenology). Evolution will take a twofold course: the original and instinctive course being the universal directional logic driving all beings, including humans, and within it and by reason of evolution itself, it will take a self-conscious, free, and directed course, based on consciousness that can act upon the original course and can manifest itself as either an enemy or friend of the surrounding environment. This is the human and noospheric level of evolution.

That level is displayed in the vast work of civilization that human beings have created during the last two million, six hundred thousand years (emergence of *Homo habilis*). In a mysterious manner, in the power of the cosmogenic and creative principle of the universe, we have created languages and monumental expressions. With the agrarian, industrial, and cybernetic revolutions we have changed the chemical and physical balance of the planet. We have projected powerful symbols to give meaning to the universe, and figures to express personally and collectively the historic trajectory of human beings. We have invented a thousand images of God—mover, animator, and attractor of the entire universe and internal flame of each consciousness. Thus as we have expressed the *sapiens* dimension of each human being we have also given free play to the *demens* dimension with images of war, ecocide, ethnocide, fratricide, and homicide. This principle of life, intelligence, and creativity can emerge in human beings only because it was first in the universe and on planet Earth. It is a product of our galaxy—our Milky Way—to whose system we belong, and our galaxy leads us to cosmic orders antedating it.

The issues of concern to human beings are not simply the immeasurable grandeur of the universe, the black holes (true cosmological hell, because they prevent any communication whatsoever), and the infinitesimal smallness of microphysics back to its initial zero point at the time of the big bang. What disturbs the human being—an abysmal depth of passions and abject sewer of miseries, as Pascal would say—are demands of the heart, wherein dwell the great emotions that at one moment make our passage through this world sad, at another make our existence tragic, at another make our life ecstatic, and at another drive us to achieve our most ancestral desires. How are we to endure the suffering of the innocent, live with solitude, accept how tiny we are? Where are we going (since we know so little of where we have come from, and only a little of what we are)? These questions are always on the agenda of human disquietude. The answers make us courageous or cowardly, happy or tragic, hopeful or indifferent.

On the level of my immediate feelings, the immensity of space matters little to me, with all its gravitons, top quarks, quarks, electrons and atoms, if my heart is not satisfied, if I have lost the meaning of love, and I find no Womb to take me in just as I am; that is, if I do not feel that I have been found by God and if I do not find God. But if I encounter God, everything becomes utterly clear. Everything is connected, since emotion and sensitivity are rooted in the universe.

All things emerge in us as articulators of a force of emotion as ancestral as the basic elements. Then even a top quark becomes a sacrament, and the universe of stars and galaxies becomes a heavenly dance for the betrothal of human and divine love. Each vibration translates the ineffable message enunciated by each being, grasped as a symphony of a thousand and one instruments. As in rites of love and friendship, so in the universe each thing has its meaning, occupies its place, and is related to the whole rhythm of feast and encounter. The entire universe shares in the emotion, communication, and ecstasy unifying the internal and the external, the tiniest with the greatest. But such an experience is given only to those who plunge into the spiritual depth of the universe.

That dimension is part of the evolutionary process. It knows its present state and is also charged with the promise of future intensifications. Everything has future. The universe has traveled fifteen billion years in order that this turmoil should occur and that the cosmic liturgy should be entrusted to the possibilities of that macro-microcosmic being that is the human being, man and woman. Planet Earth is the space and time for the celebration of the present insofar as it is seeing what is now achieved, and it is also the time and the space for celebrating the future, which is seminally at work in the totality of the promises inscribed in the drive of each being, each species, and the entire universe.

CONCLUSION:
FEATURES OF THE EMERGING PARADIGM

By way of conclusion, we present some ideas or types of thinking that characterize the new emerging paradigm:

1. *Wholeness / diversity:* the universe, the Earth-system, the human phenomenon are organic dynamic wholes. Along with analysis, which dissociates, simplifies, and universalizes, we need synthesis, by which we do justice to this wholeness. Holism seeks to express such an attitude. Holism does not mean sum, but rather totality composed of organically interconnected diversities.

2. *Interdependence / connectedness / relative autonomy:* all beings are interconnected and hence always connected among themselves; one needs the other to exist. By reason of this fact, there is an underlying cosmic solidarity, and yet each enjoys relative autonomy and has a sense of value in itself.

3. *Relationship / force fields:* all beings live in a web of relationships. Nothing exists outside of relationship. What must be grasped is not so much beings in themselves but the relationship among them; from that point we can comprehend beings ever in relationship and consider how each one enters into the constitution of the universe. Moreover, everything is within energy and morphogenetic fields, by which, as we have said, everything is related with everything, at all points and at all moments.

4. *Complexity / interiority:* everything is charged with energy at various degrees of intensity and interaction. Highly condensed and stable energy appears as matter and less stable simply as an energy field. That fact leads to ever greater complexity in beings endowed with cumulative information, especially higher living beings. This evolutionary phenomenon displays the intentionality of the universe, pointing toward an interiority, a supremely complex reflex awareness. That drive makes it possible to view the universe as an intelligent and self-organizing whole. Strictly speaking, we cannot speak of a "within" and a "without." In quantum terms, the process is indivisible and is always taking place within cosmogenesis as the overall emergence of all beings. This understanding opens the way for raising the question of a thread running through the whole cosmic process, of a common denominator unifying everything, that makes chaos generative and that keeps order ever open to new interactions (dissipative structures). Hermeneutically speaking, the God-category could supply that meaning.

5. *Complementarity / reciprocity / chaos:* all reality appears as particle and wave, energy and matter, order and disorder, chaos and cosmos, and, among human beings, as *sapiens* (intelligent) and *demens* (mad). These are dimensions of reality itself. They are complementary and reciprocal. The principle of complementarity-reciprocity is at the root of the underlying drive of the universe, which passes through chaos before arriving at cosmos.

6. *Arrow of time / entropy:* everything that exists preexists and coexists. Hence the arrow of time is stamped on all relationships and systems; it imparts to them their character of irreversibility. These marks are present in each particle and in each force field, no matter how elementary. Consequently, nothing can be understood without reference to its history of relationship and its course through time. This course is open to the future. Hence none is fully finished but rather is charged with potentialities seek-

ing to be realized. God has not finished God's work yet, and has not even finished creating us. We should therefore be tolerant with the universe and patient with ourselves, because the final word "and God saw that it was good" has not yet been pronounced. This will happen only at the end of the evolutionary process. Complete harmony is future promise, not present celebration. Universal history is subject to the thermodynamic arrow of time; in other words, it must take entropy into account along with evolution in time, in closed systems or considered by themselves (Earth's limited resources, the time of the sun, and so forth). Energies are being dissipated inexorably, and no one can do anything to stop it, but human beings can slow the effects by extending the conditions of their own life and that of the planet and by the spirit of opening themselves to the mystery beyond the thermal death of the closed system. For the universe in its entirety is an open, self-organizing system that is continually transcending toward ever higher levels of life and order that escape entropy and open it to syntropy, synergy, and the dimension of the mystery of an utterly dynamic negentropic life.

7. *Shared destiny / personal destiny:* by the fact that we have a common origin and are all interlinked we all have a common fate in a shared and ever-open future. It is there that the personal fate of each being must be situated, for each being cannot be understood by itself, without the ecosystem, other species interacting with it, and other individuals of the same species. Despite this interdependence, each individual being is unique and is a culmination of millions and millions of years of creative endeavor by the universe.

8. *Cosmic common good / particular common good:* the common good is not that of humans alone, but is rather that of the whole cosmic community. Everything that exists and lives deserves to exist, to live, and to share life. The particular common good emerges out of harmony and synergy with the thrust of the planetary and universal common good.

9. *Creativity / destructiveness:* within the totality of interactions and of beings in relationship, men and women possess a uniqueness: humans are extremely complex and co-creative beings because we can interfere with the rhythm of creation. As observers we are always interacting with everything around us, and we cause the collapse of the wave function that is solidified into a material particle (Werner Heisenberg's uncertainty principle). We enter into the constitution of the world as it appears as a realization of quantum probabilities (particle/wave). Likewise, we are ethical beings because we can weigh the pros and cons and act beyond the logic of our own interests and in behalf of the interests of weaker beings. We can assault nature and decimate species—hence our destructiveness—as we may likewise reinforce their latent potentialities, preserving and expanding the Earth-system. We may consciously coexist with nature.

10. *Holistic ecological stance / rejection of anthropocentrism:* the stance of openness and unrestricted inclusion serves a radically ecological world view (of the omni-relatedness and connectedness of everything); it helps overcome age-old anthropocentrism and helps us to be ever more unique and at the same time to be in solidarity, complementarity, and creativity. We are thereby in synergy with the entire universe and through us, it proclaims itself, advances, and remains open to new things that have never been attempted before, heading toward a Reality that is hidden behind the veils of the mystery located in the realm of what is impossible to humans. As has been said, what is possible happens repeatedly, what is impossible also happens—namely God, that all-attracting Magnet, that Moving Force animating all, that Passion producing all.

CHAPTER 2

An Ecological View of the Cosmos

Our Contemporary Story

In all cultures every major shift in the direction of history issues in a new world view or cosmology. The new ecological paradigm has had such an effect. We understand *cosmology* to mean the image of the world that a society fashions for itself by artfully combining widely varying types of knowledge, traditions, and intuitions. This image provides an overall connectedness and confers the harmony that society needs and without which individual activities are scattered and lose their meaning within a larger Meaning. A world view serves to connect all things and to map the universe, and that is usually done by means of the great cosmological narratives.

THE STORIES OF HUMANKIND: FROM THE MEANING OF THE COSMOS TO COSMOGENESIS

Every cultural group, no matter how small, even the Kayapó people in the Amazon who are on their way to extinction, has its form of the overall story. That story is how human beings represent to themselves the origin of the universe, their place in the cosmos, their sense of the human journey, how the present is the future of the past, what humankind's destiny is, and how everything is connected to the Divinity. Story overcomes the chaos of misfortunes, and a picture of the finale of the universe is sketched out. The story serves to provide human life with security and order.

We are familiar with many such stories. They generally use the language of myth and the symbolism of the imagination, which follows the logic of the collective unconscious. We will simply point to three, by way of example.

The one most widely known in our culture is the biblical story in Genesis: creation by God over the course of seven days. The story is told in two versions that differ considerably from one another in both form and content: the Yahwist account, so called because it uses the name Yahweh for God and dates from around 950 B.C.E. (chapter 2), and the second account (chapter 1) written four or five centuries later, called Priestly because it represents the liturgical theology of the Temple.[1] The differences notwithstanding, the root intention in both is to make a profession of faith in the goodness of the universe. Because the world has been created by God, it is meaningful and it has value, despite all the tendencies toward breakdown and death attested to by daily experience. Faith in the goodness of creation is a way of affirming the certainty that the cosmos is more powerful than chaos, because God its Creator has dominion over the absurd and death. This meaning is expressed in a story, namely in Genesis. Although Genesis may look like a cosmogenesis, like insight into how God created the world, it is actually narrative material that gives concrete expression to this basic claim: each thing—from the stars, plants, animals, up to human beings—is charged with goodness and meaning because it bears God's trademark within it. That is why at the end of each day of creation the text repeats, like a refrain: "And God saw that everything was good."

When chapters 2 and 3 speak of the fall, the Yahwist author does not intend to narrate the past or show what happened. Hence, we do not have here a narrative of history but a prophetic and sapiential reflection on the drama of human existence. The author wants to critique the present situation and assert that it is contrary to the Creator's original design. Man and woman (Adam and Eve) have always been sinners, both now and long ago, but the purpose of the story is to overcome that situation and to join with God in building a paradise. Maintaining the present situation means going against the Creator's will. Let us look at this in some detail.[2] The author of the story begins by laying out the evils of the present human condition, continually asking: Why are we as we are now?

Gn 3:16: ambivalence of human love. Woman, you feel drawn to your husband but he will dominate you. Why?

Gn 3:19: ambivalence of motherhood. It is a blessing but women will give birth in pain. Why?

Gn 3:19: ambivalence of life itself. The human being is alive, comes from the dust, but will return to dust. Why?

Gn 3:17-19: ambivalence of the Earth. It is meant to produce good and delicious fruits and yet it produces thorns and thistles. Why?

Gn 3:17-19: ambivalence of work. It is part of being human and it is how people earn their living, but it demands effort and a great deal of sweat. Why?

Gn 3:15: ambivalence of animals. Their origin is the same as that of human beings and hence they are fellow creatures. Why the enmity to death between life and life, human being and animal, human and serpent? Why?

Gn 3:10: ambivalence of religion. The human being lives in God's presence but runs away and hides in shame. Why?

Confronting so many questions, the author goes on to defend one idea: it is not God who causes evil, but the human being. God desires the good of the human being. The earthly paradise is what God intends, and it serves as an image to contrast with present reality, an image of the time when all evil will be vanquished. The author is accordingly providing an answer to the whys:

Relationship between husband and wife: The two will be one flesh (Gn 2:23), each turned toward the other, both conversing with and aiding one another.

Life and death: Death will be eliminated, for God will make the tree of life give fruit. Anyone who eats from it will live forever (Gn 3:22).

Fertility of the Earth: The garden will produce all kinds of good and tasty fruits (Gn 2:9). The human being was not born in paradise, but was placed there by God (Gn 2:8-15).

Human labor: It is part of life for providing sustenance, but it will be easy and creative, like working in an apple grove and garden (Gn 2:15).

Relationship with animals: The human being gives them names, indicating a shared life in family (Gn 2:20).

Relationship with God: God walks in the garden, and the human being lives in close intimacy with God and has no fear of God's presence (Gn 3:8-10).

This is how the author imagines God's will for the future of human beings. The text is about the future, not the past. Paradise is a prophecy of the future projected back upon the past. As Mesters says,

> Paradise is like an architectural model of the world. It is the building plan to be followed by the contractor, that is, the human being, man and woman. It is a project that continually challenges the faith and courage of the human being. It is placed at the beginning of the bible because before doing anything, one must know what one wants, and must draw up a workable plan to be executed. The full achievement is foreshadowed in the description of paradise, prepared using images and symbols drawn from the situation of the people at that time, to serve as a guideline and stimulus for directing human activity.[3]

All people recognize themselves in this story—in their humanly fallen situation and likewise in their desire to improve. God has endorsed this desire. God has shown how by following God's law, walking in God's presence and becoming God's friend, human beings become reconnected to everything, and that jointly with the Creator who redeems them they rebuild the paradise for which they so yearn.

This biblical story contains no cosmology properly speaking, but rather a story that presents the transcendent meaning of the universe, the human being's place in it, an interpretation of the contradictory situation of human beings, and a hint of their future. But, as E. Durkheim showed at the conclusion of *The Elementary Forms of Religious Life,*[4] the primordial religious experience also elaborates a discourse on the world and hence a measure of cosmology, but in a precise sense; it shows humankind's connectedness with the Divinity, its origin and its ultimate destiny.

Another marvelous story is that of the Maya-Quiches of Guatemala, preserved in the 1544 manuscript *Popul Vuh* (discovered by the friar Francisco Ximenez in the early eighteenth century in Chichicastenango). The story's title is "The Creation of the World, Animals, Plants, and Humans." The story is very close to that related in the Bible.

> There is not yet one person, one animal, bird, fish, crab, tree, rock, hollow, canyon, meadow, forest. Only the sky alone is there; the face of the earth is not clear. Only the sea alone is pooled under all the sky; there is nothing whatever gathered together. It is at rest; not a single thing stirs. It is held back, kept at rest under the sky.
>
> Whatever there is that might be is simply not there: only the pooled water, only the calm sea, only it alone is pooled.
>
> Whatever might be is simply not there: only murmurs, ripples, in the dark, in the night.

God's creative action begins at once. For the Maya-Quiches, God was a trinity: "So there were three of them, as Heart of the sky." They created all by the word.

> "Let it be this way, think about it: this water should be removed, emptied out for the formation of the earth's own plate and platform, then comes the sowing, the dawning of the sky-earth. But let there be no high days and no bright praise for our work, our design, until the rise of the human work, the human design," they said.
>
> And then the earth arose because of them, it was simply their word that brought it forth. For the forming of the earth they said, "Earth." It arose suddenly, just like a cloud, like a mist, now forming, unfolding.[5]

Few stories that we possess exalt human beings as much as this one of the Maya-Quiches. Sky and Earth open to aid in their birth. In the theological conception of the Maya Quiches, human beings represent the glory and grandeur of the entire creation. This understanding instilled in Maya-Quiche men and women a sense of dignity and excellence that is revealed in their marvelous cities, pyramids, poetry, and theater.

Finally, I want to present a recent story based on the biblical models that incorporates materials representing our efforts to integrate and protect the Earth. Its author, Robert Muller, is called a world citizen and father of global education. He worked in the United Nations for forty years and rose to become the assistant to the secretary general. He was one of the main architects of the UN institutional system, and he is chancellor emeritus of the University of Peace, which was created by the UN in Costa Rica in 1980. Since then Muller has devoted himself to issues of peace and spirituality. The story is called "New Genesis."[6]

And God saw that all nations of the earth, black and white, poor and rich, from North and South, from East and West, and of all creeds were sending their emissaries to a tall glass house on the shores of the River of the Rising Sun, on the island of Manhattan, to study together, to think together and to care together for the world and all its people. And God said: That is good. And it was the first day of the New Age of the Earth.

And God saw that soldiers of peace were separating the combatants of quarreling nations, that differences were being resolved by negotiation and reason instead of arms and that the leaders of nations were seeing each other, talking to each other and joining their hearts, minds, souls and strength for the benefit of all humanity. And God said: That is good. And it was the second day of the Planet of Peace.

And God saw that humans were loving the entire creation, the stars and the sun, the day and the night, the air and the oceans, the earth and the waters, the fishes and the fowl, the flowers and the herbs, and all their human brethren and sisters. And God said: That is good. And it was the third day of the Planet of Happiness.

And God saw that humans were suppressing hunger, disease, ignorance and suffering all over the globe, providing each human person with a decent, conscious and happy life, and reducing the greed, the power and the wealth of the few. And He said: That is good. And it was the fourth day of the Planet of Justice.

And God saw that humans were living in harmony with their planet and in peace with one another, wisely managing their resources, avoiding waste, curbing excesses, replacing hatred with love, greed with contentment, arrogance with humility, division with cooperation and mistrust with understanding. And He said: That is good. And it was the fifth day of the Golden Planet.

And God saw that men were destroying their arms, bombs, missiles, warships and warplanes, dismantling their bases and disbanding their armies, keeping only policemen of peace to protect the good from the bad and the normal from the mad. And God said: That is good. And it was the sixth day of the Planet of Reason.

And God saw humans restore God and the human person as the alpha and omega, reducing institutions, beliefs, politics, governments, and all man-made entities to mere servants of God and the people. And he saw them adopt as their supreme law: "You shall love the Lord your God with all your heart, all your soul, all your mind and all your strength. You shall love your neighbor as yourself. There is no greater commandment than these."

And God said: That is good. And it was the seventh day of the Planet of God.

Any story must be convincing through its beauty, its evocative power, and its ability to draw on the truest and deepest human aspirations. Only thus can it meet its aim of shaping a supreme and fulfilling meaning for human existence. This story by Robert Muller certainly does so.

We are now going to take up our contemporary ecological story. The Earth sciences enable us to compose our story on the basis of empirical observation. The cosmic epic can be told through the various stages of evolution-complexification-interiorization that have given rise to the chain of beings from the original stars, galaxies, and Earth up to the human community in its present form. As has already been noted, we are moving from the meaning of the cosmos to the meaning of cosmogenesis, that is, of the genesis and evolutionary shaping of the cosmos. Ever at work in the cosmos is a cosmogenic principle that is the origin of all beings from the simplest to the most complex.[7]

We are going to situate our cosmology within the Western experience which is our own. In our Western culture ancient cosmology projected the world as a huge *pyramid.* Beings were lined up vertically, from the simplest to the most complex: stones, plants, animals, human beings, and angels (or devils), up to and culminating in God.

Classic cosmology, which grew out of modern physics and mathematics, created the image of the world as a machine, or more precisely, a very intricate *watch.* Everything is ruled by deterministic laws that work together and that show the marvelous harmony of the universe. It is God who set this highly ordered machine in motion. It functions with no need for God to be continually stepping in.

Our own age has proposed another image of the world, that of *play* or *dance* or *arena.* This vision results from the combination of the multiple forms of knowledge characterizing our contemporary vision. On the basis of quantum physics, biology combined with thermodynamics, transpersonal psychology, and the combined knowledge provided by the Earth sciences and ecology, the cosmic reality is coming to be seen as an extremely complex network of energies that become consolidated and are then called matter or that are made manifest as pure energy forming energy fields and morphic fields. All are inter(retro)related as though in a dance or in a game, giving rise to universal connectedness.

Each cosmology comes up against the question of the ultimate basis, the crucial reference point, that link that unifies and harmonizes everything. Thomas Aquinas would say, "*et hoc dicitur Deus,*"–"and we call that God." Indeed, religions use the term *God* or myriad others for that inexpressible reality in order to identify the essential question connecting everything.

In the cosmology of the pyramid-world, God is regarded as the supreme Being. In that of the world-as-watch, God is pictured as the great Architect, creator of the machine, and as the mainspring that makes the watch work. What is the emerging image of God in our cosmology of the world-as-game-and-dance? Our task in this present reflection is to attempt to build a representation of the Divinity that may be combined with our cosmology, and at the same time may be connected with the spiritual history of humankind and of our culture. This question will be developed in greater detail in the closing chapters of this book.

ECOLOGY: SOURCE OF COSMOGENESIS

Ecology, as understood in chapter 1, encompasses and organizes current bodies of knowledge, grounds a new centrality in human activity and thought, and encourages the formation of a new covenant between the human being and the surrounding social, earthly, and cosmic reality. That understanding has been the starting point for the building of a new cosmology as cosmogenesis. We shall present an introduction to this global vision, fully aware that it is fragmentary and preliminary. Rather than answering questions, the aim is to raise the universal question of connectedness and to bring up fresh perspectives that force us to think, and so to shed light on our responsibility for protecting our planet Earth.

Ecology, as paradigm, entails taking a basic stance, always thinking holistically; that is, continually seeing the whole, which does not derive from the sum of the parts but from the organic interdependence of all the elements. This step moves beyond the thinking of modernity, which is purely analytical, split up, and disconnected.

If ecology is not holistic, it is not really ecology. *Holism,* a term popularized by South African philosopher Jan Smuts starting in 1926, means to grasp the whole in the parts and the parts in the whole, and each whole within another, ever higher, whole. Holistic ecology involves a kind of activity and thought that includes and relates all beings among themselves and with their environment from a perspective encompassing what is infinitely small (elementary energies and particles), what is infinitely vast (cosmic space), what is infinitely complex (life), what is infinitely deep (the human heart), and what is infinitely mysterious (what existed before the big bang, the unlimited ocean of energy from which everything emanates— quantum vacuum, symbol of the creator God).

An ecology-based cosmology helps us overcome an impasse found in modern cosmology, which takes its inspiration from physics and mathematics. That cosmology does not take into consideration interiority, life, and the human phenomenon, except insofar as they have a physical and mathematical dimension. Ecology teaches us to see the unity of the cosmic process, from the big bang to the appearance of the bossa nova or the computer, and to recognize that nature is not outside human beings but very much within them. Ecology helps us to raise questions such as the following: How must the overall evolutionary process and the basic thrust of primordial energies at the moment of the big bang be in order to make possible the emergence of flowers, the rainbow, hummingbirds, Vivaldi's music, the prophetic power of Martin Luther King or Archbishop Helder Camara, of the liberating mystique of Bishop Desmond Tutu and Bishop Pedro Casaldáliga? How was the arrow of time from the beginning pointing toward human beings with their ability to interfere with the rhythm of Earth, even to the point of a biological disaster brought about by the onslaught of their industry?

As is evident, our cosmology from a standpoint of cosmogenesis seeks to connect all the elements, including life and human beings, and to build a sense of journey, hope, and future for all.

OUR PRIMORDIAL WOMB:
BILLIONS OF YEARS OF FRUITFUL CHAOS

How are we to detect the connectedness of all with all? How is the snail by the roadside connected to the farthest galaxy? We must first establish the physical foundations for such relationships.

In 1924 American astronomer Edwin Hubble (1824-1953) proved that the universe is expanding. A red shift is found in the spectrum of the most distant galaxies, because light loses energy over a distance; the larger waves become predominant, and tend toward the red, thereby indicating that one body is moving away from another. Thus the most distant galaxies are moving away at a speed approaching that of light.

To better take account of this fact, in 1927 Belgian astronomer and priest Georges Lemaître (1894-1966) proposed the big-bang theory, which fascinated Albert Einstein when he heard of it during a conference at the Mount Wilson Observatory in California. It was complemented in 1980 by the theory of the inflationary universe of American Alan Guth, who argued that the expansion began at one moment out of an extremely tiny space, and continues to expand up to the present.

The big-bang theory was reinforced when background cosmic radiation was detected in 1965 by astrophysicists Arno Penzias and Robert Wilson (and further confirmed in 1992 by George Smoot). Cosmic background radiation comes uniformly from all parts of the universe, as a residual echo of the hypothetical primordial explosion or expansion that took place fifteen billion years ago. All the elements found in the most varied beings in the universe were there together at that unimaginably incandescent point of energy. As far apart as beings may be from one another, the force of gravity keeps them related and interconnected. Isaac Newton convinced the intellectual community that such gravitational interaction exists.

What is to be the fate of the universe? Unlimited expansion until it is utterly thinned out? Or, after expanding, will it reverse direction and become concentrated upon itself until it goes back to an initial point of matter-energy at an inconceivable degree of density? Opinions differ on this question, because there has not been enough research into the total mass of the universe and the interplay between the expansionary energy and the pull of gravity. There are three positions, along the following lines:

• If gravity and expansion energy are equal in force, they are in equilibrium, and then one would speak of the "critical value" or "critical density" of the universe. At some point the forces would come to a complete standoff and there would be complete stability and immutability.

• If the expansion energy should be stronger than gravity, expansion would continue indefinitely, and there would be no return.

• If gravity were to prevail over expansionary energy, a moment would come when expansion would come to a halt and a process of reconcentration would begin. The universe would sink in upon itself and be reduced to an infinitesimal point with an extremely intense energy charge. The big bang would be followed by a corresponding "big crunch."

At the current state of knowledge, matter is said to be close to the "critical value," but there is not enough information to decide which of the three possibilities is likely. In any case, from its very first moment the universe has been dynamic; its natural state is evolution rather than stability, change rather than immutability. Such is probably the prevailing logic both with regard to expansion and to collapsing upon itself. The universe displays a self-organizing capability; instead of thermal death we would seem to have more life than death, greater organization than disorder, and structures and process emerging and continually unfolding like the bud on a flower. Based on data that enjoy a broad consensus among scientists, contemporary cosmologists describe the origin of the expanding universe as follows.

In the beginning, at the zero-moment (Planck's limit) there was an extremely tiny sphere 10^{-33} centimeters in diameter (trillions and trillions of times smaller than the head of a pin). It was at an extremely high temperature, 10^{32} degrees centigrade, which means inconceivable energy density. At this phase the four basic interactions of the universe (gravity, electromagnetic force, and the strong and weak nuclear forces) made up a single undifferentiated cosmic force.

The elementary particles, the predecessors of those that are today the smallest of the small (the six kinds of quarks, beginning with the smallest of them, the top quark) made up a brew virtually containing the galaxies, stars, microbes, trees, animals, humans, and this pen with which I am writing. Using extremely intricate calculations, Steven Weinberg[8] and Stephen Hawking[9] attempt to calculate the time sequences in billionths of a second.

Immediately after the creation (astrophysicists use the term, regardless of their faith) at the 10^{-43} second (it has been possible to go back to that point, which is Planck's limit-time), the first great singularity took place. The primordial sphere underwent first an expansion or inflation, which extended for a very brief time to the 10^{-32} second. Then came the big explosion or big bang.

The initial "mathematical" point grew to the size of an atomic nucleus whose diameter was 10^{-13} centimeters. Expansion continued until it reached the size of an apple 10 centimeters in diameter. At this moment, the 10^{-32} second, there existed only the X particle, a pure energy field, before it crystallized into matter.

At the next instant, 10^{-31}, the X particle gave rise to the primordial particles of matter, the top quark and the other kinds of quarks, electrons, positrons, neutrinos, and photons and their antiparticles. In the following billionths of a second these elementary particles interacted and caused an expansion to the size of a large ball. Densities diversified, supplying the bases for the various kinds of heavenly and earthly bodies that were to follow.

Between the 10^{-11} and 10^{-5} second most of the antiparticles (antimatter) disappeared into light. After this fantastic and mysterious annihilation, there remained only a billionth of the initial mass of the elementary particles with which the whole universe (including us) was to be formed. The six kinds of quarks (the basic building blocks out of which everything that exists is made; they always exist in threes) stabilized and came together forming the atomic nuclei (neutrons and protons). Once all the particles were stabilized, permanent interconnections got underway. Otherwise, the universe would have been impossible.

Where previously everything was entirely undetermined, there now emerged symmetries and structures in particle interactions, thereby giving rise to the four original interconnections: gravity, the electromagnetic force, and the strong and weak nuclear forces. These inter(retro)connecting energies, which science has not yet been able to explain, should probably be understood as modes of primordial action through which the universe itself acts, interacts with its elements, and is self-regulating. In short, this is the cosmogenic principle, the genesis of the cosmos by means of these ongoing interconnections, which are charged with direction and rationality.

The universe continued to expand and to cool. Two hundred seconds after the primordial explosion the elementary particles in interaction gave rise to hydrogen and helium, the simplest elements of creation and the most abundant in the universe. Three minutes after the great explosion, huge clouds of hydrogen gas were formed, shot through with extremely powerful radiations. They remained incandescent and gradually cooled down, presumably for two or three billion years.

Ten or twelve billion years ago these clouds slowly condensed and heated up again, forming the first gigantic stars. Inside them occurred inconceivable nuclear reactions that created ever heavier atomic elements, which are absolutely necessary for the makeup of the universe as we have it. After millions of years these reactions culminated in a huge explosion (the star became a supernova), and the heavy elements shot out into interstellar space. These materials gave rise to second generation stars, such as our sun, which came from the huge star that some call Tiamat (the Great Mother who is the source of all, according to Assyrian-Babylonian mythology). Then the planets took shape, with all the atomic elements found through the cosmos, the stars and their satellites, the atoms with their different atomic weights out of which all the substances in the universe are composed.

As portions of the universe, we are all brothers and sisters: elementary particles, quarks, stones, snails, animals, humans, stars, galaxies. Once we were all together in the form of energy and the original particles, in the primordial sphere, then we were in the giant red stars, then in our Milky Way, in the Sun, and on Earth. We are all made of the same elements. As living beings we have the same genetic code as other living beings: amoebas, dinosaurs, sharks, monkeys, Australopithecus, and *Homo sapiens (demens)* today. A core of brotherliness and sisterliness objectively ties us together, a link St. Francis intuited in a mystical way in the thirteenth century. We make up a great cosmic community. We have a common origin and certainly a single common destiny.

OUR COSMIC HOMELAND:
THE MILKY WAY, OUR GALAXY

The primordial matter expelled by the primordial explosion and from the giant stars condensed into galaxies. They constitute huge clusters, each containing billions of stars. At a limit distance of 3×10^{33} km we can identify 10^8 galaxies and 10^4 quasars (*quasi-stars*, starlike objects rushing away from us at astonishing speeds). Our spiral-shaped galaxy, the Milky Way, has existed for ten or twelve billion years. It is 100,000 light years across (one light year = 9.46 trillion kilometers or 5.88 trillion miles) and 10,000 light years thick, and is made up of around two hundred billion stars. The Milky Way takes 200 million years to rotate. The closest galaxies are the two Clouds of Magellan, 300,000 light years from Earth, and the great spiral of Andromeda, 1,700,000 light years away. The most distant galaxy detected thus far is fourteen billion light years away.

Galaxies do not sail through the universe by themselves but form clusters of galaxies. Our local group includes around a hundred Milky Way-like systems. Other clusters contain thousands of galaxies. It is assumed that these clusters form parts of even larger clusters.

We on Earth revolve around the sun, and the sun revolves around the center of the Milky Way, while the Milky Way moves at 373 miles a second toward the constellation Serpentarius. Where is it going? We do not yet know.

American and Russian theoreticians, working independently, have postulated an "inflationary universe." According to this hypothesis our universe is like a huge ball containing all the galaxies with millions and millions of stars. But there could be other similar balls, likewise constituting other universes, that would be inaccessible to us in principle. Might there be communication between them? Such questions are entirely open but not irrelevant for a religious and theological understanding of creation and of the creator God.

The Milky Way may be regarded as our cosmic homeland within the galactic continent.

OUR COSMIC CITY: THE SOLAR SYSTEM

There is a medium-sized star (863,000 miles in diameter—as compared to the Earth's diameter of a mere 8000 miles) located 27,000 light years from the center of our galaxy inside one arm of the spiral. This star is our sun. Five billion years ago a disk-shaped cloud was spinning on an arm of Orion in the Milky Way. It condensed and formed a huge star called

Tiamat, which around 4.6 billion years ago exploded and became a super-nova. Around 4.5 billion years ago our sun was formed out of its materials.

Studies of long-term radioactive elements emitted by the sun, such as rubidium 87 which becomes strontium 76, have shown that the planets took shape about 4.45 billion years ago. The sun by itself holds 99.9% of the matter in the solar system. The sun is a ball of gas at 150 million degrees centigrade, within which thermonuclear fusion reactions (like our hydrogen bombs) are taking place, changing hydrogen into helium, a gas that represents a stable state of matter incapable of being recombined with other atoms.

Over the course of billions of years almost all the hydrogen will be turned into helium, forming an ever more dense crust. Nuclear reactions will decompose elements heavier than helium. The sun's volume and temperature will rise considerably and it will shine as never before. Mercury, Venus, and Earth will be annihilated. Billions of years later the sun's volume will become hundreds of times smaller. It will grow colder until it becomes a white dwarf. Some millions of years later it will become a black dwarf, cold like the surrounding interstellar space.[10]

This unpleasant ultimate fate notwithstanding, the solar system is for now our cosmic city. From its heat and light comes the vast multiplicity of beings, forms of life, and species. Out of it come our consciousness, our joy in living as well as our sadness, our insatiable impulse toward the infinite in all its manifestations, in the great, the small, the complex, and the deep.

OUR HOUSE: THE GREAT MOTHER, EARTH

Earth is a satellite of the sun that emerged 4.45 billion years ago; it and the moon make up a double planet. It is 93 million miles from the sun. Light from the sun, traveling 186,000 miles a second, reaches us in eight minutes. Earth's radius is 4,000 miles and its circumference is 24,800 miles. It is continually fed by the marvelous solar energy that arrives in the form of electromagnetic radiations, 1.95 calories per square centimeter per minute, or 1,360 watts per square meter. That is enough energy to light thirteen 100-watt bulbs every 1.2 square yards.

What does Earth have that other planets do not? It has some specific features that allow for a balance of gravitational and electromagnetic forces, in addition to a distance from the sun that is suitable for maintaining an optimal temperature for the emergence of complex molecules, and hence of life. For some hundreds of millions of years it has been struck by meteors and planetoids in enormous collisions.

For a billion years, under the sun's heat, the only thing on Earth is a huge sea of melting lava. Vapors and gasses break away from it forming huge clouds. They slowly become thicker and give rise to the first Earth atmosphere made up of carbon, ammonium, carbon monoxide, nitrogen, and hydrogen gasses. After millions of years it begins to cool down. Lava hardens and the first land appears. The atmospheric clouds condense, and the first torrential rains made up of many liquids pour down. Some portions remain on the land and others evaporate to nourish the atmosphere and fall once more to Earth. The rains pour down continually for ages and ages. They produce oceans, vast internal lakes, rivers, and springs. Gigantic electric storms with enormous lightning bolts sweep across the skies and strike the whole Earth for millions of years. Chemical compounds take shape, thereby allowing cosmogenesis to advance.

After four billion years, in the oceans, under tremendous lightning storms of cosmic elements from Tiamat, and from the sun in interaction with Earth chemistry taking shape over the ages, Earth takes the complexity of inanimate forms to an extreme. A barrier never before crossed is now breached: around twenty amino acids take shape. These are highly organized atoms, the basic building blocks of life. Suddenly, possibly in a huge lightning bolt striking the sea, the first living cell emerges. The newborn creature is called Aries (first sign of the zodiac, March 21-April 19: a mythological ram who saved children ordered to be sacrificed). In a qualitative leap in our space-time curve, in a corner of our galaxy, by a minor sun, on a tiny planet, the Earth, there emerges the unique cosmic novelty: life. Aries is the ancestor of all the living things with which we are familiar.

Bacteria go on to explode (they inhabit each living organism and there are billions of species of them; just a spoonful contains about fifty billion of them) and microbes and then the entire exuberant biodiversity of plants, animals, and human beings. Earth will still need millions of years to settle down, to assure conditions for life to continue despite all the cosmic attacks and extinctions to which it may be subjected. If it has its identity firmly established, it will stand and will carry the cosmogenic principle forward.

Within the sphere of Earth we can observe five subspheres:

The *lithosphere* (rock), which is made up of magma, molten rock at 1,250 degrees centigrade in the Earth's core, and of the rocky crust of Earth.

The *hydrosphere* (water), which covers three-fourths of the Earth's surface, 97% of which is oceans and seas.

The *atmosphere* (air), which surrounds the planet to a height of 620 miles (exosphere) and is made up of hydrogen, oxygen, carbon, nitrogen, and so forth, in increasingly thin layers. They function like an umbrella protecting Earth from the rain of cosmic particles (an energy of 10^{20} electron-volts) and filter out solar radiations harmful to the life system (the ozone filtering ultraviolet and carbon gas filtering infrared).

The *biosphere* (life), which consists of all those regions that make life possible, extending from under an inch within the lithosphere and 26,000 feet down into the hydrosphere up to 13,000 feet up into the atmosphere. There are millions of different living species (many still unknown) in hundreds of climates and biological niches (places suited to life) that need water, oxygen, and energy to produce and reproduce the life system.

The *noosphere*, which many are claiming is a new subsphere, the sphere of the spirit. The complexity of human brains, their growing number, the network of relationships being established between persons, continents, and cultures through all the means of communication, raise the possibility that we are laying the foundations for the emergence of a common consciousness around the Earth, which would function as the Earth's brain.

As we considered in greater detail in chapter 1, a number of scientists involved in the Earth sciences, especially those coming from biology and astronautics, argue that the Earth makes up a single system, a living superorganism, which they call Gaia. All the living and nonliving elements are interconnected and make up an organic whole in dynamic equilibrium: the great living being, Earth.[11] It is indeed, as the indigenous peoples and the mystics have always called it, the great and good Mother, Nurse, and Pacha Mama.

If we think about it, the quantitative side of the universe fills us with fear. The distances are inconceivable. Some people have tried to make a somewhat less unsettling representation by changing the measurements. For example, we can make a million light years one millimeter (four-hundredths of an inch!). The entire universe then looks small to us, an area 22 by 22 by 22 yards. At this scale our Milky Way would be almost invisible, about the size of a fine grain of sand. However, it must be said that this Milky Way, this grain of sand, contains 100 billion suns, one of which—a medium-sized one—is our sun, a sun out in the suburbs, and the Earth spinning around it, which is utterly invisible. There would be no way to represent individual persons. With such mathematics we can represent the macrocosmos, but we completely lose sight of our own perception of the cosmos we have around us, let alone our bodies, oceans, and forests, not to speak of the microscopic world.

Likewise, if we were to take time instead of space, we can reduce things in a way that would make the reality of our universe easier to perceive. A million years would equal one second. The universe would then be 5.5 hours old. The history of Earth would be a bit more than an hour, the history of humankind a few seconds, and our individual stories would be so insignificant that they could not be measured. Nevertheless, no matter how insignificant we might be, here we are to think and to say all this about ourselves and about the entire universe, in keeping with the anthropic principle mentioned earlier.

If there is an infinitely tiny and an infinitely vast, there is also the infinitely complex. We stand at the brink of the phenomenon of life.

LIFE: SELF-ORGANIZING MATTER

The fact that we have a common origin does not mean that we are all alike. As the expansionary process moves forward, the matter and energy in the universe tend to become ever more complex. In other words, we are within systems that are open, and to the extent that they become organized, ever higher levels of complexity can be reached. The upshot is that each system is set within a movement of interactivity, in a dance in which energy and matter are exchanged in an ongoing dialogue with their milieu, from which they receive, store, and exchange information. The systems are not fixed once and for all but fluctuating.

Biologists and biochemists like Ilya Prigogine claim that there is a continuity between nonliving and living things. We do not need to invoke a transcendent external principle to explain the emergence of life, as the religions and classic cosmology generally do. It suffices that the principle of the complexification and organization of all, and hence also of life, namely the cosmogenic principle, is present in the infinitesimally small primordial sphere—which, however, is created by a supreme intelligence, an infinite love, and an eternal passion.

Indeed, this principle was already at work at the very beginning, after the great explosion or the inflationary phase. From the outset everything interacts and establishes a creative dialogue with everything around it. Starting from the initial matter and energy, the universe is created and differentiated as it advances. As we have already noted a number of times, the cosmogenic principle and *autopoiesis* (self-organization) are continually at work within the universe, driving evolution and the emergence of all beings.

Life thus represents the realization of a possibility present in the original matter and energy; that marvelous event has actually come to pass on a tiny planet of the solar system, our still fresh Earth.

We noted above the process by which the first living cell, Aries, emerged out of the twenty amino acids in the sea. They become organized in stable structures and give rise to proteins, glycines, lipids, and nucleic acids, the main components of living organisms.

The code of the nucleic acid gives rise to the DNA molecule, which reproduces copies of itself, and RNA, which also reproduces itself. RNA's specific function, however, is to transmit the genetic information that is absolutely necessary for making proteins, which are required for nourishing life. These chemical systems become stabilized and cling together, forming larger molecules in water. From them arise colloids, more or less fluid jelly-like substances, which absorb molecules from their surroundings. They gather more energy internally and form a membrane by which they are protected from the environment and through which they select materials necessary for maintaining their equilibrium.

The origin of the explosion of life remains ever mysterious. It involves both chance and necessity,[12] and the logic of complexification of evolution, governed by the cosmogenic principle.

There is a complex continuum that is physical and chemical in nature, but this continuum is broken by leaps, such as the one mentioned above, the separation between the internal and external milieu, energy exchanges, and primarily the leap from a chemical organization to a self-organization, self-repair, and self-reproduction in dialogue with the environment.[13]

Everything seems to support the idea that life is the result of a highly complex evolutionary process that created enormous probabilities, deriving from cumulative chance events favorable to this unique explosion. One of the discoverers of the DNA/RNA chain, Dr. Crick, proposes the hypothesis that the source of life might be extraterrestrial. Spectroscopic astronomy has identified more than sixty different kinds of gas molecules in interstellar space, especially on the flattened disks of dust surrounding young stars. These molecules range from the simplest, such as hydrogen and carbon monoxide, to complex molecules such as ethanol and long acetylene chains. Among all the molecules identified can be found everything believed to be essential for setting in motion the process of biological synthesis.[14] Meteorites have been shown to have amino acids, which are the eventual bearers of the proto-bacteria of life. There were probably numerous beginnings of life that were frustrated before one finally perdured.

It is assumed that all the diverse forms of life grew out of a single living thing, Aries, four billion years ago. It reproduced, was changed, and spread in all directions, adapting to the most varied ecosystems in water, on land, in the air. Around 600 million years ago, there began to take place a startling diversification of the kinds of life, plants, invertebrates, and vertebrates, reptiles and mammals.[15] Mammals signal the rise of a new quality of life, emotional sensitivity in the sexual bond and in the mother-child bond, which leaves an indelible mark on the psychic structure of creatures with a central nervous system. Among mammals, around seventy million years ago, the primates become prominent, and then around thirty-five million years ago, there appeared the first higher primates, our genealogical grandparents, followed seventeen million years ago by our predecessors, the hominids, until finally around eight to ten million years ago the human being, Australopithecus, emerged in Africa.

Man and woman are the most recent shoot on the tree of life, the most complex expression of the biosphere, which is in turn an expression of the hydrosphere, and the geosphere, and ultimately of the history of Earth and the history of the universe. We do not live upon the Earth; we are sons and daughters of Earth but also members of a vast cosmos. The billions of particles that go into our identity emerged fifteen billion years ago; others have wandered through the universe for millions of years, coming from the most distant stars. The carbon atoms that are necessary for life were formed in the churning ovens of suns prior to our own sun. *Homo sapiens (demens)* whose immediate heirs we are, finally emerged fifty thousand years ago bearing the billions of years of history of the entire universe in the fabric of their body and in the incisions in their soul.

The characteristics of life are its *self-organization*: the parts are within an organic whole and the functions are differentiated and complementary; *autonomy*: each being exists in itself, but at the same time it exists from others and for others, and hence it is not independent, because it is always interacting with its milieu; *adaptability* to the milieu: that is how the life-system assures its fragile equilibrium, survives, and expands; *reproduction*: this is life's most original quality, for it transmits itself identically within a single species; and finally *self-transcendence*, always open to new levels of evolution and new forms of expression.

Ilya Prigogine describes living beings as "dissipative structures." As we have previously explained, he uses this expression to describe their characteristic drive. They are open systems, with an equilibrium that must be continually reachieved through self-organization and an ever-higher level of internal organization. Living beings consume energy from the milieu and thereby generate entropy, but through their internal order and self-regulation they also in some fashion elude entropy (second law of thermo-dynamics). They dissipate the forces leading to increasing disorder (hence the expression "dissipative structures") toward utter chaos. Living beings tend toward being ever more well ordered and creative, and hence they are counter-entropic. Disorder itself is an index of a new order that will emerge. Chaos is generative.[16]

With life, matter is seen to be no longer inert. Each particle that goes into the formation of life has had a history (hence the importance of time along with the four fundamental energies and the other universal cosmic constants), which is the result of interactions with other particles and of irreversible changes. Hence matter possesses interiority and life.

Contrary to what Jacques Monod says, life is not *purely* and solely the result of chance.[17] Biochemists and molecular biologists (using computers and random numbers) have demonstrated that it is mathematically impossible for life to be the product of pure and simple chance. In order for the amino acids and the two thousand underlying enzymes to come together and to establish an orderly chain and form a living cell, more time would be needed than the age of the universe—indeed trillions and trillions of years. The possibilities are 10^{1000} to one. If chance is significant, it is in the sense of the indeterminacy principle of quantum physics introduced by Werner Heisenberg.

Hence, life is among the possibilities of the primordial energy and matter. As the philosopher Jean Guitton aptly put it, "What we call chance is simply our inability to understand a higher level of order" as manifested by the phenomenon of life.[18]

CONSCIOUSNESS IS COSMIC AND PERSONAL

Consciousness is the highest form of life. Like the universe itself, life and every being have their own genealogy. The same is true of consciousness. It also has its place in the universe and is an expression of the relationships between primordial matter and energy at a most intense degree of complexity and relatedness. In this sense, as we will see, it shares the ancestry of the cosmos.

Thinkers from the new physics, such as David Bohn, H. Frölich, J. Crook, I. N. Marshall, and D. Zohar, who combine various kinds of knowledge derived from modern cosmology and from philosophical traditions, argue that consciousness is a quantum phenomenon. Hence, we conscious human beings are an integral part of the universe and not some peculiar being originating from somewhere other than the cosmic "we." Today it is not difficult for us to admit the evolution of our physical being and its cosmic origin. We should just as readily identify the origin of our mental being, including its origins in the elementary particles. Let us attempt a brief explanation of such an understanding.

Quantum physics (mechanics) is the scientific theory worked out in the early years of this century that goes beyond the classic vision of the atom (as the ultimate indivisible particle of matter) to analyze the elementary particles that make up the atom, the nucleus (composed of protons and neutrons, which are in turn made up of quarks and around one hundred subparticles; the name for all the particles taken together is hadrons) and the electrons dancing around the nucleus.

Actually quantum theory moved beyond particles to energy waves, for they are made up of intensified energy, called *quantum* energy (*quanta* = wave packages). What exists is an energy field (relativistic quantum theory of fields). It represents a kind of picture resulting from the continual interactions of particles. They never exist in themselves but always as related to one another. The field is precisely the result of this ongoing web of relationships.

When intending to highlight the energy dimension (wave) of the field, one speaks of *bosons*. When it is the matter dimension (particle) of the field that is being emphasized, one speaks of *fermions.* Bosons refer to the relationship and fermions to the thing related. Everything is made up of bosons and fermions–human beings included. The fermions within us are our individual and bodily dimension, while bosons are our relationships and spiritual dimension.

What is new about this relativistic quantum theory is that it claims that every phenomenon is a quantum reality. Reality always appears under a twofold aspect; it is simultaneously wave and particle. Particle and wave come from something even more basic that cannot be detected by any instrument but is deduced from the very dynamic of the field, which continually points to something more fundamental than itself. It is called, quite inadequately, *quantum vacuum.* It is not empty, as the word *vacuum* suggests. As we shall see, it represents the field of fields, the abyss of energy, the ocean of forces in which everything happens and from which everything emerges. What emerges at one point seems to be an energy wave, and at another a material particle, and again as wave and particle simultaneously and in a complementary fashion. Everything comes from the quantum vacuum and everything returns to it.

Einstein's relativity theory showed that mass and energy are convertible. Energy can become matter and matter can become energy. Or rather, matter is concentrated stable energy that can be turned back into energy. Thus, for example, the conversion of a mere gram of matter into energy releases enough heat to evaporate 34 billion grams of water (or 34 million liters of water).

How does consciousness emerge when reality is thus understood to be entirely composed of particles and waves? We must first define how we understand consciousness. In quantum thinking, it is taken in the broadest and most all-encompassing possible sense. It represents what is called a *relational holism.* That is, the essence of consciousness is an ongoing and indivisible totality or a coherent unity resulting from the entirety of relationships (hence it is called holism = unity in diversity and diversity in unity) that a point establishes with everything around it, coming from the past and pointing toward the future. Consciousness is essentially relationship on all sides and in all directions (as the philosophical traditions of a number of cultures have tended to claim, particularly the Western tradition, as it sought to understand the meaning of *person* as "being of relationships").

Now, as we have already seen, we find this relationship structure at the very first moment of the primordial expansion/explosion. When two protons at that very initial state relate, they are superimposed, share the same field, and make up a tiny unit. Hence they appear as bosons (relationship particles).

The evolutionary expansion of matter-energy consists of exponentially increasing the relationships and the creation of ever more complex units.

Hence that which constitutes the basic structure of consciousness—relationship and creation of unity—is already present at the origins of the universe.

It has been observed that when this unity reaches a certain highly complex level, as the result of greater superimposition of waves (bosons), living material emerges. In quantum physics this phenomenon of living unity is called the *Bose-Einstein condensation.* When living matter in turn attains even much greater complexity with the appearance of the brain, at a certain moment it happens that the material components of the nerve network (neurons) begin to vibrate in unison; they do not simply act as a whole but they actually become a whole. It is as though all the instruments in the orchestra were to play a single note in unison.

In other words, the bosons in relationship become totally superimposed and form an ongoing field of unity. This relational holistic unity is in contact with its milieu, and it receives all kinds of information and organizes it into its basic unity. This is the emergence of human consciousness. In technical quantum physics terms, it means that there has emerged a Frölich-type Bose-Einstein condensation (Frölich is the British scientist who identified these vibrations in the neurons over twenty years ago).

Consciousness is, by analogy, like a basic black box. Through interaction with the environment, consciousness gathers information and records it in this black box. It works on it, and so enriches its own basic unity. As Prigogine has shown, all living systems are open, taking unstructured matter from their milieu and establishing dialogue and activity with it. By the self-organizing capability that is proper to all living beings, they create a higher new order. Within this order, matter realizes potentialities that are inherent in it and that are only attained in living beings and conscious beings (Frölich-type Prigogine systems).

The difference between living and nonliving beings lies in the intensity of their relationships. In "nonliving" beings, the bosons are not so clustered and fermions (things in themselves, although always within a web of relationships) prevail. In living things, the bosons become more intense, forming Bose-Einstein condensations up to the maximum concentration of the Frölich type, producing an indivisible, harmonic unity: human consciousness. The difference between one and the other is not a difference of principle but of degree. The principle of relationship and of the capability to establish unities is inherent in creation. It is at work from the beginning.

Consciousness thus has a long ancestry, and it is part of the cosmos itself. In its most rudimentary form, it began in the primordial unity of the first two elementary particles that interacted and related to one another. It gradually rose in proportion to the growth of the range of relationships, in a dynamic dialogue with the milieu (with the fermions), until it came to the ultimate complexity that was transformed into reflex consciousness. From that moment the field of consciousness (bosons) and the field of matter (fermions) are in an ongoing dialogue, bringing about ever richer and more open and more rapid levels of organization in all fields of culture, society, religions, and all of humankind.

Consciousness is driving the universe toward accelerating the pace of evolution, toward being more highly organized and more directed, even while the direction could reverse, given the *demens* side of the human being. The thrust is upward, however, not downward. When consciousness becomes an act of communion with the whole and with every expression of being, the universe comes to itself and is most fully realized. The ecological covenant of integration and reconciliation is sealed.

Consciousness is thus not a quality of matter but a relationship between elementary particles (in their wave aspect) so complex and of such an intensity that they are all superimposed and create a single and stable whole.

We are accordingly made of the same matter and are the result of the same cosmogenic drive that permeates the entire universe. Consciousness is a special type of relationship, a relationship that constitutes all that is extra in the cosmos. Through our consciousness human beings fully mesh with the overall scheme of things. We are not outside the ascending universe but inside it, part and parcel of it, and accordingly we are able to know ourselves and others, to feel them, and to love them.

HUMAN BEINGS: CO-CREATORS OF THE COSMOS

The fundamental discovery of the new physics subsequent to the modern physics deriving from Newton and Galileo lies in the demonstration that everything can be matter and energy, that energy and matter are convertible (Einstein). In other words, matter can be specified more and more: from the physical beings that we can feel we go on to the atom, to elementary particles, to quarks, until we reach the energy field, which means an interplay of particles and energies, and finally to the quantum vacuum, which is the ultimate womb from which everything comes and to which everything goes. By its very nature it is indescribable; before it all language falls silent. Language comes only afterward—it cannot speak of what comes before. It is not theologians who are using such language but contemporary scientists, astrophysicists, and cosmologists.

Another discovery of the new physics is that it has established that the entire subatomic and elementary reality from which our universe comes (as we do ourselves) always takes the form of energy wave and particle matter (the quantum theory of Niels Bohr and Max Planck). Each elementary entity can be described either as solid particles (billionths of millimeters in size down to immeasurable particles that can be grasped only by their effects) or as waves like those in the ocean (they appear in packets called *quanta* of energy). However, neither description is complete unless we take *both* perspectives into account together. There is a basic duality in reality, but this duality does not establish a dualism because the two poles of the duality are complementary. Hence matter manifests itself through this particle-wave duality; it is this duality.

Light, for example, can be described either as material particle (photons) or as energy, but we only grasp the phenomenon of light well if we consider both possibilities together, that is, wave/particle. Analogously, human beings are body and spirit, but we understand humans comprehensively only if we take body and spirit to be reciprocal and complementary realities. Both together constitute the single unique human being.

Pursuing their inquiry further, atomic physicists have found that the elementary entities are neither entirely wave nor entirely particle but a mixture of both. The particle has a wave aspect, and the wave has a particle aspect. Hence wave and particle are always together and complement one another. At one point the particle aspect is more prominent and so one speaks of particle; at another, the wave dimension predominates, and so one speaks of a wave.

Although they are absolutely necessary for providing us with a complete picture of reality, waves and particles cannot be examined at the same time. Either the exact position of the material particle is measured and one loses the velocity of the wave, or the wave is measured and the position of the particle is lost. In 1927 Werner Heisenberg formulated what is called the uncertainty principle.

Things are that way not because we lack more accurate instruments for making an examination but because reality itself is undetermined and is probabilistic in nature. Anything can happen one way, or another, or yet another. Predictions can be made only on the basis of what is most probable given certain overall conditions in reality.

Here the question arises: if that is how things are, everything based on uncertainty, who determined that we should cease to be probable and should come to really exist, we mountains, sea, trees, human persons? How is it that anything can exist?

Here is where the role of consciousness becomes crucial. It can be the bridge between the world of elementary particles and our everyday world, as Danah Zohar has sought to show in *The Quantum Self*.[19] Consciousness, as we have indicated above, becomes the co-creator of the universe. The more consciousness there is, the more creation there is, the more evolution accelerates, and the higher order develops. That has been the case since the great initial explosive expansion.

Heisenberg has convincingly shown that the observer enters into the determination of the object observed. If I want to capture particles and I set up a device for detecting particles, I capture reality as particle. If, on the other hand, I want to register waves and I set up the device for waves, I actually observe waves. In other words, the subatomic world is defined only when we apply a measuring instrument to it. Before that it remains uncertain and probable; it can be wave and it can be particle.

When we are not observing it, elementary reality remains permanently open to all probabilities and options. The world takes on a specific shape only at the last moment, at the instant when it is observed. Prior to that it is not real. Our reality is constituted only on the basis of dialogue with the observer.

Why is that so? Because we make up an interconnected whole. There is no being apart from the other. The observer is united to the object observed even if it is not aware of that fact—and the object observed is plainly connected to the observer. They interact, establish a creative dialogue-activity, connectedness emerges, and thereby all of reality breaks forth.

Einstein initially made fun of this view, saying, "God does not play dice." Someone else shot back, "Einstein should stop giving God advice. Actually, God and consciousness are playing dice, and the dice are sure to come up the ways that are most probable at each moment." Or, "God is playing dice there where we can't see."[20]

When we speak of an observer, we are not thinking only of a human being observing and investigating reality. The idea is epistemological; that is, it is a tool for understanding that enables us to comprehend and clarify the interdependence of cosmic phenomena. Observer means any entity that dialogues and interacts vis-à-vis another. Thus a proton interacts with another proton, they mutually exchange energies, and together they create a system of relationships that surrounds them. One does not stand without the other. Both hold information from this encounter. As far apart as they may be, whether in the subatomic world or in the macrocosmos, they make up a single system. The information is carried forward in time (the irreversibility of the time-encounter analyzed in detail by Ilya Prigogine) and goes into other encounters and qualifies those realities with these cumulative experiences. Thus a dialogue between entities—a connectedness, and a covenant of exchanges—is always taking place. Similarly, a bacterium questions the world and decodes the chemical signs by which it finds direction. Both it and the protons are observers in this epistemological sense.

We said that when the first encounter between two or more elementary entities takes place, an initial unity is already beginning to be formed that we called the lowest degree of consciousness. The richer the encounter, the more complex the reality and the more transparent the degree of consciousness. All these processes of relationship signify the "observer," the "consciousness" in the material world, the animal and vegetable worlds, and the human world. Rocks, plants, and animals, insofar as they are within the network of interactions, are also co-creators of the universe.

At bottom what exists primarily is an undetermined number of prob-abilities of beings–quantum physicists call these *wave packets*–each with its own speed, its position, and its trajectory. At the moment when it is observed, there is a *wave function collapse*; in other words, only one par-ticle, the one observed, is materialized and comes into existence. All other possibilities go into collapse and disappear, returning to the quan-tum vacuum.

Our earthly reality, then, has undergone observation (encounter, dia-logue, interaction). Who has observed it? With the data that we have gathered above we can answer that the one observing has been the consciousness existing from the first moment of creation and by the kind of consciousness that has constituted human consciousness. As the great physicist John Wheeler saw very clearly, the universe is participatory; it is a most intricate web of relationships, enveloping everything, and human beings in particular.

There remains one final question: has the universe as a whole itself not been observed? There was a universal wave–and by the action of the out-side observer it entered into wave collapse, likewise universal. The result was the emergence of this specific universe that we have, of which we are a part, resulting from the universal collapse of the universal wave.

But, in the end, who is this absolute outside observer who made the universal wave collapse thereby giving rise to the vast universe? In chap-ter 7 we are going to attempt a stammering response. Its name must be uttered with absolute respect, for It is ineffable and hence it does not fit in any word. Its nameless name is God-Mystery.

However, it is important to first grasp the uniqueness of each personal and conscious individual, a most unique wave collapse.

THE UNIQUENESS OF EACH HUMAN BEING

As much as we are part of the universe (collapsed universal wave), an axis in the vast current of beings and of living things, each individual human being possesses his or her own irreducible uniqueness. Indeed, each being possesses its uniqueness, but in the human being this unique-ness is twofold: the human being is unique and consciously knows that he or she unique. Each has its own *haecceitas*, said a medieval philosopher and theologian, one of the most subtle and brilliant, John Duns Scotus (d. 1346). *Haecceitas* means "this clearly defined embodiment here" or "hereness" (from *haec* = this [here]).

Individuality is not a number. It is rather the negation of number inso-far as the individual is singular and irreplicable in a conscious manner. Each one is himself or herself (thisness) in an original way never experienced before and never to be repeated again. Of course he or she shares an infrastructure with the elements of the universe—oxygen (65%), carbon (18%), hydrogen (10%), nitrogen (3.3%), and other elements that, with the exception of hydrogen, were all produced in the stars billions of years ago—and shares the same genetic code with all living beings. That is the foundation on which our cosmic kinship is based; we bear the same biological, sociological, and anthropological stamp.

Let us connect the levels. The human being is an animal of the mammal class, of the primate order, of the hominid family, of the genus *Homo*, of the *sapiens (demens)* species, endowed with a body made up of 30 billion cells, procreated and controlled by a genetic system that has been formed over a four and a half billion year period, whose psyche, which has the same ancestry as its body, is able to fashion overall visions and detailed analyses and to constitute indivisible unities based on the vibration in unison of around ten million of the ten billion neurons in the brain, thereby enabling it to symbolically create and re-create the universe and to decipher an ultimate and all-encompassing meaning.

Each human being is a conscious and unconscious bearer of this wealth of nature and culture, but he or she is so in a manner that is *sui generis*, unique, and unrepeatable. Each one makes his or her synthesis of the whole. Each can transform his or her entire experience and knowledge in his or her way in an act of love, in other words, in an act of acceptance and affirmation of the universe, in a selfless surrender to the other and in an unlimited openness to the Mystery that religions are accustomed to call God. Each person can also refuse all of this, make his or her life-project one of rebellion against the meaning of the universe, and assume exclusionary stances. Such is human grandeur and tragedy.

Here we are not dealing with quantities but with a new quality of creation expressed through human *pathos* (feeling), *logos* (reason), *eros* (passion), *nomos* (law), *daimon* (inner voice), and *ethos* (ethics). It is only on this level that there can be tragedy or fulfillment, feelings of frustration or of bliss, insofar as human beings discover their place in this complex whole or remove themselves and withdraw from it.

The individual or person, in other words, an irreducible being (individual) but one ever in communication (person), is the basis for a miracle in the universe and a profound mystery. The most fitting and adequate stance toward the individual person—miracle and mystery—is admiration, reverence, openness, and attentiveness, so as to grasp his or her message and unique novelty. It is there that we may understand that as an individual person each one stands before God immediately; ultimately each answers only to God. This human being existentially raises the radical question about the universe, about its where and its whither, about what meaning it has and what meaning we ourselves have with our inquiries and our irrelinquishable impulse toward the absolute. That is the point at which the question of God is raised, a topic to be taken up later.

Human beings are today fearfully raising the question of the major danger weighing on the Earth-system. The thread that once interconnected all things, shaping a unity of meaning and life (the uni-verse), has been lost. Let us now take up this central question.

ESSENTIAL BIBLIOGRAPHY FOR THIS CHAPTER

Alonso, J. M. *Introducción al Principio Andrópico* (Madrid: Encuentro Ediciones, 1989).

Barbour, I. *Religion in an Age of Science* (San Francisco: Harper & Row, 1990).

Barrère, M. *Terra, Patrimônio Comum* (São Paulo: Nobel, 1992).

Barrow, J. D., and F. J. Tipler. *The Anthropic Cosmological Principle* (New York: Oxford University Press, 1986).

Benjamin, C. *Diálogo sbore Ecologia Ciência e Política* (Rio de Janeiro: Nova Fronteira, 1993).

Bohm, D. *Causality and Chance in Modern Physics* (Philadelphia: University of Pennsylvania Press, 1971).

Brillouin, L. *Science and Information Theory* (New York: Academic Press, 1965).

Capra, F. *The Turning Point: Science, Society and the Rising Culture* (New York: Simon & Schuster, 1982).

Charon, J. E. *O Espírito, Esse Desconhecido* (São Paulo: Melhoramentos, 1990).

Ferris, T. *Coming of Age in the Milky Way* (New York: Morrow, 1988).

Freitas Morão, R. R. *Ecologia Cosmica: Uma Visão: Cósmica da Ecologia* (Rio de Janeiro: Francisco Alves, 1992).

Fritsch, H. *Von Urknall zum Zerfall, Erzeugnung und Schöpfung* (Wiesbaden, 1976).

Gleick, J. *Chaos: Making a New Science* (New York: Penguin Books, 1988).

Gribbin, J. *Future Worlds* (New York: Plenum, 1981).

Guitton, J., and I. and G. Bogdanov. *Deus e a Ciência* (Rio de Janeiro: Nova Fronteira, 1992).

Hawking, S. *A Brief History of Time: From the Big Bang to Black Holes* (New York: Bantam Books, 1988).

Heisenberg, W. *Physics and Beyond: Encounters and Conversations* (New York: Harper & Row, 1971).

Laborit, H. *Deus Não Joga Dados* (São Paulo: Trajetória Cultural, 1988).

Lemaître, G. *The Primeval Atom: An Essay on Cosmogony* (New York: Van Nostrand, 1950).

Longair, M. *The Origins of Our Universe* (Cambridge: Cambridge University Press, 1992).

Lovell, B. *Emerging Cosmology* (New York: Columbia University Press, 1981).

Lucchini, F. *Introduzione alla Cosmologia* (Bologna: Zanichelli, 1990).

Massoud, Z. *Terre Vivante* (Paris: Odile Jacob, 1992).

Morin, E. *La Méthode I, II, III* (Paris: Seuil, 1977-1979).

_____. *Science avec Conscience* (Paris: Fayard, 1990).

_____ . *Terre-Patrie* (Paris: Seuil, 1993).

Müller, H. A. *Naturwissenschaft und Glaube* (Berne: Scherz, 1988).

Nick, H. *Quantum Reality: Beyond the New Physics* (New York: Doubleday/Anchor, 1985).

Ohlig, K.-H. *Die Welt ist Gottes Schöpfung: Kosmos und Mensch in Religion, Philosophie und Naturwissenschaften* (Mainz: Grünewald, 1984), 88-111.

Overbye, D. *Lonely Hearts of the Cosmos: The Scientific Quest for the Secret of the Universe* (New York: HarperCollins, 1991).

Pagels, H. *The Cosmic Code: Quantum Physics as the Language of Nature* (New York: Simon and Schuster, 1982).

Prigogine, I. *La Nascita del tempo* (Milan: Bompiani, 1991).

Prigogine, I., and I. Stengers. *Entre o Tempo e a Eternidade* (São Paulo: Companhia das Letras, 1992).

Sagan, C. *Cosmos* (New York: Random House, 1980).

Schroeder, G. L. *Genesis and the Big Bang* (New York: Bantam Books, 1991).

Swimme, B., and T. Berry. *The Universe Story: From the Primordial Flaring Forth to the Ecozoic Era—A Celebration of the Unfolding of the Cosmos* (San Francisco: HarperSanFrancisco, 1992).

Toolan, D. *Facing West from California's Shores: A Jesuit's Journey into New Age Consciousness* (New York: Crossroad, 1987).

Toulmin, S. *The Return of Cosmology: Postmodern Science and the Theology of Nature* (Berkeley: University of California Press, 1982).

Weber, F. *A Dança do Cosmos* (São Paulo: Pensamento, 1990).

Weber, R. *Diálogos como Cientistas e Sábios* (São Paulo: Cultrix, 1988).

Weil, P. *A Consciência Cósmica* (Petrópolis: Vozes, 1989).

Weinberg, S. *The First Three Minutes: A Modern View of the Origin of the Universe* (New York: Basic Books, 1977).

Weizsacher, C. F. von. *La Imagen Física del Mundo* (Madrid: BAC 366, 1970).

Whitehead, A. N. *Process and Reality: An Essay in Cosmology* (New York: Harper Torchbook, 1957).

Zohar, D. *The Quantum Self: Human Nature and Consciousness Defined by the New Physics* (New York: Morrow, 1990).

Zohar, D., and I. Marshall. *The Quantum Society* (New York: William Morrow, 1994).

CHAPTER 3

The Ecological Crisis

The Loss of Connectedness

The ecological crisis demands explanations that are accurate, radical, and persuasive, just as an illness requires that the causes be identified, for it is only by attacking the causes—not the symptoms—that the patient can be cured. The same is true of the Earth, which now lies gravely ill. Where is the clinic and the medical specialist for it? How can it be cured? What is to be the prescription for it? Obviously, the clinic and the specialist are the human community. The medicines are to be found on the Earth itself; the cure will be effected through the care devoted by each member of the human species and by the species as a whole toward Gaia.[1] We intend to identify the causes for the sake of a therapy for the Earth and not out of mere historical curiosity.

Before undertaking any analytical effort we must ask how we could have come to our present situation of open warfare between the human being and nature. It must have been a deep mistake, some grave error in cultures, religions, spiritual traditions, and in the pedagogical processes of socialization of humankind that failed to avoid this current dramatic situation.[2]

The Jewish and Christian traditions, for example, claim that the human being was created to be the caretaker of Earth as the garden of Eden. These traditions proclaim the kindness of the God of the oppressed; the playfulness of the Word, who assumed human flesh in its utter frailty and through it the whole cosmos; and the presence of the Spirit dwelling within the entire universe with its energies. Their self-understanding includes the spiritual legacy of St. Francis of Assisi, who felt like brother to every creature from the most distant star to the snail along the road.

With so many ideals and such marvelous values, why has Christianity been unable to educate humankind, to prevent us from reaching our current critical juncture?[3] Instead of doing so, it soothed the conscience; in dominating and exploiting the Earth people thought they were carrying out a divine command and that the perverse effects of the *dominium terrae* were more due to divine providence than to human responsibility.[4]

Why have indigenous peoples like the Yanomamis, the Apapocuvas-Guaranis, and the Bororos of Brazil, or the Kunas in Panama, or the Sioux peoples in the United States proven to be much more civilized than we, in the sense that they manifest a more all-embracing way of incorporating the human into the universe and of delving into the archetypal powers of the collective unconscious, a way that is more harmonious than all our contemporary ways of individuation (spiritualization). Why are we losing ground instead of moving ahead toward our own heart in tune with the heart of all things?[5] Franciscan missionaries in Mexico at the outset of the evangelization/conquest testified that the Olmecs and Toltecs were such sages that they were able to hear their own heartbeats.[6]

This process of enmity between human beings and Earth is marked by guilt and sin. A condition for reconciliation and lasting peace must be an acknowledgment and shift of direction on the part of all.

CAUSES AND EXCUSES

In identifying causes we must be alert to a common mechanism in personal and group psychology: inventing excuses that serve to avoid accepting guilt and responsibility. We attempt to show that Earth's deteriorated condition is inevitable. We are going to list some of the numerous factors that can explain the crisis of the planet without pausing over any of them but rather attempting to see how they are linked together. Our goal is to get to the bottom of the matter, the ultimate mechanisms that actually account for our present situation.

Technology and Ecology:
The Attacking Virus Will Not Bring Healing

It is often said that the imbalance of the Earth-system is due to *technology*, which is still primitive, destructive, and polluting. Present-day technology certainly collects a high tax in the form of ecological evil. It brings about the systematic exploitation of natural resources, soil poisoning, deforestation, atmospheric contamination, chemicals in foods, and so forth.[7]

Indeed, classical technology is energy-hungry, dirty, and ecologically destabilizing. High-technology countries are using it less and less within their own borders, but they sell it to peripheral countries. Recently, more advanced and less devastating technologies have been devised, but they are practically limited to the wealthy countries. In the currently globally integrated system, technology is not socially integrated; that is, it does not produce benefits for all societies but only for those that control scientific and technical production, and it excludes others or grants them information by exacting heavy tribute (royalties). It is not even ecologically appropriate, for at a certain point it burdens ecosystems and does not assure their reproduction for future generations. Nevertheless, many are quite optimistic about the relationship between technology and ecology. Their argument is that if the application of technology has brought ecological problems, it has the ability to resolve those problems with new technologies, such as genetic technology, lasers and other types of rays, computers, and so forth.[8] Is it not an illusion to think that the virus attacking us can be the principle by which we will be made well?

Finally, we must realize that technology does not exist in itself and for itself. No matter how much technological progress is made, any technology is adopted within a model of development. That is what must be questioned.

Development and Ecology:
The Contradiction of Sustainable Development

Thus we are pushed back to a second cause: the current model of *development* as responsible for the ecological crisis. Indeed, for four centuries all societies in the world have been held hostage to a myth, the myth of progress and of uninterrupted and unlimited growth. Countries must show higher rates in the production of goods and services every year. That is the standard for judging whether a country is developed, underdeveloped, or just plain backward.

Such progress follows the iron logic of maximizing benefits while minimizing costs and the use of time. A truly amazing industrial productive apparatus has been built up in the pursuit of this aim. All productive forces have been harnessed to draw from the Earth all that it can provide. It has been subjected to a true Procrustean bed (people were stretched or shortened to fit the bed, thereby breaking their arms and legs)—researched, tortured, and punctured to make it surrender all its secrets. A systematic assault has been mounted on its wealth in the soil, the subsoil, the air, the sea, and the outer atmosphere. War has been waged on all fronts. Victims have been produced on an unprecedented scale: the working class oppressed worldwide, peripheral nations exploited, the overall quality of life in decline, and nature plundered.

From an ecological standpoint, the dream of unlimited growth means the invention of destructive (rather than productive) forces and the historic and social production of illness and death of Earth's species and of everything composing the Earth.[9]

This is no longer a matter of labor seeking to generate enough for social needs and a surplus for human enjoyment but of production aimed at making labor as productive as possible to meet the demands of the market and to generate profit. The driving concern is not the particular work but the merchandise placed in the circuit of the local, regional, and world markets with a view to earnings and profit.

It is true that starting in 1987 with the Brundtland United Nations Report (also called "Our Common Future") based on research carried out from 1983-1987 on the ecological state of the Earth, the ideal of *sustainable development* is gaining ground. *Sustainable development* is defined as "a process of change in which the exploitation of resources, the orientation of investments, the paths of technological development and institutional change are in accordance with current and future needs." That ideal incorporates ecological reason, but as is clear from the terms used, it still remains a captive of the development-and-growth paradigm, which is assumed to be inherently valid. No matter which terms are tagged onto such development, whether *self-sustaining* or *self-generating*, it never gets away from its economic origins, namely, rising productivity, accumulation, and technological innovation.

The report's assumption, detected by most critical first- and third-world analysts, is that poverty and ecological deterioration mutually affect one another and occur in tandem. What pollutes, so the thought goes, is extreme poverty. Therefore the more development advances, the less dire poverty there will be, and the less dire poverty there is the less pollution there will be, to the betterment of ecology. The development process must accordingly be accelerated in order to assure an optimal ecological balance.

A very grave error is at work here. The real causes of poverty and environmental deterioration are not being examined. They are the result of precisely the kind of development being practiced, one that is highly concentrating and that exploits people and nature's resources. Hence, the more intense this kind of development that benefits some, the greater the dire poverty and deterioration produced for the vast majority. Indeed, that is the situation around the world, where a tiny number of countries have a great accumulation of goods and services at the cost of the two-thirds who are marginalized or outcast. As a rule, it can be said that whenever conflicts arise between the two sides, the decision falls on the side of development and growth and against arguments for ecological sustainability. The category of *sustainability* has been worked out in the realm of ecology and biology to define the trend of ecosystems toward dynamic equilibrium sustained in the web of interdependencies and complementarities flourishing in ecosystems.

Can the term *sustainability* be applied to the kind of modern development and growth whose logic is based on plundering Earth and exploiting the labor force? *Sustainable development* is an oxymoron. This is especially true of capitalism, which is based on private appropriation of nature and its resources; it is especially against nature.[10]

The expression *sustainable development* masks the modern paradigm operative in both capitalism and socialism, even of the green sort, always with its all-devouring logic. A Brazilian analyst puts it well: "The expression 'sustainable development' creates confusion and does not symbolize a new way of conceiving the world."[11]

The term used should not be *development* at all but rather *growth,* which is sought for its own sake within a single quantitative and linear model. What is sought is not development in the sense of the flourishing of human potentialities in their various dimensions, especially that spiritual dimension proper to *Homo sapiens (demens),* ever tied to the global interactions of human beings with the cosmos or the Earth in its immense diversity and in its dynamic equilibrium. Only those potentialities that serve the interests of profit are sought. Development in this model is merely material and one-dimensional—mere growth. Sustainability in this context is nothing but rhetoric and illusion.

Society and Ecology: Ecocapitalism and Ecosocialism

We must also recognize that development does not exist in itself; it points back to a *model of society* that provides itself with the kind of development it wants. It is therefore imperative that we briefly examine the kind of society from which we all suffer ecologically.

This is the third causal mechanism for Earth's deficit. All societies in history, at least since Neolithic times (12,000 B.C.E.), are energy devouring and ever more consuming of nature's energies. That is especially true of modern society because it is built around the core of economics, understood as the art and technique of unlimited production of wealth through the exploitation of nature's resources and the technological ingenuity of the human species. Hence, in modern societies economics is no longer understood in its original sense—the rational management of scarcity—but rather as the science of unlimited growth.

All modernity, in both free-market-capitalist or Marxist-socialist variants, lives on this common assumption: it is imperative to grow, expand markets, and fill them with goods and services. There is one significant difference: in free-market capitalism, those goods and services are accessible to an elite of countries or social groups within countries, while socialist society strives to distribute the benefits of economic growth built with the labor of all to the largest number of persons. That is the socialist ideal.

This difference flows from the fact that the modes of production are profoundly different in the two types of society. In free-market capitalism private property is central and the individual is overvalued. In the organization of social relations, control lies in the hands of those who have capital (the means of production, such as technology, factories, land, money), and they hold in subjection those who live off their labor alone, whether from muscle or intellect. The driving force of the production process is profit, achieved by productivity and competition. In socialism, on the other hand, the core is social property, managed by the state through one party (real socialism of the Marxist-Leninist type) as the only owner and the champion of the common good. Land is socialized but any of its enchantment has been banished, and land itself is demoted to the status of original capital.[12]

Economic growth does not produce social development in either model of society.[13] The former type of society (free-market capitalism) has led to great social disparity; class, gender, and generational struggle; injustice; and overall poor quality of life. In the latter type (socialism) the result has been a great deal of massification, authoritarianism, and lack of participation and creativity on the part of citizens. The socialist state can provide benefits but participation is meager. It has brought women into the work world, but it has not overcome macho patriarchal culture. It socializes the means of production but not the means of power (democracy) and of leisure. Moreover, human beings want not only to receive but to give and to work together in building what is collective; it is human nature to be creative and co-creative and to express gratuity and lovingness.

Both these models of society have broken with the Earth. They have reduced it to a supply of raw materials and natural resources. Persons have been reified as human resources or human capital, constituting the great reserve army at the disposition of the owners of the means of production (state or capital). The Earth and the cosmic community are no longer heard in their myriad voices and tongues. The code for deciphering their symbolic and sacramental message has been lost. The complex superorganism Gaia is viewed as a lifeless machine composed of hundreds of physical and chemical elements to be disassembled by the greed of science harnessed to technology. Humans, who are the most recent arrivals in the chain of beings, do not respect other beings in nature for their inherent worth, even though their ancestry goes much further back.

At the root of these two types of society are profound dualisms. Capital has been separated from labor, work from leisure, person from nature, man from woman, body from spirit, sex from affection, efficiency from poetry, wonder from organization, God from the world. One of these two poles has come to dominate the other, thereby giving rise to anthropocentrism, capitalism, materialism, patriarchy, machismo, secularism, and monarchical un-trinitarian monotheism. The worst has indeed happened: human beings have become separated from the cosmic community and have forgotten the web of interdependencies and the synergy of all the cosmic elements that enabled them to emerge in the cosmic process.[14] They have withdrawn into themselves, and have become alienated from their own dignity and function at this advanced stage of the cosmic process.

The kind of society now in place is profoundly anti-ecological. That is one of the reasons for the current deterioration of the Earth-system. We are accordingly pushed to even deeper levels.

Anthropocentrism: The Human Being, Earth's Satan?

From society we are pushed back to the *human being.* What image of the human being underlies the kinds of societies mentioned above: Does the primary cause of our present *status terrae corruptus* lie in the human being? The human being is accused of being the Satan of Earth. Is this another excuse mechanism or does it properly assign blame?

The image that human beings (understood personally and collectively) have of themselves and their place in the universe is decisive for defining their relations with nature, with the Earth as a whole, and toward their own destiny. There is no denying that in contemporary societies human beings have made themselves the center of everything. Everything must start from them and return to them; everything must be at their service. They feel like a modern Prometheus, with enough ingenuity and power to overcome all obstacles standing in the way of their aims. And their aim is the *dominium terrae,* the conquest and domination of Earth. Nietzsche said it well, The will to power-domination characterizes human beings in modern societies.[15] Prior to this great prophet, who denounced the culture of arrogance, surely no other text from the Western cultural tradition better embodied this will to conquest and domination than the papal bulls that legitimated the Iberian imperial powers. In the late fifteenth and early sixteenth centuries they set out to create a world civilization by conquering lands, plowing through previously unsailed seas, subjecting peoples, and devastating previously unknown cultures in the name of God and the church—and succeeded in their venture.

In the bull *Romanus Pontifex,* Pope Nicolas VI (1447-55) promises rule over the Earth to the Portuguese monarchs in these terms:

> We, giving due consideration to each and every one of the things indicated, grant full and free authorization to invade, conquer, battle, defeat, and subject any Saracens, pagans, and other enemies of Christ, wherever they may be, and the kingdoms, duchies, principalities, dominions, possessions and the fixed and moveable property as they have and possess; and to reduce to perpetual servitude their per-

sons, and to set apart for themselves and their successors, and take possession of and apply for their own use and utility and that of their successors, their kingdoms, duchies, principalities, dominions, possessions and property. Having obtained this power, King Alfonso accordingly justly and legitimately possesses the islands, lands, ports and oceans which correspond and belong by right to King Alfonso and to his successors.[16]

In terms even more arrogant, Pope Alexander VI (1492-1503) with the bull *Inter Coetera* grants the monarchs of Castile and Leon the same powers over "islands and mainlands found and to be found, discovered or to be discovered . . . by the authority of almighty God conferred on us in Saint Peter, and as of the vicariate of Jesus Christ which we exercise on Earth in perpetuity."[17] These texts speak for themselves; they require no exegesis whatsoever. Such a will to worldwide domination is buried in the collective unconscious of Western culture, which has now spread around the world, whether it comes in the name of God, Christian culture, enlightenment rationality, science and technology, the knowledge society, or democracy. It is always a matter of dominating and enclosing everyone within the dictates of the Western paradigm of power and domination, especially those who are different. It has now transferred the conquest of the Earth to the conquest of outer space and the stars. It is profoundly against nature.[18]

The imperial and anti-ecological anthropology at work in the contemporary dreams, projects, ideals, institutions, and values can be summed up in one word: *anthropocentrism*. The term means that everything throughout the fifteen-billion-year story exists solely for the human being, man and woman. Hence, everything culminates in the human being. Nothing has intrinsic value, nothing has otherness and meaning apart from the human being. All beings are at the disposal of human beings, to serve as their property and under their control, so that humans may attain their desires and projects. Human beings feel that they are *above* things rather than *alongside* and *with* things. They imagine themselves as an isolated single point, outside nature and above it. They arrogantly excuse themselves from respecting other beings.

Humans are forgetting, however, that the universe and the Earth are not the result of their creativity or their will. They were not present at the birth of the universe, nor did they set the arrow of time, nor did they invent the primordial energies that continue to stir in the vast evolutionary process and are acting in human nature itself as part of universal nature. They are in the rear guard, the last to arrive at the enormous creation party. Being prior to them, the universe and the Earth do not belong to them. Indeed, they belong to Earth and to the universe. If Earth is not the center of the universe, how can human beings, sons and daughters of Earth, regard themselves as its center and purpose? Anthropocentrism is unaware of all this and does not want to know.

The classic formulation of such anthropocentrism is the statement of Protagoras of Abdera (c.485-10 B.C.E.), "The human being is the measure of all things."[19] This attitude violates the first universal law; namely, that we constitute an immense cosmic and planetary community, and we must live in harmony and solidarity with one another because we are all interdependent and have the same origin and destiny.[20]

As indicated in chapter 1, such *anthropocentrism* when considered historically is exposed as *androcentrism.* It is the male rather than the female who proclaims himself lord of nature. He regards woman as a part of nature that he must possess exclusively, domesticating her and subjecting her to his rational, objective, and voluntarist logic. Hence, the male, centered on his own exclusionary masculinity, tends to repress what is connected to the feminine and, in it, to woman: the spontaneity of nature, the emergence of vital and free energies, sensitivity, the logic of the heart and of tenderness, the ability to grasp the message of things, and the *esprit de finesse* for the dimensions of mystery and the sacred. He is governed by the *esprit de géométrie,* as Blaise Pascal marvelously expressed it, that is, by the iciness of the concept, by rational calculation, and the strategy of efficacy. He has forced into women this same overall self-understanding of the human being, alienating them from their uniqueness as women.[21]

Human beings thus interpreted are lost in the thicket of relationships that they have created with themselves; they are impoverished, drained of life, enclosed in their own limits, which today threaten their very life and future. Finally, they display a boundless aggressivity, for they are threatened on all sides.[22] They use power in order to have more power and so feel more secure. This is sheer illusion. Taking away and thwarting the power of others does not make them more secure but only more vulnerable, because they are surrounded by enemies on all sides. That leads to even greater insecurity, which in turn opens the way to further seeking of power. An oppressive vicious circle ensues.

Within this logic, starting from a position of power, human beings deeply disrupt nature, always for their own exclusive benefit. A unique civilization has arisen as a result, our modern civilization. Its organizing axis is not life—the wonder of life, and the defense and expansion of life—but rather its own power and the means for greater power, which is domination.[23]

Civilization against Nature

From human beings we are driven back to their primary work, androcentric and dominating *civilization,* which is certainly one of the decisive causes for the current ecological crisis. A civilization arises out of the sense of being that human beings have worked out and from the practices that they have attempted in order to embody that sense with regard to themselves, nature, the past, and the Divinity, the ultimate dream of all strivings. A civilization is composed of the interaction of four major systems: the system of representation, the normative system, the system of expression, and the system of action. This last has gained special prominence in modernity[24] because it is directly tied to the logic of power. We accordingly come to the fundamental characteristics of our civilization, power and domination, which have become historically and socially embodied in technology. Ours is unquestionably a technological civilization. That means that we use the tool (*techno*) as our primary way of relating to nature. We treat nature and everything in it as an instrument for our own aim of power and domination. This instrumental approach disrupts immediacy, direct contact, feeling nature on our skin. The instrument stands between us and nature, and thus the basic solidarity uniting us to everything in the cosmos and on Earth is also broken. Human beings claim a position of sovereignty as those who have at their whim the things that are within reach of their hand or the extension of their hand, arm, eye, or desire, namely, the tool.

The tool, in turn, demands a kind of rationality suited to it, namely, instrumental-analytic rationality. Instrumental reason is a subjective reason; it is only in human beings and in their interests. It establishes the reasons suited for those interests, especially reasons of power. It demotes the objective reason that is unfolding in the cosmic process throughout billions of years, in the inter(retro)relationships of all with all. When this latter reason is grasped it has already been subjected to subjective reasons, that is, to the interests of power, with no regard for the intrinsic value of the beings of nature, and it accordingly makes them means (instruments) for the ends of human subjectivity, generally profit and individual well-being.

Technology means an operational knowledge in the sense that science operates as an analytical, critical, and systematic study of reality which takes the form of knowledge. Technology is simply applied science. Such science provides the leverage for all kinds of transformations occurring in nature, society, and in the human body and mind.

However, modern science, as Jürgen Habermas has pointedly demonstrated, is guided by interest. It uncovers even the most subtle structures of the real, creates the structure of knowledge in order to put it into practical operation for the sake of progress, industrial growth, and more profit. It thus unfolds in the form of technique, transforming ecological relations.[25] It has unquestionably brought countless human conveniences, ranging from household appliances to the transformation of the two categories that frame existence in the world, namely, space and time. Both have been deeply modified: space fantastically shortened by the means of communication and transportation, and time drastically reduced to the point of simultaneity through television and the fax machine.

In large areas of the world there is too little of the technology needed to improve food production, handle the health conditions of populations, develop safe and decent transportation. In a few other areas there is excessive technology, to the point where it unnecessarily complicates domestic and social relations, damaging the quality of life and pouring contaminants into the biosphere. Chlorofluorocarbon (CFC) produced by aerosols, refrigerators, and air conditioners is particularly harmful because it is destroying the ozone layer (already reaching 50% in Antarctica) that provides protection from ultraviolet rays, which cause skin cancer and even changes in the genetic code (DNA).

The ecological crisis means two basic imbalances in society: too much consumption by the rich and too little consumption by the poor. It means the global crisis of the life-system, from the destruction of forests, the spread of urban neuroses, to the contemporary indifference toward the drama of millions of starving people and the nihilism of the heavy rock music that excites youth.

Things have not always been thus in human history, nor must they inexorably be so. For centuries science and technology traveled separate paths without influencing one another, as A. Koyré has shown convincingly. But the project of techno-science has created a close association at the service of the obsessive will to power and domination. This association has created the basis for the efficacy and power of modernity's imperial project. It is the characteristic feature of our age and what is unique about contemporary life, initially in the West and then everywhere, including other types of civilizations. There are those who say with some justification that Jewish and Christian theology has served as a framework that has made possible the association between science and theology, since this theology claims that nature's only purpose is to be at the service of human beings, and that it can therefore be exploited and dominated to the utmost of human understanding,[26] a point we will now discuss.

Power always raises disturbing questions: whose power? what for? over whom? Power, as is clear, always has to do with things that are not power, and it serves them or is used to attain them. Power thus belongs to the order of means rather than of end. Toward what end are human beings striving through power? That is the question to be answered and that occupies us in this book.

The fact is that power has come to stand by itself. Power has emerged as an end in itself. Is it right for a means to become an end? The consequences of such *hubris* are at the root of the ecological crisis and the destruction of the links that held the human being together. It will not be overcome until this question is faced radically, and until alternatives are found.

The will to power is not necessarily perverse. It can mean the will to be, to defend one's integrity, and to establish a possible relationship, a relationship of sharing, synergy, and self-limitation of power in order to live with other powers. The issue is the will to power as domination. This will to domination is sometimes manifested as annihilating the power of the other (oppression), sometimes as subjecting it (subordination), and sometimes as coopting and harnessing it (hegemony). Power is established as the point around which everything is organized. This domination strategy stirs the impulses to command everything, control everything, force everything, make everything fit, and subject everything. It encourages ontologized (rather than functional) hierarchies, subordination, dualisms (who orders whom), and disruptions of solidarity, which is the dynamic of all beings in the universe. Only the male human being speaks; he does not listen to the woman and to what the woman has to offer based on her experience. He turns a deaf ear to all the other creatures and to the age-old stories that they have to tell, loaded with wise lessons for the spiritual development of the human being.

With power and domination we are accordingly dealing with a proposal for civilization, a voluntary decision, and an ethic responsibility. The inspired North American ecologist Thomas Berry has rightly observed that "in Western civilization our cultural coding has set itself deliberately against our genetic coding and the instinctive tendencies of our genetic endowment are systematically negated. Such is the origin of our present situation."[27] In other words, power and domination have displaced life from its absolutely central place and have set themselves up as an absolute reference point. Life is turned into a mere function. Its demands—demands for integration on all sides, demands for internal balance (for all life is vulnerable and demands care, and on the conscious level, tenderness), demands that conditions be maintained so that life may not only reproduce but continue to expand and develop creatively—are all ignored.

Power and domination continually conspire against life; peaceful coexistence and a synergistic energy between them is impossible. A worldwide effective policy to reduce demand for material goods (collective control of desire) or to take a strong hand in managing available natural resources is not enough. Doing so does not yet overcome the anti-ecological paradigm of dominating power that has the effect of a killing machine spreading destruction.[28]

Ultimately, however, we are approaching the unavoidable moment of reckoning. Either we continue in our model of civilization—and along that path head toward a planet-wide cataclysm—or we shift directions (new paradigm) and in so doing safeguard Gaia, her sons and daughters, and our common future.

This is an immeasurable challenge, one larger than any that has ever appeared in human history. It is so urgent that there is no room for equivocation or mechanisms of delay or excuses. Time is pressing.[29] We know how much our ways of speaking, our institutions, our legal system, our spiritual dreams, our religions and churches, our methods of socialization and of nourishing our imagination are replete with elements of power, authoritarianism, machismo, and anthropocentrism. We will need generations of Paulo Freire (the Brazilian educator who envisions education as the practice of freedom) and Robert Muller (the high UN official who conceived the content and method for a global and planetary education) to fashion ourselves a civilization for which education is a creative practice of participatory freedom and a shared life, an ongoing exercise of universal solidarity and synergy. "Unless we attempt the impossible," wrote a revolutionary youth on the walls of Paris in 1968, "we will be condemned to face the inconceivable." That is why we have to seek whatever new and alternative approach could be saving and liberating.

We truly need a new foundational experience, a new spirituality that would make possible a unique and astonishing new reconnection of all our dimensions with the vast diversity of our planetary, cosmic, historic, spiritual, and transcendental reality. Only then will the dream of a new way of being become possible, a dream that will be the starting point for a new sense of living alongside the entire global community.

Thus we are pressed back toward a deeper reason for the contemporary ecological disaster and its possible redemption: that dimension that brings to expression and always seeks to keep alive the human being's connectedness to the rest of the universal process, namely, religion.

Religion: Connectedness Distorted by Power

How much does religion share the responsibility for this loss? How much has it been responsible for rescuing and saving Earth? This is not the place for a detailed analysis of religion or of the great religions to ecology.[30] We simply want to indicate the most visible historic line of the religious phenomenon, and to pause on some of the specific features of the Jewish and Christian tradition, since it has been the symbolic space in which Western civilization, now worldwide, was created. It is largely responsible for the destructive thrust of the ecological dinosaur of dominating power. Finally, we will take up what we regard as the absolute disaster in the human realm that led to the loss of connectedness. How shall we recover the innocence and enchantment that will lead us back along the path to universal ecological peace?

There have been three major periods in the process of the connection between human beings and nature: the era of the spirit, the era of the body, and the era of life.

The *era of the spirit* has flourished in indigenous and ancestral cultures. Human beings discovered the spirit, as we will see in greater detail in chapter 9, and felt carried along and guided by forces acting in them and in the cosmos—numinous, fascinating, and all-encompassing realities that granted them an experience of protection and safety. This grounding experience connected them in kinship with all things, creating a *union mystique* with beings and giving rise to a deep spiritual development that was translated into symbol-rich languages and calls to the depths of human consciousness and the unconscious. That was the time when great myths were projected and the deities were born. These divinities represent not so much entities focused toward the outside but powerful energy centers in human life and nature, with which human beings must coexist and which they must confront, internalize, heed, and follow. This experience of connectedness and integration became part of the great ancient historic religions in India, Sri Lanka, China, Japan, and also in the Near East and in the Americas of the Sioux, Toltecs, Incas, Mayas, Quiches, Tupis-Guaranis, Kayapos, Long Belts, Krenakacores, and in all ancient cultures that were centered on the sacred, the religious, and the spiritual. These peoples also fought wars and shared all the ups and downs of human life, but the mark of the Spirit and the cosmic Sacred permeated all these embodiments. That path of civilization has profoundly stamped the collective unconscious to our own day. Archetypes represent this symbolic capital and accumulated spirituality.

Second comes the *era of the body*. Human beings discover the body, the physical force of the Earth and the cosmos. It was a marvelous shift when human beings became aware that they could manipulate that force for their advantage. Neolithic agriculture represents the first great worldwide revolution assimilated by all peoples. The founding masters of the modern paradigm—Galileo, Copernicus, Newton, and Bacon—brought the invention of science and its practical use in technology. At this point human beings have the impression that they can refashion the lost paradise of happiness. They feel like a god, or at least a demiurge, capable of transforming creation. A systematic conquest of Earth thereupon ensues, with the exploitation of its resources as means for satisfying the unlimited human desire for consumption, well-being, and happiness. The powers of spirit and soul from the previous period come under suspicion and are relegated to the field of subjectivity, to the world of magic and superstition. Each individual organizes those powers as he or she wishes or restrains them. The upshot of this focus on the body and its controllable powers is that the experience of numinosity and sacredness that so filled the archaic world with enchantment and intimacy during the age of the spirit is lost. God has been placed outside the world. A God without the world ushers in a world without God, as has happened in European modernity. The technical and transformative capability of human intelligence is now a marvel. Initially, the era of the body brought so many advantages that they seemed to be fulfilling a messianic mission of making human life easier and turning human beings truly into kings and queens of the universe. But the unfolding of the paradigm has revealed its contradictions: weapons of death have been invented and have been tested with vast destruction of human life; perverse changes in the rhythm of nature and of human life have occurred. Earth as a whole has begun to lose its immunity and to become ill. Such is the current situation, which has been criticized at length in previous pages. A new revolution of civilization is imperative.

Now we are entering into *the era of life*. Life connects body and spirit. Life assumes the web of interdependencies throughout the universe and objectively reveals the connectedness of living and nonliving beings, of biosphere and hydrosphere, atmosphere and geosphere. From the biosphere arose the noosphere, the specifically human sphere, whose characteristic features are reflex consciousness, the responsible spirit, and the role of serving as copilot of the evolutionary process. The result is a new sense of the meaning of human beings and their place in the universe. Everything is synergistic. Everything is ecological, the expression of this entire synergy and perichoresis. Human beings are at last discovering their return path to the great community of living beings under the rainbow of cosmic kinship. How is the life of Gaia, of humans, and of all species to be protected? That is the great challenge of our age, the challenge of the era of life and of ecology.

How can religions, especially those of the Jewish and Christian traditions, aid in this task? The debate on this religious stream's possible shared responsibility for the crisis of the Earth-system takes two main approaches.

The first claims that the book shared by Jews and Christians—the sacred scriptures—is the expression of God's explicit revelation, valid for all times and for all human beings, and therefore, it can contain no error. By reason of that faith these religions cannot be anti-ecological, because the good and beneficent creator God could not have revealed anything hostile to life and life systems. Any passages that may have pointed in that direction were misread, insufficiently explained, or misinterpreted. We must go back, so it is said, to the original meaning, which deeply integrates the human being with creation and its Creator. God is "green,"[31] and hence God's revelation is good for nature.

The second approach regards the position we have just sketched as dogmatic. It holds that even from a dogmatic standpoint (that of faith) the texts must be understood in their literary form as they are written down, and that the kind of mindset that they have nourished and encouraged with their unmistakably anti-ecological connotations must be taken into account. It therefore humbly admits the shared responsibility of Judaism and Christianity for our present jeopardy but strongly resists the idea that this is the *main* reason for ecological imbalances, as claimed by the American historian Lynn White, Jr.,[32] and the brilliant German essayist Carl Amery.[33] This religious factor, this view holds, is merely one among several, others of which may have had even more impact. But it has been powerfully at work creating a general framework paving the way for secularization, lack of reverence for the Earth, and the rise of the schemes of technology and science; this whole complex is one of the main reasons for the Earth's current flawed condition. There are six points of an anti-ecological accent in the Jewish and Christian traditions.

The first is *patriarchy*. The Hebrew and Christian scriptures express their message within the shared cultural framework of classical antiquity, which is patriarchy. Male values are most prominent. Even God is presented as Father and absolute Lord. Female, especially maternal, characteristics of pre-neolithic deities, which tend to be matriarchal, are delegitimized. The female dimension of existence accordingly becomes invisible, for it cannot be objectively eliminated. Women are marginalized and confined to private space. This reductionism assaults gender balance and represents a break in social and religious ecology.[34]

Second, the Jewish and Christian traditions are profoundly *monotheistic*. Their root intuition consists of bearing witness that underneath, before, and after the cosmic process there is at work a single creative and universal providential principle, namely, God. Monotheism is sustained by reasons of a philosophical and theological nature.[35] What is of concern to ecology lies not in this area, but rather in the psychological and political formulation that monotheism has received throughout history.[36]

As is widely known, the Jewish and Christian traditions struggled tirelessly against any sort of polytheism. As well founded as it might be philosophically, that struggle made it impossible to safeguard the element of truth in polytheism, which was rescued much later by St. Francis of Assisi (as we will see in the final chapter). That truth is that the universe with its variegated beings, mountains, fountains, forests, rivers, firmament, and so forth, is permeated with powerful energies and hence is the bearer of mystery and sacredness. Indeed, human beings are inhabited by many powerful energy centers overflowing them on all sides and with the universal Energy shaping the cosmos for billions of years, centers that impart a profound meaning to existence. Throughout history, these transcendent forces have been hypostatized in the form of male and female deities. A substantialist vision of the sacred and the spiritual took shape and gave rise to the world of gods and goddesses as subsistent entities, but originally they translated the interior churning of the drive of the universe and of each human being regarding the radical meaning of his or her personal and social life. The deities functioned as powerful archetypes of the depths of the human being. The radicalization of monotheism, as it battled poly-theism, closed many doors of the human soul. It desacralized the world in confronting it with, and distinguishing it from, God. Monotheism thus established too great a separation between creature and Creator, world and God. Because of the battle with paganism and its polytheism, Chris-tianity could not discern the presence of the divine energies in the uni-verse and specifically in human beings themselves. It failed to draw out sufficiently the sacramental nature of the world and of history by which it could have created a bridge between God and world, for everything would be permeated with the ineffable presence of Mystery. That was not the prevailing tendency, although over the centuries one such vein did de-velop a cosmic mysticism. Overall there was a massive destruction of the many-colored universe of polytheism and its anthropological significance.

Monotheism has also had political consequences. It has frequently been invoked to justify authoritarianism and centralized power. The claim has been that just as there is a single God in heaven there must be a single lord on Earth, a single religious head, a single head keeping order in the fam-ily.[37] This linear vision has destroyed the dialogue, equity, and universal community resulting from our being sons and daughters of God, sacra-ments of God's goodness and kindness. It became even more reductionist when only the human being, man and woman, came to be regarded as the representative of God in creation. Only humans are said to be divine im-age and likeness (Gn 1:26). Only they are believed to extend God's cre-ative act and so to have a centrality that is denied to the other beings, who are also image and likeness of God and by their evolutionary activity embody and extend the divine creative will. The great cosmic community that bears the Mystery and hence reveals the Divinity is forgotten.

Anthropocentrism derives from this arrogant interpretation of the human being. The biblical text leaves no doubt when it says, "Be fertile and mul-tiply; fill the earth and subdue it. Have dominion over the fish of the sea, the birds of the air" (Gn 1:28). These texts present a clear call to limitless demographic growth and unrestricted *dominium terrae*. That same empha-sis on dominating and populating the Earth can be seen clearly in the flood story. In the new order of the world, established after that vast eco-logical catastrophe, the text says, "Be fertile, then and multiply; abound on earth and subdue it" (Gn 9:7). This domination is spelled out in a prior verse, "Dread fear of you shall come upon all the animals of the earth . . . into your power they are delivered" (Gn 9:2). Even Psalm 8, which is de-voted to God's glory in creation, maintains the bible's radical anthro-pocentrism: "You have made him a little less than a god. . . . You have given him rule over the works of your hands, putting all things under his feet: All sheep and oxen, yes and the beasts of the field, the birds of the air, the fishes of the sea" (Ps 8:6-8).

There is no getting around the meaning of these texts. The learned exegesis of so many who keep trying to situate and re-situate such texts in the context of Middle Eastern anthropology in order to dispel their anti-ecological tenor[38] will not do. No matter how much apologetic effort is made, their tenor remains. And that is how these texts were understood and assimilated by the modern mindset (starting in the seventeenth century)—as a divine legitimation of the savage conquest of the world and the subjection of all the beings in creation to humanity's self-willed ambitions.

Of course, there is another reading of the creation account in the scriptures, one where the human being has a different role, that of being guardian and gardener in Eden (Gn 2:15). This interpretation supports a basic ecological perspective. At the proper place we shall have to draw from the Jewish and Christian traditions other perspectives that are helpful for re-connecting all things with themselves and with their source. Thus, we will be referring to original grace, the covenant with all living things symbolized by the rainbow after the flood, the dance of creation, the gospel of the cosmic Christ, the indwelling of the Spirit in the energies of the universe, the sacramental nature of matter by reason of the incarnation and the sacraments, the recapitulation of all things so that they may be, as it were, God's body. Here, however, we want to indicate the shortcomings of a religion that in history has failed to satisfy its reconnecting function and hence has contributed to the disaster that we are now suffering.

Something else shared by the heirs of Abrahamitic faith (Jews, Christians, Muslims) and that is troubling for an ecological conception of the world is the *tribal ideology* of election. Whenever a people or an individual feels chosen to be the bearer of a unique message, it risks arrogance and gets caught in the logic of exclusion.[39] Indeed, the sense of Jews, Christians, and Muslims that they are chosen by God has led them to make war against everyone else or to strive to subject others and bring them into their vision of things. They have made their convictions dogmas to be imposed on everyone else in the name of God and God's plan in history. That was why at certain periods in the West a true brotherhood of terror against all diversity of thought has been established (inquisition, fundamentalism, religious wars). Nothing is more hostile to ecology than this fissure in universal solidarity and the denial of the covenant whose rainbow extends over all, not just some.

Nevertheless, of all the things that distort ecology none outweighs that which derives from belief in the *fall of nature*. This doctrine refers to the belief that the whole universe has fallen under the power of the devil due to original sin introduced by the human being. The universe has lost its sacred character; it is no longer the temple of the Spirit but the harvest field of the demons; it is corrupt, sinful, decadent matter.[40]

The biblical text is explicit, "Cursed be the ground because of you" (Gn 3:17). God tells Noah, "I have decided to put an end to all mortals on earth; the earth is full of lawlessness because of them" (Gn 6:13). The idea that the Earth with all that exists and moves on it must be punished because of human sin denotes a limitless anthropocentrism. Earthquakes, annihilation of species, and death already existed before human beings even appeared on the face of the Earth. Hence, human behavior cannot be made accountable for everything that happens, good and evil. But this demonization of nature because of the fall has led people to have little appreciation for this world, and for centuries it has hindered religious persons from having a project to carry out in the world. It has impeded scientific research and made life harsh, because it made heavily suspect any pleasure, achievement, and fulfillment dealing with and enjoying nature. In this way of seeing things, original sin outweighs original grace.

For many people this coupling of sin and redemption is what Christianity is all about. Certain traditions, which go back to doctrines of St. Paul, St. Augustine, and Luther, make sin become so central that the human being feels more closely tied to and dependent on the old sinful Adam than on the new liberating Adam, Jesus Christ.

ULTIMATE ROOT OF THE CRISIS: THE DISRUPTION OF UNIVERSAL CONNECTEDNESS

Thus we are pushed back to an ultimate basis for the current ecological impasse: the ongoing *disruption* of the basic connectedness with the whole of the universe and with its Creator that the human being has introduced, fueled, and perpetuated. Here we are touching on a deeply mysterious and tragic dimension of human and universal history. The Jewish and Christian traditions call this basic frustration *original sin* or *sin of the world*.[41] *Original* here does not refer to the historic origins of this negative phenomenon and hence to bygone times; rather, it has to do with origins in human beings, their grounding and radical sense of being, today and always. Nor may *sin* be reduced to mere moral dimensions or to an isolated act of the human being. It has to do with an overall stance and hence an overturning of all the relationships in which the human being is placed. This is an ontological dimension that has to do with the human being understood as a node of relationships in all directions. Sin therefore has to do with the human condition today.

It must be emphasized that original sin is an interpretation of a fundamental experience. It is a response to an enigma that is always challenging the human being and any reading of history. What is that fundamental experience?

When we contemplate the universe we have a twofold sensation: we marvel and are astonished, and at the same time we feel strange and perplexed. We and all things seem to be governed by the law of *mors tua, vita mea*—your death is the price of my life. Beings devour one another. The cat will always hunt the mouse; it is pointless to preach to the cat to show mercy to the mouse. From the victim's viewpoint, that of the mouse, we have a universe that is dramatic and tragic. The cat, in turn, is the victim of the dog, which is the prey of the tiger, and so forth up the chain.

Few in modern times have captured with piety and perplexity the fundamental experience that the expression *original sin* sought to translate better than Lord McLeod of Fuinary, with this prayer intended for the Iona community:

> Almighty God, Creator of all. Yours is the morning that advances toward fullness. Yours is the summer that slips lazily toward autumn. Yours is the eternity that has entered into time. The green pastures, the fragrances of the flowers, the lichen growing on the rocks, the algae populating the depths of the sea, all are Yours. And we live happily in this garden that You have created. Even so, creation is not enough. Decline also spreads over beauty. The lambs feeding without a care will soon, soon, be taken to the slaughterhouse. Nature, exuberant and verdant, also bears the marks of a thousand scars. It is a garden where there are always thorns and thistles. Creation is not enough. God, redeemer and all-powerful: Yours is the sap of life that nourishes our bones and our whole being and leads us to ecstasy. Nevertheless, in the midst of beauty, in our own minds, we always bear the bitter taste of sin: the long dead dry lichen of sins that have left scars in the soul. In the garden that is each one of us there are always thorns and thistles.[42]

People sense that something is not working in human beings and nature. Reality is not all that it could be; it could be better, more beautiful, and more harmonious. The scriptural account that closely ties original sin to the account of creation and the new covenant after the flood hints at this ambiguity between original blessing and original sin that affects humans and the universe.

Without going into all the possible interpretations of the original fall,[43] we assume one that seems to shed more light and that is gaining wider acceptance among religious thinkers: the fall as a condition of all things within an evolutionary process. What has been called original sin would thus simply be nature itself in a state of becoming, as an open system moving from less complex to more complex levels. God did not create the universe as something completed, an event in the past, something utterly perfect and finished forever. Rather, God set in motion an open process that is to journey toward ever more highly organized, subtle, and better ways of being, of life, and of consciousness. The imperfection that we observe in the cosmogenic process in the course of evolution does not betray God's ultimate design for creation and does not signify God's final word about God's creatures but is only a moment within a vast and ever open process. Within this approach, the earthly paradise does not mean nostalgia for a vanished golden age but the promise of a future that is still to come. The first page of scripture is actually the last. It is presented as a kind of model of the future, to fill us with hope about our destination and the fate of the universe that is one day to be attained.

In the evolutionary process, as we reflected previously, there are falls, but they are falls on the way up. The emergence of chaos means the opportunity for more complex and rich forms of life to appear.[44] Quantum physics offers us a metaphor for understanding this process of ascent by means of another, descending, process. It speaks of the particles and waves in continual movement that make up all beings. They make up the world of probabilities. When a wave decays a probability is realized and matter arises. The decay was an ascent, that is, the initiation of a being that has arisen from probability to reality, from chaos to order, in short, that came into the world of existence.

St. Paul saw the fallen condition of creation as a subjection "to vanity" (*mataiótes*), not by reason of the human being but by reason of God. The exegetical meaning of *vanity*, according to many interpreters, suggests a maturing process. Nature has not yet reached maturity; it has not yet come to its final abode. It is journeying because God wanted it that way. In its current phase it feels frustrated, as it were, far from the goal, "subject to vanity." Hence, Paul rightly says that "all creation is groaning in labor pains even until now" (Rom 8:22). The human being shares in this maturing process, likewise groaning (Rom 8:23). The whole creation is anxiously awaiting the maturing of the sons and daughters of God. When that takes place, it also comes to its maturity, along with humans, for, as Paul says, it will "share in the glorious freedom of the children of God" (Rom 8:21).

This is where God's final design is achieved. Only then will God be able to say of God's creation "and all was good." At present these words are prophetic and hold promise for the future. The human being and the rest of creation show a deep interdependence and connectedness. Delay on the part of human beings in their maturing entails delay of creation; their advance entails an advance for the whole. It is an instrument by which the evolutionary process is either liberated or becomes bogged down.

What we have described thus far represents the objective situation of the evolutionary process, independent of the human will; it is the logic of cosmogenesis. But there is a drama taking place. When evolution reaches the human level, it attains the explicit level of conscious freedom. By comparison to other living beings, human beings are extremely complex. They gather an extremely rich store of information. They can speed up the evolutionary process enormously and become involved in it. What needed millions of years to happen spontaneously in accordance with the guiding forces of the universe can take place in a short space of time due to human intervention.

Human beings have the uniqueness of copiloting the whole process together with nature; they have been created as creators. They grasp that which could be but is not yet. Dwelling in them is a demon, that of desire, a machine manufacturing utopias. Through their imagination and the principle of utopia, human beings know what could be. They organize their activities so as to approach their dream of reality. No matter what they do, the dream ever remains on the horizon, impossible within history. Human beings, men and women, can pause and take a biological siesta, as it were, resting on their laurels after arduous conquests. They may close themselves to the evolutionary process, stand opposed to the universal drive in which they are inserted, whether they like it or not. Or they can flee to a golden past or toward the imagined future dream, withdrawing from their tasks in the present. They thus fail to accept their condition of becoming, of an achievement ever open to new and higher forms of life, and hence moving from the imperfect toward the perfect. They want to leap now to the goal of their desire without traversing the rocky path of the evolutionary process and its maturing. They do not joyfully accept its imperfection and process character.

Beyond the entire process there is always a chasm between dream and reality. Humans feel the desire for endless life, and they realize that life has an end, that they really die. That is the objective condition of the human being–spirit open to the infinite but condemned to live in the finite. This is the source of the frustration between what we are, mortal, and what we would like to be, immortal.

This is where the challenge to human freedom comes in. Human beings can accept this situation and accept their mortality. They can surrender their life to Someone greater who can make their yearning for endless life a reality. Death is not the negation of life or absence of relationship; it is the passage to another kind of relationship and of life. The human being is transformed through death. We do not really live to die; we die in order to live more fully and better–to be resurrected.

On the other hand, human beings can rebel against this condition. They want the unattainable immortality at any cost, without having to pass through death. They disrupt the basic solidarity of all things in the universe, which emerge, make their way, and in death are transfigured. Death is thus not loss but a transition that must be made in order that life may achieve its purpose and reach another level of the evolutionary process. Death is thus seen to be a higher kind of connectedness with the whole. Brazilian novelist Guimarães Rosa says that we do not die, we are enchanted.

To be closed to the evolutionary process, to refuse to accept mortality, to refuse to accept death in oneself as a necessary transition toward life beyond this life—that is what original sin means in human beings. This sin disrupts connectedness with all things and with God's design, which has so disposed the trajectory of everything that issues from God's heart, passes through time, and through death returns to that heart.[45]

In their striving to secure life and its reproduction, create as abundant means of life as possible, and avoid general entropy, human beings become organized in a way that is centered on themselves. Anthropocentrism takes root.[46] They make everything—nature, living beings, plants, animals, and even other human beings—serve them. They take possession of those things and subject them to their own interests. They disrupt the natural kinship with all things, for we all live off the same cosmic humus and we are all involved in the same universal adventure. Such self-centeredness does not bring the immortality we desire but rather the disruption of all connections and connectedness. To the extent that human beings do not feel and assume everything joyfully and lightheartedly in cosmic solidarity and in the community of the living, in an open process, in maturation and transformation through death as well, and thereby in connection with all, they will become isolated and overcome by fear, and out of fear will utilize power against nature, breaking the covenant of loving peace with it. This is what gives rise to the basic anti-ecological stance, which underlies all the others, nourishing and sustaining them.

Nevertheless, all spiritual traditions and religions of humankind hold that the last word is not that of disruption and solitude but of connection and connectedness, not original sin but original grace. Everything therefore can be saved. The covenant of peace and of kinship among humans, nature, and God is the absolutely necessary horizon for any effective ecological commitment.

Let us examine the Amazon, a concrete case showing how this basic connectedness can be broken.

CHAPTER 4

All the Capital Sins against Ecology

The Amazon

The Amazon is the place where Gaia displays the lush riches of her body; it is also where she suffers the greatest violence. If we want to see the brutal face of the capitalist and industrial system, we need only visit the Brazilian Amazon. That is where all the capital sins (mortal sins and sins of capital) are committed. There we see in unvarnished form the pursuit of bigness by the spirit of modernity, the rationalizing of the irrational, and the crystal-clear logic of the system. We likewise witness the clear contradiction between capitalism and ecology. To add the prefix *eco* to capitalism or to development projects–ecocapitalism or ecodevelopment– simply masks the inherent perversity of capitalism and its development paradigm. The internal logic of the system suggests that there is no such thing as ecology, or, if it does exist, it must be rejected.

The world strategists for capitalism have tried to apply the most advanced technologies to the largest nature reserve on Earth. The Brazilian government, Brazilian companies, and multinational companies have set up a powerful tripod. They have given rise to what has been called "the Amazon mode of production,"[1] which may be defined as an extremely predatory kind of production with an intensive application of technology against nature–declaring war on the trees, exterminating indigenous people and later arrivals, and exploiting the labor force in order to export and supply the world market. Rather than an Amazon mode of production, we have here an Amazon mode of destruction, because the major projects set up there "bring about social, cultural, and economic destruction of the native populations, indigenous or otherwise."[2] Thus the Amazon reveals how imperative it is that there be alternative development, a kind of development for all of humankind, whose starting point is the centrality of ecology, which provides the basis for dealing with economic, political, cultural, and other aspects of a civilized society.

Euclides da Cunha, a classic Brazilian writer who was one of the first to analyze the situation of the Amazon early in this century, said, "Human intelligence would not bear the weight of the vast reality of the Amazon. It will have to grow with it, and adapt to it, in order to dominate it."[3] Chico Mendes, a martyr of the ecological struggle in the Amazon and a symbol of the forest peoples, saw very clearly that human beings would have to grow along with the forest; he maintained that only a technology that is subject to the rhythms of the Earth, and an extractive approach to developing the incomparable wealth of the Amazon would preserve this ecological heritage of humankind. Anything else is insufficient and dangerous.

THE AMAZON: TEMPLE OF THE PLANET'S BIODIVERSITY

Spanning the continent, the Amazon contains 2.5 million square miles. It covers two-fifths of the area of Latin America (half of Peru, a third of Colombia, and a larger part of Bolivia, Venezuela, Guyana, French Guiana, and Suriname) and three-fifths of the area of Brazil, (1.35 million square miles).

The Amazon basin is located between two plates that represent the oldest lands on the planet (Pre-Cambrian age, 600 million years ago): to the north the plate of the Guianas, and to the south the Brazilian plate. In geological terms, throughout the entire Paleozoic period (550-230 million years ago) the whole proto-Amazon was underwater and made up a huge gulf open toward the Pacific. South America was still connected to Africa. During the Mesozoic age (230-55 million years ago) the land rose up and the rivers ran opposite to the way they do today, that is, toward the Pacific. At the end of this age, South America separated from Africa. During the Cenozoic age at the beginning of the Tertiary period, 70 million years ago, the Andes began to rise and continued to do so throughout the whole Pliocene and Pleistocene ages (5 million-72,000 years), blocking the outflow of water to the Pacific. The whole Amazon depression remained a watery landscape until an exit toward the Atlantic was found, bringing the Amazon to its present configuration.[4]

The Amazon region houses the river system with the largest mass of water on the globe, draining more than 2.7 million square miles of land. The Amazon River is the longest river in the world, 2,200 miles, longer than the Mississippi/Missouri and the Nile. It begins in Peru between the city of Cuzco and Lake Titicaca. It carries by far the largest volume with an average discharge of 7 million cubic feet per second. By itself it handles between one-fifth and one-sixth of the water mass emptied into the oceans and seas by all the rivers on Earth. The main river bed is 2.5 or 3 miles wide and varies in depth from 328 feet at Óbidos to 13 feet at the mouth of the Xingu. The drop is tiny: during the last 1.5 to 930 miles it falls just 49 feet (.6 inch per mile), but it has currents that move from 1.5 to 6.5 feet a second.

The Amazon is the site of the largest tropical rain forest on the planet, so much so that the great nineteenth-century naturalist Alexander von Humboldt (1769-1859) called it Hiléia (the Greek name meaning "wild forest region"). It contains 30% of the broad leaf forest reserves in the world and indeed the greatest genetic wealth. The various kinds of forests and soils existing there (riverbanks, dry earth, swamp, farmland, brush, pasture, and mangroves) house an astonishing biomass: more than 60,000 species of plants, 2.5 million species of arthropods (insects, spiders, centipedes, etc.), 2,000 species of fish, over 300 mammal species, and an inconceivable number of microorganisms. As Eneas Salati, one of our best researchers on Amazon issues, says, "In a few hectares of the Amazon forest there is a larger number of species of plants and insects than among all the flora and fauna of Europe."[5] We should have no illusions, however. This luxuriant forest is very frail, because it grows out of one of the poorest and most leached soils on Earth.

In pre-Colombian times around two million Amerindians lived in the Amazon region (according to the historian Pierre Chaunu, there were eighty to one hundred million inhabitants in South America and five million in Brazil). In the sixteenth century several indigenous groups had chiefdoms that displayed a significant degree of development, and their craft work was similar in some ways to that of the Andean and Mesoamerican civilizations. They made major developments in forest management, respecting its uniqueness while at the same time modifying the habitat to encourage vegetation useful to humans. The groves of vines, the stands of chestnuts and palms, for example, and the well-known "dark lands of the Indians" point to the civilizing work of the Amerindians mentioned in chapter 3. Human beings and forest evolved together in profound reciprocity. As the anthropologist Viveiros de Castro says, "The Amazon that we see today is the result of centuries of social intervention, just as the societies living there are the result of centuries of life shared with the Amazon,"[6] thereby dispelling the notion that the forest was wild and lacking in civilization.

In pre-Cabral Brazil (that is, before the arrival-conquest of Cabral in 1500), there were around 1,400 tribes, 60% of them in the Amazon. The languages they spoke belonged to 40 trunks subdivided into 94 different languages. This is impressive since a single trunk, the Indo-European, encompasses languages as different as Sanskrit, Greek, Latin, German, and Slavic. The ethnologist Berta Ribeiro was led to say that "nowhere else on Earth is there a linguistic variety similar to that found in tropical

South America."[7] Of the five million Amerindians in Brazil in the year 1500, only 220,000 remain today; around 100,000 now live in the Amazon region, divided into 160 tribes.

The river was given its name by Dominican friar Gaspar de Carvajal. He served as a chronicler for the Spanish captain Francisco Orellana, who, from the imperial standpoint of the Europeans, is regarded as the discoverer of the Amazon. In 1541-42 he spent eight months navigating up the river from the mouth to its sources. The chronicler saw full-bodied women who looked like warriors; he was reminded of the Amazons of ancient mythology, who cut off their left breast so as to be able to handle their bow and arrow more easily. The river thus came to be called the Amazon.

UNDOING MYTHS ABOUT THE AMAZON: NEITHER THE WORLD'S LUNGS NOR ITS STOREHOUSE

Before entering into the anti-ecological aspects of the current situation of the Amazon we must disabuse ourselves of three myths.

The first is to regard the Amerindians in general and especially those in the Amazon as *wild, genuinely natural beings*, representatives of the peoples of the virgin forest and hence in perfect harmony with nature. They are regarded as integrated into the environment like the manatee in the Amazon lakes and the tapir in the brush. They are thought to be governed by natural as opposed to cultural norms, and to be in a kind of biological siesta vis-à-vis nature, effortlessly adapted to nature's rhythms and logic. It is also believed that the indigenous peoples are bearers of an ancestral knowledge of the secrets of nature and of the healing power of herbs and plants unknown to modern science. Such an ecologizing of indigenous peoples is the fruit of the urban imagination, which in a second- or thirdhand way is overwhelmed by the extravagance of nature and would like to return to its original state. This is a projection of the crisis of the social paradigm, in ancestral guise, by James Redfield in his widely read novel *The Celestine Prophecy*.[8]

The Amazon Indians are human like any other human beings, and hence they are always in interaction with their environment, even one as rich as that of the Amazon. Research is increasingly showing the interplay between the forest peoples and their surroundings; they mutually condition one another. The relationships are not "natural" but cultural in an intricate web of reciprocity. Indigenous peoples are as cultural as we are, but their culture is of a different type. Perhaps what makes indigenous people unique, different from modern human beings, is that they feel and see nature as part of their society and culture, as an extension of their personal and social body. For them, nature is a living agent, one charged with purposiveness; it is not what it is for modern people, more in the nature of an object, mute and neutral. Nature speaks and Indians hear its voice and message. Hence they live a true ecological and cosmic sharing. Nature belongs to society and society belongs to nature. They see nature-as-subject and human-as-subject having exchanges such as always exist between subjects. In this play of their inter(retro)relationships human beings and nature are co-evolving. They are always adjusting to one another, always in a process of mutual adaptation. Hence the indigenous peoples are much more integrated into the Earth and the universe than we are. Their posture leads to the preservation of nature, and if we assume such a posture ourselves—as we urgently need to do—it will also save our planet.

The second myth holds that the Amazon is the *lungs of the world.* Specialists say that the Amazon forest is at a climax state. In other words, it is at an optimum state of life, in a dynamic equilibrium in which everything is utilized and hence everything is in balance. Thus the energy fixed by the plants through interaction with the food chain is completely utilized. The oxygen released by photosynthesis of the leaves by day is consumed by the plants themselves at night and by the other living organisms. That is why the Amazon is not the world's lungs.

It does act as a large carbon dioxide filter, however. A large amount of carbon is absorbed in photosynthesis. Carbon is the main cause of the greenhouse effect, which is warming the Earth (it has risen by 25% during the last hundred years). Should the Amazon be totally cleared, fifty billion tons of carbon a year would be sent into the atmosphere. Living beings could not withstand such amounts, and there would be mass death of live organisms.

The third myth is that the Amazon could be the *storehouse of the world* as early explorers like von Humboldt and Bonpland and the Brazilian planners during the period when the military was in power (1964-83) thought. It is not. Research has shown that "the forest lives off itself" and largely for itself.[9] It is lush, but its soil is poor in humus. That seems to be a paradox, but it becomes understandable when we consider the way the forest is formed. The great Amazon specialist Harold Sioli says that "the forest actually grows *over* the soil not *out of* the soil."[10] He explains that the soil is only the physical support for an intricate web of roots. Plants are interconnected by the roots and support one another at the base. They are like an immense balance scale; the whole forest moves and dances. When one tree is brought down, it brings down several others with it.

The forest remains lush because the chain of nutrients is closed. Materials are decomposing on the soil, its covering, which is composed of leaves, fruits, small roots, and animal excrement. These things are enriched by the water dripping from the leaves and running off the trunks. It is not the soil that nourishes the leaves, but rather the trees that nourish the soil.

These two kinds of water wash and carry off the excrement of birds, monkeys, coatis, and the myriad insects whose habitat is in the tree cover. There are also huge numbers of fungi and another countless number of microorganisms that along with the nutrients resupply the roots. It is through the roots that the food substance passes into the plants, thereby assuring the giddying exuberance of Hiléia. This is a closed system, however, and its balance is complex and fragile. Any small deviation can bring disastrous consequences. The topsoil is generally no more than a foot or so in depth. With torrential rains it is carried off, and soon there is nothing but sand. Without the forest the Amazon could become a huge grassland or even a desert. The Amazon can never be the world's storehouse, but must remain the temple of the greatest biodiversity on the planet.

The two greatest threats to the Amazon are clear cutting (with chainsaws or bulldozers) and burning. In 1978 Shelton Davis, a major international expert on Amazon issues, wrote with immense sadness, "At this moment a silent war is being waged against aboriginal peoples, innocent peasants, and the whole ecosystem of the Amazon basin."[11] The forest was almost intact up to 1968. Since then, the forest has been brutalized and plundered by the introduction of huge industrialization and colonization projects, especially under military governments.

During three centuries of colonization, no more than 39 square miles were cleared. In a mere thirteen years of the military dictatorship 117,000 square miles were mowed down.[12] The extent of deforestation is now estimated to be 9 to 12%. That may seem small, but in absolute terms it is an area of over 234,000 square miles, which is larger than the reunified Germany, larger than all the land producing soy, wheat, or corn in Brazil.[13] Researchers estimate that the Amazon tropical forest requires at least a thousand years to recover its previous splendor.[14] Moreover, deforestation upsets the entire regional ecosystem, damaging what were intended to be development projects.

For example, in 1927 Henry Ford received from the Brazilian government 2.5 million acres of the Tabajós River in Pará with the right to grow rubber trees to export rubber to the world market completely tax free for fifty years. Around 275,000 trees were planted, but because they were located outside their natural habitat, they were attacked by a devastating fungus and a large portion had to be cut down. The project failed.[15]

In 1967 the American billionaire Daniel Ludwig set up a huge project on the Jari River near the mouth of the Amazon, a six hundred million dollar investment that occupied almost 9 million acres (larger than Belgium or Israel). It was conceived as a large forest project to produce wood pulp and a large agricultural project to export beef, rice, and soybeans. He cleared the native forest and on half a million acres he planted a hundred million plants of *Gmelina arborea* (brought in from Africa, within six or seven years it grows to seventy feet and is excellent for wood pulp) and *Pinus caribea* (from Honduras, within six to nine years is good for wood pulp, and after twelve years for lumber). The trees were outside their own ecosystems, however, and they were attacked by a fungus (*Cylindroncladium pteridis*) and devastated. The project had to be abandoned and was sold to a group of twenty-two Brazilian companies. The failure was the result of ecological carelessness and ignorance.[16]

In 1975 Volkswagen of Brazil created a company (Cia. Vale do Rio Cristalino–Agropecuária, Comércio e Indústria) in the southern part of the state of Pará. It bought 144,000 acres and cleared 55,000 of them using napalm and defoliants that had been used in the Vietnam War. Grass seed was dropped by plane to create huge pasture lands. The company placed 86,000 head of cattle there. In order to prevent desertification and preserve pasture lands it set aside 3,600 square yards for each head of cattle. Nevertheless, it suffered huge losses and the project was abandoned.

These events show how delicately the Amazon is balanced and demonstrate that disregarding ecological matters results in enormous failures.

THE AMAZON MEGAPROJECTS: WAR ON THE TREES

The Amazon is regarded as the last frontier for those who are looking for land to work and the final refuge of 60% of the indigenous people left from the great biological tribulation that has battered them for five hundred years (with the result that only one in twenty-two has survived).[17] For the government the Amazon has always represented the challenge of integrating the nation. The new expansion into the Amazon began with the building of the 1,340-mile Belém-Brasília highway (begun in 1958 and completed in 1960).

Although the Amazon soil is generally poor, there are regions of great mineral wealth, especially in the eastern part between the Xingu and Araguaia rivers. One of the largest mineral concentrations in the world is located within one 39 square mile area. It is calculated that twenty-five to thirty billion tons of metals, such as iron, bauxite, magnesium, nickel and copper, are lying in a 23 square mile area. The advantage is that these mines are on the surface and relatively close to the Atlantic, and hence the products can be shipped out.

In order to utilize this wealth, the Brazilian government moved to establish thirty-three large projects involving billions and billions of dollars, especially after 1970 when the National Integration Program was set up (the official slogan was *integrar para não entregar*, "incorporate so as not to surrender"). It is said that these projects are second in magnitude only to the NASA projects in the United States. All are supported by a tripod of investors: the Brazilian government in combination with private Brazilian companies and transnational capital, which now comes from the United States, Japan, Germany, England, Italy, and elsewhere, all of which operate globally.

The Major Roads: Creating Rural Slums

Six major roads cut through the Brazilian Amazon. Their main objective is to facilitate colonization and integration and the shipping of products. The Belém-Brasília road has already been mentioned. The others are the 3348-mile Transamazon highway, south of the Amazon River, linking the Amazon and Northeast Brazil; the 2480-mile Northern Perimeter Highway, yet to be built, which will follow the borders of Suriname, Guyana, Venezuela, Colombia, and Peru; the Cuiabá-Santarém highway, connecting the Amazon to the Center-South of Brazil; the Manaus-Boa Vista highway, a branch of the Transamazon highway, which would run south from the Northern Perimeter Highway; and the Cuiabá-Porto Velho highway, connecting the capital of Mato Grosso to the capital of Rondônia. A 973-mile railway running north and south has also been built between Goiás and Maranhão.

These roads have led to a large influx of settlers who with government encouragement have occupied lands along the roads. In the terminology of the National Integration Program they are settled into *agrovilas* (45-60 families), twenty-two of which make up an *agropolis* (a set of 22 *agrovilas*) and a *rurópolis* (an urban center with industry and commerce). The 213,000 inhabitants in 1960 grew to 360,000 in 1970, and 452,000 in 1975, and then dropped to 404,000 in 1980. They have pushed out the indigenous peoples and *caboclos* (people of mixed blood), cleared forests with abandon, contaminated rivers, and caused vast poverty and ecological devastation. It was assumed that five million people from the Northeast would settle in the Amazon; the official slogan was, "Land without people for people without land." These efforts to occupy the land with human beings were a failure due to unpreparedness, lack of help from government agencies, poor soil fertility, and difficulties with storage and transportation of products. Huge rural slums were the result. The next step was to attempt to occupy the land with cattle.

In a short period of time over five hundred large farming and ranch projects were set up. Instead of paying taxes, large companies could open huge investments in the Amazon. Entrepreneurs received deeds and tax incentives if they agreed to clear land and begin to set up cattle and lumber operations. Thus ecological crime was sanctioned by the government. Fifty-two million acres of Brazil were offered to business people, and the resulting projects led to the clearing of 5.12% of the total area of the Brazilian Amazon. Similar projects resulted in the clearing of almost 15 million acres in the Peruvian Amazon and 70 million in the Colombian Amazon.

The Large Hydroelectric Projects: Poisoning the Waters

Large projects are energy intensive. There are seventy-nine hydroelectric projects planned for the Amazon up to the year 2000, and they produce 17,000 megawatts, by flooding 2% of the entire Amazon. The energy potential of the Amazon basin is 100,000 megawatts, or 60% of the total capacity in the country. Of the various plants, we want to pause briefly over two, Balbina and Tucuruí, because they are enough to show how irrational modern technology is when it is applied with no consideration for the specific ecological setting.

The Balbina dam project on the river Uutumã, near Manaus, was planned for 1985, but it did not go into operation until 1989. It was intended to serve the city and the industrial pole in the Manaus Free Zone. It was not preceded by planning and geotechnical feasibility studies (proper slope and placement), nor were ecological factors and the affected populations taken into account. Since the lands are sedimentary and have little slope, the dam flooded too much land—920 square miles. Hence, average depth is a scant 24 feet and over 312 square miles it is barely 13 feet. With a low outflow because the slope is so slight, and the appearance of unanticipated leaks (caves that absorb water), energy yield is one-third less than expected. Since there was little prior clearing of land (barely 2%) in a large part of the lake the forest cover is sticking through the water surface. Since the forest is dead and decomposing and the water changes very slowly (it needs a year), the water is for practical purposes poisoned and is harming the fauna and the turbine operation. In short, "Balbina is technically inadequate, disproportionately expensive, ecologically disastrous, and profoundly disrupting for the local populations, including the Uaimiris-Atroaris, who have practically disappeared. It is an example of what not to do."[18]

We find these same irrationalities even more dramatically in the Tucuruí plant, which stands along the Tocantins River in the Marabá micro-region. It is part of the Grande Carajás Project, about which we will speak below. This is the fourth largest plant in the world and the largest built in tropical rain forests. It costs around 4.6 billion dollars to generate 8000 megawatts and floods 950 square miles. It is intended to meet the energy demands of the major aluminum and iron project in the region, and also to supply electricity to the city of Belém, the capital of Pará, and large portions of northern Brazil. At the height of its construction in 1982, it employed around thirty thousand people, but that figure fell to seventeen thousand in 1983, and by the end of 1985 it was just four thousand. After being laid off by the Carajás industrial projects, these workers formed several cities of impoverished slum dwellers. During the four years of dam construction the city of Tucuruí rose from a population of four thousand to eighty thousand with consequent grave problems of social ecology.

The creation of the Tucuruí reservoir had a series of ecological consequences. One grave omission was failure to remove the vegetation from the areas flooded, something that must be done to avoid causing the growth of harmful water plants, water acidity, and death of the fish. Only a few areas were cleared, mostly to protect the turbines and the spillways.

In fact, the decomposition of organic materials is killing fish at an astonishing rate. Water acidity has corroded the turbines and other equipment. The spread of harmful plants like hyacinths and samambaias is threatening to clog the turbines. The water plants are becoming ideal hatcheries for mosquitos and small parasitic worms that transmit diseases such as yellow fever, malaria, and schistosomiasis, which is made worse by the creation of 350 square miles of marsh and swamp areas.[19] Located near the cities, the water reservoir has led to an astonishing spread of flies and mosquitos to the point where in 1991 the mayor of Tucuruí "in view of the fact that no human being can live in the area, declared a state of emergency."[20]

Here again we can see the same perverse result of a linear paradigm that is blind to the ecological whole and insensitive to any humanistic or ethical dimension toward the subjectivity of nature and of the persons living in the area.

The Grande Carajás Project: Pharaonic Approach to Technology

The Grande Carajás Project is being set up in the state of Pará for the mining of strategic ores and minerals, and for agroindustries and tree farming. The project is on a giant scale, in keeping with the spirit of the imperial modernity that dominates the Earth: it covers a 351,000 square mile area, that is, the area of England and France combined; it has a 62 billion dollar price tag; and it was set up in thirteen years (the inauguration was in 1980) with a demographic explosion that will rise by 400 to 800 percent by the year 2000. A 552-mile railway has been built in record time, going from Paraupebas (Carajás) to Porto Madeira in Sao Luis de Maranhão (Itaqui). Factories, cities, villages, roads, and parks have sprung up overnight, thus creating the largest integrated project in the world's tropical areas.

Four major projects make up the Grande Carajás Project: a deposit of iron ore, two aluminum factories, and the Tucuruí dam. In the hills of Carajás in Pará, west of the city of Marabá, lies one of the richest mineral deposits on Earth: 20 billion tons of iron, 66% pure, one of the highest rates in the world; 65 million tons of manganese; 1 billion tons of copper; 40 million tons of aluminum; 100 million tons of nickel; 100,000 tons of tin; and 100,000 tons of copper.[21] The project is headed by the Companhia Vale do Rio Doce, one of the largest state-owned companies in Brazil, in conjunction with large multinational mining companies such as Alcoa, an American company that is the largest producer of aluminum in the world (60%); Nalco (Nippon Amazon Aluminum Co.); Alcan (Aluminum Company of Canada); Alusuisse; Billiton-Schell; Patiño Englardt; and others. Thirty foundries producing pig iron, iron alloys, and processing units for other metals have been set up along the railway, all powered by charcoal. That involves taking 34 million cubic yards of wood from 3.7 million acres. That is equivalent to 86 acres cleared per day. As has been said, the Amazon forest is being exported in the form of cast iron and charcoal; that is why the soils are being leached, thousands of species of life are facing extinction, river beds are choking, and the environment is generally being degraded.[22]

It is worth noting that the Companhia Vale do Rio Doce, which is overseeing the project, set up a group of nine scientists and specialists in Amazon issues to oversee the ecological impact of the various programs. They carried out outstanding work, for example holding an international congress entitled "Economic Development and Environmental Impact in the Brazilian Rain Forest" in the city of Belém in 1986. A section of the city of Carajás was built in which ten thousand administrative employees live with all the infrastructure of a modern first-world city. All ecological requirements were strictly observed in a 1 million acre area. Beyond that area, however, the land is being cleared at an unprecedented rate for the agroindustrial and animal raising projects, such as rice, beans, corn, manioc pellets for animal feed, palm products, and so forth, all of it for export. The ecologists were in continual communication with the technicians and engineers who showed little sensitivity for such issues. As usually happens, at Carajás maximizing short-term profit took precedence over any long-range ecological considerations.[23] The brutality of the technicians won out over the sensitivity of the ecologists.

Heavy industry has been set up in the Amazon in response to the demands of international capitalism. Since 1972 oil has risen from two dollars to thirty-two dollars a barrel, thereby making electric power more expensive, especially in Japan, where it is generated by crude oil. It also made shipping minerals more expensive, especially bauxite, the source of aluminum, which is basic to industry. A third of the related industries in Japan, the United States, and Europe were forced to close. The solution was to transfer these industries to parts of the world that had vast amounts of energy, large bauxite deposits, and cheap labor. The Amazon fulfills those requirements splendidly. Thus the main multinationals involved in steel have come here and have enjoyed a further benefit: they kept the clean industries in their own countries and got rid of their harmful industrial wastes, which they dumped in the Third World. For example, "red mud," the waste from bauxite, which is highly toxic, is stored in artificial lakes. That also explains why the projects have been accelerated to meet world demand by employing a huge labor force: 140,000 workers (27,000 in the Ferro Carajás Project; 63,000 to build the Tucuruí dam; and 50,000 prospecting in the Serra Pelada).[24]

The primary acts of aggression against nature in the Amazon have been perpetrated by the Grande Carajás Agrícola company in conjunction with JICA (the Japan International Cooperation Agency, which is comprised of twenty-two Japanese investment companies). Although the Japanese agency recommended that ecological precautions be taken to harmonize agricultural development with environmental preservation, the government's decision-making machine went in a strictly technocratic direction. Ignoring the wisdom of the native populations, acquired over thousands of years, it praised the virtues of mechanization and pursued the destruction of the forest on a scale unprecedented in Brazil. It pushed out Indians and mixed-race people. The government only gave subsidies when the companies proved that they had "cleared the ground"—that is, cleared the trees and bushes, pushed the native populations out, and brought in others from the South, who had the illusion that they were better prepared for modern agroindustry because they were descendants of Europeans. The farming projects sought to create a herd of two million head of cattle for export. Along with the projects, however, came wild speculation involving major Brazilian companies like Café Cacique, Varig, Sul América Seguros, as well as multinationals like Volkswagen, Liquifarma (an Italian pharmaceutical chemical company), Atlântica-Boavista (Rockefeller group), and others.

To speed up the clearing, many ranchers used the defoliant Tordon 155-Br (Agent Orange) or Tordon 101-Br, which is even more destructive, sprayed from a plane, thereby polluting soils and river, and killing many people, especially the Nhambiquara Indians, who were almost wiped out.[25] The peasants who were expelled or threatened became organized and formed many rural unions. The implementation of these projects in the hills of Carajás provoked a real war in the countryside. In 1985 around one hundred were killed, and in 1986 the figure rose to two hundred; in the following years the figure declined but still remained high. The thirteen thousand Indians from thirty-four different tribes in the region saw their lands invaded by cattle growers and lumbermen and many Indians were killed.[26]

Such agroindustry and cattle projects have not proven sustainable. Large crops and cattle raising on vast pastures are causing permanent damage to the Amazon ecosystem: erosion, compacting, and leaching of the soil, silting of rivers and dams, air pollution produced by huge fires, some of them so large that they were detected by American and Russian satellites, running the risk of turning the eastern Amazon into a "red desert." On a single day in 1988 the Discovery space shuttle detected 8,438 fires in the Amazon. Once again the government planning machinery has ignored the enormous potential for economic and social progress offered by the traditional technologies of the native groups. Research on the Kayapó tribe in southern Pará, for example, has shown that they have a careful classification of species and skillful forest management. They were able to define more than forty kinds of forests, fields, and soils with their associated insects, animals, birds, winds, and climates, thereby enabling them to meet their needs while preserving the balance of the regional ecosystem.[27] That knowledge should have been utilized by the technicians and strategists of the major projects for managing the Amazon forest and preserving species, but it was haughtily and arrogantly dismissed.

Indians and Prospectors: The Holocaust of the Innocent

At any one time in Brazil there are around 600,000 prospectors (the number reached a million in 1988). They are made up of the unemployed, landless peasants (most of them teenagers, as young as 14 or 15) who have emigrated from the droughts in the Northeast, and adventurers from everywhere who come seeking gold and diamonds in the river beds and in mineral-rich zones. Washing used to be done by hand, but today prospecting is done with heavy and expensive equipment. At the well-known mine on the Madeira River in the Amazon, five hundred boats pulled up 6.4 tons of gold from the river bed in 1987 alone, polluting the river with one hundred tons of mercury.

The Serra Pelada mine associated with the Grande Carajás is famous. Forty thousand prospectors work out in the open, hauling up the gold ore—a human anthill comparable only to the building of the great pyramids of Egypt. Forty tons of gold were taken out in 1986, each prospector climbing the steps of the six-hundred-foot hole. The hunger for gold and the miserable quality of life in the slum cities of Curionópolis (30,000 inhabitants) and El Dorado (20,000) next to Serra Pelada led to very violent social relations, heightened by inhalation of mercury vapor, which causes irritability, loss of self-confidence, hallucinations, suicidal depression, and manic-depressive psychosis. As it is washed down rivers, mercury kills fish, affects fishermen, and is especially dangerous for native peoples. Hundreds and hundreds of Yanomamis have become sick and died as a result of the pollution that the 35,000 prospectors have produced in their lands on the Brazil-Venezuela border.[28]

It is the indigenous people who suffer most from the exploitation and internationalization of the wealth of the Amazon.[29] The slogan of FUNAI (National Foundation of the Indian), the body that should be protecting them, was "A hundred thousand Indians can't hold up Brazil's progress." FUNAI has been an accomplice in the way of the cross of these primordial peoples. Let us note only a few stations.

First station: The slaughter at parallel 11 in Rondônia (at the far western end of the Amazon) in 1963. Large ranches and tin-mining operations were being set up. Around ten thousand indigenous people lived in the area, in a hundred different villages. To make it easier to move in, the Arruda e Junqueira company ordered sacks of sugar dropped into a village during a ceremony. The Indians happily picked up the sugar, and then a plane flew over, dropping dynamite, and slaughtered them.[30]

Second station: The slaughter of the Nhambiquaras, also in Rondônia. Early in this century there were around ten thousand Nhambiquaras in the Guaporé River area. To ease the introduction of livestock from the south, they were transferred to the clearing of the Parecis where land is arid. Those who did not die of hunger caught smallpox, a disease of whites. The entire Nhambiquara population was decimated in less than fifteen years. Those who remained in the fertile Guaporé Valley were hit with defoliants sprayed from planes. In 1980 there remained only 650 representatives of the ten thousand. One of them outlines their tragic tale very well: "At first there was only the Indian. There was no American, Brazilian, FUNAI—nothing. Then, the American missionary came in 1964. Three moons went by and then came the Brazilian: machine, bulldozer, road, they knocked down a lot of forest, they spread fire and it began: grass, grass, grass, cattle, cattle, ranch, wire, wire."[31]

Third station: The sacrificing of the Uaimiris-Atroaris in the outskirts of Manaus. This is perhaps the tribe that has suffered most in recent decades. They numbered six thousand in 1905 but had declined to three thousand by 1968. By 1982 there were only 517 left, and only 350 in 1984. That rate of extermination is like that of the conquest-invasion of Europeans into South America. Such a biological catastrophe is the result of the various development policies implemented in the Amazon near Manaus. The building of the Manaus-Boa Vista road, the mining operation Taboca S.A. (a subsidiary of the Paranapanema company, which mines casitterite and tin), and the building of the Balbina plant directly affected the Uaimiris-Atroaris' lands. Matters went so far that the rivers were renamed in order to cheat them and in order to say that the lake formed by damming the Uatumã River with the Balbina dam would not affect their lands. The Uatumã River, which runs along the Indian reservation, was renamed the Pitinga River and the name Uatumã was switched to a smaller tributary. While the Manaus-Boa Vista road was under construction the Indians were attacked by government helicopters and light planes, and their settlements were set on fire, killing many Indians. In at least one case, the military command in the Amazon ordered the use of chemical weapons against unarmed Uaimiris-Atroaris. As a result of the various attacks they underwent only ten of the original sixty Indian villages were left by 1987. Their situation has been accurately called ethnocide.[32] Today these Indians are lost in the forest, reduced to silence, buried in the forgetfulness of our culture, which practices ecocide and devastates the primordial populations.

No number of pages would be enough to tell the tragic tale of the indigenous peoples of the Amazon, such as the Kayapó, the Paracanã, the Txucarramãe, the Crenacarores, the Gavião, and so many others. However, the survivors trust in the power of the Earth and in the justice of sacred things. In 1975 the World Council of Indigenous Peoples issued a solemn declaration in Port Alberni, expressing its hope against all hope: "They have not been able to eliminate us, or to make us forget what we are, for we are a culture of Earth and heaven. Our ancestry is thousands of years old and there are millions of us. And even if our whole universe were to be destroyed, we would live longer than the empire of death."[33]

In all these resistance struggles, indigenous peoples and small farmers have had a crucial ally, the churches committed to the poor and to liberation. The Catholic church in particular, with Christian base communities, the Pastoral Land Commission (CPT), and the Indigenous Missionary Commission (CIMI), has played a prophetic and public role in denouncing the violence in Brazil and internationally. The church has also played a crucial political and social role by providing strategic aid to the victims by way of medical and legal assistance, establishing independent rural unions and human-rights commissions, and creating a far-reaching consciousness-raising program to serve the resistance and liberation of the forest peoples and oppressed populations in the city and countryside. Liberation theology expresses in theoretical form the concrete commitment of the churches to the cause of the downtrodden and oppressed. That theology has attained a popular and international character because the cause it has taken on is just and because there is a pressing ethical urgency to do something about the vast human and ecological disaster being perpetrated in areas as important as these in the Amazon.[34]

THE DREAM OF CHICO MENDES AND THE FUTURE OF THE AMAZON

The observations we have made about the Amazon—and that we could also make about the Pantanal in Mato Grosso and the Atlantic forest in

Brazil—are overwhelming proof of how misguided it is to pursue development along the lines of modernity. Such development ignores nature and
is carried out against it, for it sees nature as an obstacle instead of an ally.
As we have already indicated, the underlying question lies not in making
development sustainable, but rather in starting from the sustainability of
nature to create an alternative to the straitjacket of such development.
Instead of speaking of development, we must speak of society, defending
life, and promoting the quality of human life. Sustainability, as we have
seen, is eminently an outgrowth of ecology, just as the category of *development* derives from the economic realm. Sustainability has to do with the
dynamic and self-regulating balance (homeostasis) that is inherent in nature as a result of the chain of interdependencies and complementarities
among all beings, especially living things that depend on resources that
are continually recycled and hence are sustainable without limit. The
Amazon is the greatest example of such natural sustainability. We must
learn from the technology and sustainability of nature—something that the
Amazon megaprojects have denied and continue to deny. This economy
of nature must inspire the human economy, which thereby comes to participate in the sustainability of nature.

This was precisely the underlying intuition of Chico Mendes, a genuine
representative of the forest peoples and a sharp observer of the logic of
nature. Those of us who were close friends with him were aware of how
deeply identified he was with the Amazon forest, with its vast biodiversity,
with the rubber tappers, with the animals, and with the slightest sign of life
in the bush. He was a secular and modern St. Francis. He divided his life
between the city and the jungle, but while in the city, he could hear the
powerful call of the forest in his body and soul. He experienced himself as
part and parcel of the land, and so he used to go back to the rubber area
and commune with the wild and the cosmos. It was there that he felt he
was in his habitat, his true home. His ecological awareness prompted him
to leave the forest temporarily in order to organize rubber tappers, establish labor union cells, and take part in resistance struggles (the famous
"standoffs," a strategy by which the rubber tappers, together with their
children, old people, and other allies, stood peacefully in the way of those
clearing the forest and their machines, preventing them from toppling
trees).

In view of the ecological crisis being forced on the Amazon, and speaking for the movement of forest peoples, he suggested that extractive reserves be created. His idea was accepted by the government in 1987. Very
realistically he said,

> We understand—the rubber tappers understand—that the Amazon
> cannot be turned into an untouchable sanctuary. However, we also

understand that there is an urgent need to avoid the clear cutting that is threatening the Amazon and thereby threatening the life of all the peoples of the planet. Hence we are thinking of an alternative for preserving the forest that can be economically productive at the same time. That is why we are thinking about creating an extractive reserve.[35]

He explained how this mode of production would work:

> In extractive reserves we ourselves are going to sell and manufacture the products that the forest generously grants us. The university must be part of the extractive reserve. It is the only way to keep the Amazon from disappearing. Furthermore, this reserve is not going to have owners. It is going to be the shared property of the community. We will have use but not ownership.[36]

It would thus be possible to devise an alternative to the savage extraction, whose only beneficiaries are speculators. A mahogany tree cut down in Acre costs from one to five dollars; sold on the European market it costs from three to five thousand dollars.

On Christmas Eve 1988, Mendes was murdered with five shots, felled by the enemies of humankind. He departed from life in the Amazon to enter into universal history and into the collective unconscious of those who love our planet and its vast biodiversity. As an archetype Chico Mendes drives the struggle to preserve the Amazon and the forest peoples that has now been assumed by millions of people around the world. A poet of the forest of Pará put it well when he sang, "Ay! Amazon! Amazon! They have buried Chico Mendes, but hope just won't be buried" (João de Jesus Paes Loureiro).

The Amazon megaprojects are a conclusive argument against the kind of development that has been imposed as a scourge on all the Earth's cultures for four hundred years. Such only produces growth, which is appropriated by a few at the cost of a great deal of sacrifice and misery for the many. That is why it is inhuman and a monstrosity. It is against human life and is inimical to the Earth; it is the fruit of an insane rationality. Such Pharaonic projects demand that information and decisions be made in frigid offices full of papers and cold data, far from the enchanting paradise, away from the beseeching countenances of the people of the backlands, indifferent to the naive eyes of the Indians, without any link to compassion and to the sense of human and cosmic solidarity. What takes place in those offices is an abstract rationality disconnected from human space and time. That is why such stupidity produces economic disaster and cultural degradation.

The people are poorer today than they were when the megaprojects began. Pará, the site of the Grande Carajás Program, is the number three state in exports in the country (after São Paulo and Paraná), but the people around the projects are living in slums without any infrastructure and no safe drinking water. Seventy percent of the population of the capital, Belém, earns less than a minimum wage (in 1995, a hundred dollars a month). Only one out of every three working age people in Pará has a job; the other two live off the informal economy.[37]

This "development" has not been carried out for the people or with the people. No one was asked to give his or her opinion, no one was listened to. The very people whose wisdom has accumulated over hundreds of generations and who live there and know their habitat were not only disregarded but actually killed. This growth produced by capital for capital took as its starting point the perverse assumption that the primordial peoples and the forests alike must be wiped out as a condition for entering into modernity.

Studies have shown that there is no need to destroy the Amazon forest to draw wealth from it. The extraction of the palm products (cabbage-palm, wine-palm, the *bacaba* palm, *pupunha* palm, and so forth), Brazil nuts, rubber, oils, and vegetable dyes, alkaloid substances for medicines, powerful herbicide and fungicide substances, yield more than turning it into pasture—which even now is taking place at the rate of thirty-seven acres per minute. Profits from livestock are so small that any kind of extraction is equal or better. Medicine around the world would have a great deal to gain if it were wise enough to listen to the *caboclos* and the Indians, who are masters in their knowledge of medicinal herbs. The ten percent of the red soil already identified as very fertile could become one of the most productive agricultural areas in the world. Exporting mining and wood products could go hand in hand with ongoing reforestation so as to assure that the areas affected would be kept green.[38]

The Amazon is the place that refutes modernity's development paradigm—unsustainable development full of capital sins (that is, sins of capital) and sins against ecology. But it is also the place for testing a possible alternative, in keeping with the rhythm of its lush natural endowment, by respecting the ecological wisdom of the primordial peoples who have been living there for centuries, drawing out riches without destroying the forests, rivers, and soils, and thus engaging in activity that benefits nature and humankind. Here lies its universal paradigmatic value, a point of meditation for all those who love this beautiful, shining planet and who refuse to accept the type of relationship that breaks the cosmic covenant it took millions and millions of years to stitch together, a covenant that has been handed down to us as a precious inheritance to be preserved and used in keeping with the logic that it dictates itself, a logic of solidarity and sobriety. It is to be used so that all may enjoy a generous sufficiency.

CHAPTER 5

Liberation Theology and Ecology

Rivals or Partners?

Liberation theology and ecological discourse have something in common: they start from two bleeding wounds. The wound of poverty breaks the social fabric of millions and millions of poor people around the world. The other wound, systematic assault on the Earth, breaks down the balance of the planet, which is under threat from the plundering of development as practiced by contemporary global societies. Both lines of reflection and practice have as their starting point a cry: the cry of the poor for life, freedom, and beauty (cf. Ex 3:7), and the cry of the Earth groaning under oppression (cf. Rom 8:22-23). Both seek liberation, a liberation of the poor by themselves as active subjects who are organized, conscious, and networked to other allies who take on their cause and their struggle; and a liberation of the Earth through a new covenant between it and human beings, in a brotherly and sisterly relationship and with a kind of sustainable development that respects the different ecosystems and assures a good quality of life for future generations.[1]

Now is the time to bring these two discourses together, to see to what extent they are different, or in opposition, or complementary. We begin with ecological discourse because it represents a truly comprehensive standpoint. We are going to take up once more the perspectives presented thus far—with some risk of repetition—so as to bring these two major movements together.

THE ECOLOGICAL AGE

Ecology was first understood to be the subheading of biology that studies the inter(retro)relationships of living beings among themselves and with their environment. That was how it was understood by Ernst Haeckel, who first formulated it in 1866. Soon, however, that understanding spread into three ecologies.[2] *Environmental* ecology is concerned with the environment and the relations that various societies have with it in history, whether they are easy or harsh on it, whether they integrate human beings into or distance them from nature. *Social* ecology is primarily concerned with social relations as belonging to ecological relations; that is, because human beings (who are personal and social) are part of the natural world their relationship with nature passes through the social relationship of exploitation, collaboration, or respect and reverence. Hence social justice—the right relationship between persons, roles, and institutions—implies some achievement of ecological justice, which is the right relationship with nature, easy access to its resources, and assurance of quality of life. Finally, *mental* ecology starts from the recognition that nature is not outside human beings but within them, in their minds, in the form of psychic energies, symbols, archetypes, and behavior patterns that embody attitudes of aggression or of respect and acceptance of nature.

In its early stages ecology was still a regional discourse, concerned with the preservation of certain endangered species (whales, panda bears, and so forth) or the creation of nature reserves to guarantee favorable conditions for the various ecosystems. In short, it was concerned with what is green on the planet, such as forests, and particularly tropical forests, which are the sites of the greatest biodiversity on Earth. However, as awareness of the unwanted effects of the industrial development process grew, ecology became increasingly a global discourse. It is not just species or ecosystems that are threatened; the Earth as a whole is ill and must be treated and healed. The alarm went out in 1972 with the well-known report of the Club of Rome, *The Limits to Growth.* The death machine is unrelenting. By 1990 ten species of living beings a day were disappearing. By the year 2000 the rate of disappearance will be one an hour, and by that time twenty percent of the life forms on the planet will have disappeared.[3]

A vigorous social critique has arisen out of ecology.[4] An arrogant anthropocentrism is at work, one which lies at the root of contemporary societies. Human beings understand ourselves as beings above other beings and lords of life and death over them. During the past three centuries, scientific and technical advances have provided us with the tools for dominating the world and systematically plundering its riches, which are reduced to "natural resources" with no regard for their relative autonomy.

The Earth sciences that have developed, especially since the 1950s with the deciphering of the genetic code and of various kinds of knowledge drawn from space projects, present us a new cosmology, that is, a unique image of the universe, a different perspective on Earth and on the role of the human being in the evolutionary process, which many now call *cosmogenesis.*[5]

To begin with, we have attained an absolutely new vision. For the first time in the history of humankind, we can see the Earth from outside, as the astronauts do.[6] "From the moon," said astronaut John Jung, "the Earth fits on the palm of my hand; on it there are no blacks and whites, Marxists and democrats; we must love this marvelous blue and white planet, because it is under threat."

Second, from a spaceship it is obvious that the Earth and humankind are a single entity, as Isaac Asimov noted in 1982 on the twenty-fifth anniversary of the launching of Sputnik, which began the space age.[7] Such is perhaps the most fundamental intuition of the ecological perspective: the discovery of Earth as a living superorganism called Gaia.[8] Rocks, waters, atmosphere, life, and consciousness are not just put together side by side, separated from one another, but have always been interconnected in an entire inclusion and reciprocity, constituting a single organic reality.

Third, human beings are not so much beings on Earth as beings of Earth. We are the most complex and unique expression of the Earth and the cosmos thus far. Man and woman are the Earth—thinking, hoping, loving, dreaming, and entering into the phase in which decision is no longer by instinct but conscious.[9] The noosphere (the specifically human sphere, that of the spirit) represents an emergence from the biosphere that in turn entails an emergence from the atmosphere, the hydrosphere, and the geosphere. All is related to all at all points and at all times. A radical interdependence of living systems and of apparently nonliving systems is at work. This is the basis for cosmic community and planetary community. Human beings must discover our place in this global community along with other species, not outside or above them. There is no justification for anthropocentrism, but that does not mean ceasing to regard the human being as unique, as that being of nature through whom nature itself achieves its own spacial curve, breaks out in reflex awareness, becomes capable of copiloting the evolutionary process, and emerges as an ethical being assuming responsibility for bringing the entire planet to a happy fate (the meaning of the anthropic principle). As the great American ecologist Thomas Berry says, "This is the ultimate daring venture for the Earth, this confiding its destiny to human decision, the bestowal upon the human community of the power of life and death over its basic life systems."[10] In other words, it is the Earth itself that through one of its expressions—the human species—takes on a conscious direction in this new phase of the evolutionary process.

Finally, all these perceptions create a new awareness, a new vision of the universe, and a redefinition of human beings in the cosmos and their practices toward it. We therefore face a new paradigm. The foundation is laid for a new age, the ecological age. After centuries of confronting nature and being isolated from the planetary community, human beings are finding their way back to their shared home, the great, good, and bountiful Earth. They wish to initiate a new covenant of respect and kinship with it.

HEARING THE CRY OF THE OPPRESSED

Where does liberation theology stand with regard to ecological concern? We must acknowledge that the initial setting within which liberation theology emerged was not that of ecological concern as we have sketched it above. The most salient and challenging fact was not the threat to Earth as a whole but to the sons and daughters of Earth exploited and condemned to die prematurely, the poor and oppressed.[11] That does not mean, however, that its basic intuitions have little to do with ecology. The relationship to ecology is direct, for the poor and the oppressed belong to nature and their situation is objectively an ecological aggression. But all of this was considered within a more restricted historical and social framework and in the context of classical cosmology.

Liberation theology was set in motion back in the 1960s by ethical indignation (true sacred wrath of the prophets) in the face of the dire poverty of the masses, especially in the Third World. This situation seemed–and still seems–unacceptable to the Christian conscience, which reads in the faces of the poor and the outcast the reembodiment of the passion of the Crucified One, who cries out and wants to arise for the sake of life and freedom.

The option for the poor, against their poverty and for their liberation, has constituted and continues to constitute the core of liberation theology. To opt for the poor entails a practice; it means assuming the place of the poor, their cause, their struggle, and at the limit, their often tragic fate.

Never in the history of Christian theologies have the poor become so central. To seek to build an entire theology starting from the perspective of the victims and so to denounce the mechanisms that have made them victims and to help overcome those mechanisms by drawing on the spiritual storehouse of Christianity, thereby collectively forging a society that offers greater opportunity for life, justice, and participation: this is the unique intuition of liberation theology.

That is why for this theology the poor occupy the epistemological locus; that is, the poor constitute the point from which one attempts to conceive of God, Christ, grace, history, the mission of the churches, the meaning of the economy, politics, and the future of societies and of the human being. From the standpoint of the poor, we realize to what extent current societies are exclusionary, to what extent democracies are imperfect, to what extent religions and churches are tied to the interests of the powerful.

From the beginning Christianity has cared for the poor (cf. Gal 2:10) but never have they been accorded so central a place in theology and for political transformation as they have been given by liberation theology.

The understanding of the poor in liberation theology has never been reduced to a single focus on them as poor. The poor are not simply beings made up of needs, but they are also beings of desire for unrestricted communication, beings hungering for beauty. Like all human beings, the poor– as the Cuban poet José Roberto Retamar puts it nicely–have two basic hungers, one for bread, which can be sated, and another for beauty, which is insatiable. Hence, liberation can never be restricted to the material, social, or merely spiritual realm. It is only true when it remains open to the full sweep of human demands. It has been the merit of liberation theology to have maintained its comprehensive scope since its origins; it did so because it was correctly interpreting what human liberation is about, not because of the demands of doctrinal authorities in the Vatican.

To be genuine, liberation must not only remain comprehensive in scope, but it must also and primarily be achieved by the poor themselves. Perhaps this is one of the unique features of liberation theology when compared with other practices of tradition, which have also shown concern for the poor. The poor are generally regarded as those who do not have food, shelter, clothes, work, culture. Those who have, so it is said, must help those who do not, so as to free them from the inhumanity of poverty. This strategy is full of good will and is well meaning; it is the basis for all assistance and paternalism in history. However, it is neither efficient nor sufficient. It does not liberate the poor, because it keeps them in a situation of dependence; worse yet, it does not even appreciate the liberating potential of the poor. The poor are not simply those who do not have; they *do* have. They have culture, ability to work, to work together, to get organized, and to struggle. Only when the poor trust in their potential, and when the poor opt for others who are poor, are conditions truly created for genuine liberation. As people sing in our Christian base communities: "I believe that the world will be better, when the child who suffers believes in the child." The poor become the agents of their own liberation; they become free persons, capable of their own self-determination with others who are different from them, so that together they may be free in a society that is more just, family spirited, and ecologically integrated.

Hence we should insist that it is not the churches that liberate the poor, nor the welfare state (whether socialist or social democrat), nor those classes that aid them. They may be allies of the poor, provided that they do not deprive them of their leading role and leadership. We can speak of liberation only when the poor themselves emerge as the primary agent of their journey, even when they have support from others.

Certainly one of the permanent merits of liberation theology flows from the method that it has brought into theological reflection.[12] Its starting point is not ready-made doctrines, not even what is revealed or Christian traditions. All of that is present on the horizon of the Christian and the theologian as background to illuminate convictions and as the starting point of reflection. It is what we call the horizon prior to any knowledge that becomes known thematically. But liberation theology's starting point is the anti-reality, the cry of the oppressed, the open wounds that have been bleeding for centuries.

Its first step is to honor reality in its more stark and problematic side. This is the moment of *seeing*, of feeling and suffering the impact of human passion, both personal and social. This is an overall experience of compassion, of protest, of mercy, and of a will to liberating action. This entails direct contact with the anti-reality, an experience of existential shock. Without this first step, it is difficult to set in motion any liberation process intended to change society.

The second moment is the analytical *judging* in a twofold sense, in the sense of critical knowledge (analytical meditation) and the sense of illumination on the basis of the contents of faith (hermeneutic mediation). It is important to decipher the causes that produce suffering, to seek their cultural roots, in the interplay of economic. political, and ideological power. Poverty is neither innocent nor natural; it is produced. That is why the poor are exploited and impoverished. It has been the merit of Marxist rationality to have shown that the poor are oppressed, people who have been dehumanized by an objective process of exploitation that is economic, political, ecological, and cultural in nature.

The data of revelation, the faith tradition, and Christian practice over the centuries condemn this situation of poverty as sin; that is, as something that also has to do with God, insofar as it denies the historic realization of God's design, which goes by way of the mediation of justice, of kindness toward the poor, and of participation and communion. From the standpoint of faith, the poor represent the suffering Savior and the supreme and eschatological judge. That is why they have an unsuspected theological intensity, especially in view of the degradation caused by dire poverty. Within the logic of faith, it is precisely this degradation that prompts God to intervene and that as a countermovement initiates a sacramental presence of God.

The third moment is transformative *action*, the most important moment, for that is where everything should culminate. Christian faith must make its contribution in the transformation of relationships of injustice into relationships that foster greater life and happiness due to living in participation and in a decent quality of life for all. Christian faith has no monopoly on the idea of transformation, but it joins other forces that also take up the cause and the struggle of the poor, contributing by means of its religious and symbolic uniqueness, its way of organizing the faith of the people, and its presence in society. Where faith and the church come into play is not in the economic realm or in what is directly political, but rather in the realm of the cultural and the symbolic. The church bears powerful messages that can create solidarity movements and project values for resistance, protest, and commitment to the specific liberation of the oppressed; it can organize celebrations and nourish their imagination, so that through that imagination they may be able to reject the present oppressive situation and dream of some new situation that is yet to be achieved by historic practice.

Finally, there is the moment of *celebrating*. This is a decisive dimension for faith, for it is here that the more gratuitous and symbolic side of liberation emerges. In celebration the Christian community recognizes that the specific advances achieved through commitment go further than the social, community, or political dimensions. Besides all that, those advances also signify the anticipatory signs of the goods of the Reign, the advent of divine redemption, embodied in actual liberations in society, the moment when the utopia of integral liberation is anticipated in frail signs, symbols, and rites. Faith identifies the spirit in action in liberation processes. It discerns the power of resurrection acting in the salvaging of a minimally worthy life. It sees the Reign taking place as process within the history of the oppressed. All this is uncovered in celebration and transformed into material for praising God.

Because of its liberating commitment, which is the basis for theological reflection, Christianity has shown that the idea of revolution (liberation, transformation) is not a monopoly of the "left" but can be a summons from Christianity's central message, which proclaims someone who was a political prisoner, was tortured, and was nailed onto the cross as a result of the way he led his life. If he rose, it was likewise to show—in addition to its strictly theological content—the truth of this practice and the utopian realization of the drives for life and freedom.

THE MOST THREATENED BEINGS IN CREATION: THE POOR

At this point the discourses of ecology and of liberation theology must be brought together for comparison. In analyzing the causes of the impoverishment that afflicts most of the world's population, liberation theology became aware that a perverse logic was at work. The very same logic of the prevailing system of accumulation and social organization that leads to the exploitation of workers also leads to the pillaging of whole nations and ultimately to the plundering of nature. It no longer suffices merely to adjust technologies or to reform society while keeping the same basic logic, although such things should always be done; the more important thing is to overcome such logic and the sense of being that human beings have held for at least the last three centuries. It will not be possible to deal with nature as our societies have tried to do, as though it were a supermarket or a self-service restaurant. It is our common wealth that is being mercilessly plundered, and that inheritance must be safeguarded.

Moreover, conditions for nature's further evolution must be assured for our own generation and for those to come, for the whole universe has been working for fifteen billion years so that we could come to the point at which we have arrived. Human beings must educate themselves so that far from being the Satan of Earth they may serve as its guardian angel, able to save Earth, their cosmic homeland and earthly mother.

The astronauts have accustomed us to see the Earth as a blue-and-white spaceship floating in space, bearing the common fate of all beings. Actually, on this spaceship Earth, one-fifth of the population is traveling in the passenger section. They consume 80 percent of the supplies for the journey. The other fourth-fifths are traveling in the cargo hold. They suffer cold, hunger, and all kinds of hardships. They are slowly becoming aware of the injustice of this distribution of goods and services. They plan rebellion: "Either we die passively of hunger or we make changes that will benefit everyone," they say. It is not a difficult argument: either we are all saved in a system of participatory common life in solidarity with and on spaceship Earth or in an explosion of wrath we could blow up the ship, sending us all falling into the abyss. Such an awareness is on the rise and can be terrifying.

The most recent arrangements of the world order led by capital and under the regime of globalization and neoliberalism have brought marvelous material progress. Leading-edge technologies produced by the third scientific revolution (computerization and communications) are being employed and are increasing production enormously. However, they dispense with human labor and hence the social effect is perverse: many workers and whole regions of the world are left out, since they are of little relevance for capital accumulation and are met by an attitude of the cruelest indifference.[13]

Recent data indicate that today globally integrated accumulation requires a Hiroshima and Nagasaki in human victims every two days.[14] There has been huge progress, but it is profoundly inhuman. The individual and peoples with their needs and preferences do not stand at its center, but rather the commodity and the market to which everything must submit. Hence, the most threatened creatures are not whales but the poor, who are condemned to die before their time. United Nations' statistics indicate that each year fifteen million children die of hunger or hunger-related diseases before they are five days old; 150 million children are undernourished, and 800 million go hungry all the time.[15]

This human catastrophe is liberation theology's starting point for considering ecology. In other words, its starting point is social ecology, the way human beings, the most complex beings in creation, relate to one another and how they organize their relationship with other beings in nature. At present it all takes place under a very exploitative and cruelly exclusionary system. We are faced with the cry of the oppressed and the excluded. A minimum of social justice is most urgently sought in order to assure life and the basic dignity that goes along with it. Once this basic level of social justice (social relationship between human beings) has been achieved, it will be possible to propose a possible ecological justice (relationship of human beings with nature). Such justice entails more than social justice. It entails a new covenant between human beings and other beings, a new gentleness toward what is created, and the fashioning of an ethic and mystique of kinship with the entire cosmic community. The Earth is also crying out under the predatory and lethal machinery of our model of society and development. To hear these two interconnected cries and to see the same root cause that produces them is to carry out integral liberation.

The social and political framework for this kind of integral liberation is an extended and enriched democracy. Such democracy will have to be biocracy, socio-cosmic democracy; in other words, a democracy that is centered on life, one whose starting point is the most downtrodden human life. It must include elements of nature like mountains, plants, water, animals, the atmosphere, and landscapes as new citizens participating in human common life and human beings sharing in the cosmic life in common. There will only be ecological and societal justice when peace is assured on planet Earth.

Liberation theology should draw from ecological discourse the emerging world view or cosmology; that is, the vision that understands Earth as a living superorganism connected to the entire universe in cosmogenesis. It must comprehend the mission of human beings, man and woman, as expressions of Earth itself and as manifestations of the principle of intelligibility existing in the universe, that the human being—the noosphere—represents a more advanced stage of the cosmic evolutionary process at its conscious level, one of copiloting it, utilizing the guiding principles of the universe that have governed the whole process since the moment of expansion-explosion fifteen billion years ago. Human beings were created for the universe—not vice versa—so as to attain a higher and more complex stage of universal evolution, namely, in order to be able to celebrate and glorify the Creator who wanted to have companions in love.

This background should first of all lead to a broader understanding of liberation. It is not only the poor and oppressed who must be liberated but all human beings, rich and poor, because all are oppressed by a paradigm—abuse of the Earth, consumerism, denial of otherness, and of the inherent value of each being—that enslaves us all. We all must seek a paradigm that will enable Gaia to live and all beings in creation, especially human beings, to exist in solidarity. We suggest the paradigm of the connectedness of all with all, which allows for the emergence of a religion, convergence in religious diversity, and will achieve peace between humans and Earth.

Second, the starting point must also be redefined, namely, the option for the poor, including the most threatened beings in creation. The first of these is planet Earth as a whole. It has not become widely enough accepted that the supreme value is the preservation of planet Earth and the maintenance of conditions for the fulfillment of the human species. Such a way of looking at things shifts the central focus of all issues. The basic question is not the future of Christianity or of Christ's church. Nor is it the fate of the West. Rather, the basic question is what kind of future there will be for planet Earth and the humankind that is its expression. To what extent does the West with its applied science and its culture and Christianity with its spiritual resources assure this collective future?

Third, it is urgent to reaffirm an option for the poor of the world, those huge masses of the human species who are exploited and slaughtered by a small minority of the same species. The challenge will be to bring human beings to realize that they are a large earthly family together with other species and to discover their way back to the community of the other living beings, the community of the planet and the cosmos.

The final question is how we are to assure the sustainability not of a particular type of development but of planet Earth, in the short, medium, and long term. This will happen only through a non-consumeristic type of cultural practice that is respectful of ecosystems, ushers in an economy of what is sufficient for all, and fosters the common good not only of humans but also of the other beings in creation.

LIBERATION AND ECOLOGY:
THE BRIDGE BETWEEN NORTH AND SOUTH

Two major issues will occupy the minds and hearts of humankind from now on: what is the destiny and future of planet Earth if the logic of pillage to which the present type of development and consumption have accustomed us continues? What hope is there for the poor two-thirds of humankind? There is a danger that "the culture of the satisfied" will become

enclosed in its consumeristic selfishness and cynically ignore the devastation of the poor masses of the world. There is also a danger that the "new
barbarians" will not accept their death sentence and will set out on a des-
perate struggle for survival, threatening everything and destroying everything. Humankind may find itself facing violence and destruction at levels
never before seen on the face of the Earth unless we collectively decide to
change the course of civilization and shift its thrust from the logic of means
at the service of an exclusionary accumulation toward a logic of ends serving the shared well-being of planet Earth, of human beings, and of all
beings in the exercise of freedom and cooperation among all peoples.

These two issues, with different accents, are shared concerns in the North
and South of the planet. They are also the central content of liberation
theology and of ecological thought. These two directions of thought make
possible dialogue and convergence in diversity between the geographical
and ideological poles of the world. They must be an indispensable mediation in the safeguarding of everything created and in rescuing the dignity
of the poor majorities of the world. Hence liberation theology and ecological discourse need each other and are mutually complementary.

SONS AND DAUGHTERS OF THE RAINBOW

Theologically speaking, a truly ecumenical challenge is opening up: to
inaugurate a new covenant with the Earth in such a way that it will signify
the covenant that God established with Noah after the destruction wrought
by the flood. There we read: "I set my bow in the clouds to serve as a sign
of the covenant between me and the earth . . . everlasting covenant that I
have established between God and all living beings—all mortal creatures
that are on earth" (Gn 9:13-16). Human beings must feel that they are sons
and daughters of the rainbow, those who translate this divine covenant
with Gaia, the living superorganism, and with all the beings existing and
living on it, with new relationships of kindness, compassion, cosmic solidarity, and deep reverence for the mystery that each one bears and reveals. Only then will there be integral liberation, of the human being and
of Earth, and rather than the cry of the poor and the cry of the Earth there
will be common celebration of the redeemed and the freed, human beings
in our own house, on our good, great, and bountiful Mother Earth.

CHAPTER 6

Reclaiming the Dignity of Earth

With the ecological age we are crossing the threshold into a new civilization. It will take a firm hold only if basic changes take place in people's minds and in patterns of relationships with the whole universe. A new paradigm calls for a new language, a new imagination, a new politics, a new pedagogy, a new ethics, a new discovery of the sacred, and a new process of individuation (spirituality). We want to indicate some absolutely necessary points spelling out such a change. They can point toward the healing of Earth and the recovery of its ravaged dignity. These are the paths over which people are now called to journey.

RECLAIMING THE SACRED

Beginning a new covenant with the Earth absolutely requires a reclaiming of the dimension of the sacred. Without the sacred, affirming the dignity of Earth and the need to set limits on our desire to exploit its potentialities remains empty rhetoric. The sacred is a founding experience. It underlies the great experiences on which the cultures of the past and indeed the underlying identity of the human being have been built.

The one fact on which there is consensus among scholars of the sacred is that the sacred always has an essential connection to the cosmos—that is where it is born. The universe becomes a sacrament, a space and time where the energy permeating all beings is made manifest, the opportunity for the revelation of the mystery dwelling in the totality of all things.

If in recent centuries we have been victims of a model of civilization that has systematically assaulted the Earth and has led us to close our ears to the music in things and turn our backs on the majesty of the starry sky, it is because the experience of the sacredness of the universe has been lost. That is why we speak of the need for a true retrieval of the sacred. "Dehallowing" has reduced the universe to something lifeless, mechanical, and mathematical, and the Earth to a mere warehouse of resources made available to human beings. The word present in all things has been removed, so that human beings alone can be in charge. If we do not manage to retrace our journey and access the sacred, we will not guarantee the future of Earth. Ecology will become merely a technique for managing human voracity but never for overcoming it. The new covenant will mean only a truce so that Earth may bandage the wounds it has sustained, and then go on to be wounded again, because the pattern of relationships has not changed nor has the human mindset changed. The first step to be taken is thus to recover Earth's sacredness, reenchantment, and reverence for the universe. The American astronaut Edgar D. Mitchell expressed as much in 1971 on board Apollo 14 on its way to the moon when he said in astonishment,

> Thousands of miles away from here the Earth displays the incred-
> ible beauty of a marvelous blue and white jewel, floating in the vast
> dark sky. . . . It fits in the palm of my hand.[1]

What is the sacred? It is not a thing but a quality of things–that quality of things and in things that in a comprehensive way completely takes hold of us, fascinates us, speaks to us of the depths of our being and gives us the immediate experience of respect, fear, and reverence. St. Augustine describes the emergence of the sacred in his *Confessions*. "What is it that shines through me and that strikes my heart without injuring me, and that both repels and attracts me? I feel repelled to the extent that I am different from it, and attracted to the extent that I see that I am similar to it." He is talking about the sacred.

Rudolf Otto describes the experience of the sacred in two key words: *tremendum* and *fascinosum*. It is the *tremendum*, that is, that which makes us tremble by its greatness because it overflows our capacity to bear its presence, a presence that with its overwhelming intensity sends us fleeing. At the same time, it is the *fascinosum*, that is, that which fascinates us, draws us like an irresistible magnet, makes us experience what is of absolute concern to us.[2] The sacred is like the sun; its light overwhelms us and fills us with enthusiasm (*fascinosum*). At the same time, it obliges us to turn our gaze away and to run into the shade because it could burn and blind us (*tremendum*).

It is this ambivalent experience that traditional indigenous groups have had in contact with life, with the Earth, with the cosmos, with people, with children, with the loving attraction between a man and a woman, and with the mystery of the universe. They have felt an irresistible force communicated in these things, which researchers have classically expressed with the Melanesian word *mana* or with that of African religions in the Americas, *axé*. All things are potentially bearers of mana or axé, which has great transforming energy. They are the revelation of the sacred par excellence. Actually they are only sacraments, vehicles, and signs of the Ultimate Reality, the Divinity, the Creator who is within and beyond the cosmos, the Earth, and life, but Ultimate Reality announces its epiphany and diaphany through such realities.[3]

Indigenous peoples grasped with their own peculiar instinct what we grasp empirically through science and reflection: the cosmic energy (mana or axé or energy fields) connecting everything, the ordering principles of the universe, and the action of the arrow of time that points ever forward and upward. We grasp it through a science that has consciousness and through an objectivity that also manifests subjectivity. We reclaim the sacredness of the Earth as a whole; we are recovering the dignity of Earth.

Today we allow the sacred to break in if we appropriate what is in our cosmology and turn it into emotion and experience. It is not enough to know things about the world and the universe—books and multimedia are full of such information. What we need is to be stirred and to have a deep experience. We need to enter into this knowledge about the cosmos, Earth, and nature, because it is knowledge about ourselves, about where we come from, about our deepest reality. It is in being stirred by such feelings that we change our lives. They ground the seminal experiences that nourish our other everyday experiences.

How shall we not fall into ecstasy over the immense outpouring of energy in the singularity of the big bang, in the formation of the first relational units, the top quark, protons, electrons, neutrinos, the first atoms, the formation of the gas clouds that led to the first generation of gigantic stars grouped in galaxies and clusters of galaxies? How shall we fail to be in awe of their burning for millions and millions of years and forming within themselves the hundred elements that make up the building blocks of the universe until they exploded as supernovas, thereby forming the billions and billions of second generation stars like our sun? If they had not sacrificed and surrendered the wealth that they had accumulated within themselves, we would have no solar system and no planet Earth, and we would not be here to ponder and celebrate all this. This is the *fascinosum.*

What is more tremendous and mysterious than the massive destruction of the initial matter by antimatter, leaving barely a billionth of it, from which the whole universe and we ourselves take rise? Here the *tremendum* joins the *fascinosum* .

Who could fail to experience the *tremendum* upon learning of the fantastic collisions of galaxies and galaxy clusters with their myriads of stars? The thundering and lightning, the astounding energy produced, the fusion of masses, the ejection of matter in all directions, the production of light (photons) of such intensity that it would attract the attention of even the most heedless observer in the most distant reaches of the universe?

Is not the rise 3.9 billion years ago of the cell Prometheus, which invented photosynthesis and so utilized carbon and freed oxygen, which for it was terribly toxic, both the *fascinosum* and the *tremendum*? And that another organism two billion years ago, called Prospero, learned to handle oxygen and made it a principle of new life rather than death?

Is not the self-organization of the universe fascinating, an inner drive manifested in the four known basic interactions that no one can define (gravity, electromagnetic energy, and the strong and weak nuclear forces)? Is not the fact that everything comes out of a vast chaos, the big bang, and the fact of violence on all levels of the universe the *tremendum*? Is not the fact that from this primordial chaos and this violence there should come new orders of beings and ever more elaborate complexities, including life and human consciousness, the *fascinosum*?

Is not the balance of all the elements giving rise to the optimal situation for life that we find on Gaia—in the atmosphere, the soils, the seas, the biosphere, and the noosphere—the *fascinosum*? Are not the various massive extinctions that Gaia suffered and in which almost all its genetic inheritance was lost the *tremendum*? And how can its ability to regenerate and withstand the aggression by the species *Homo sapiens (demens)* not be the *fascinosum*?

Is not the *fascinosum* manifest in the creativity of human beings, in the diversity of their cultural manifestations, the dreams they project, in their accumulating historic achievements, in their ability to decipher the Reality that sustains, drives, and draws all—God?

Does not their capacity for destruction, geocide, ecocide, ethnocide, homicide and suicide express the *tremendum*?

All these experiences situate us before a reality that overflows us, that lets itself be known but that also pulls away from any rationality and manipulation. This is the sacred, and it calls for respect, care, and reverence. The best way to approach it is to enter into its logic, which is dialogical (that is, it includes its opposite and makes opposites complementary), to accept its rhythm, and to feel that we are part and parcel of it. We only become integrated and feel at home when we join with this symphony (and cacophony), when we understand that the violin can get along with the Brazilian drum, the *bumbo,* and when we use our creativity to act along with nature and never against it.

When taken on in this manner, the sacred brings us back from our exile and awakens us from our alienation. It brings us back to the home that we had left, and we begin to treat Earth, each thing in it, and the whole universe, as we treat our body, each of our organs, every emotion of our soul, and each thought of our mind. Only a personal relationship with Earth makes us love it. We do not exploit but respect and reverence the one we love. A new era may now begin, not one of truce but of peace and true connectedness.

A PEDAGOGY FOR GLOBALIZATION

Having a new cosmology is not enough. How are we to spread it and bring people to internalize it so as to inspire new behaviors, nourish new dreams, and bolster a new kindness toward the Earth? That is certainly a pedagogical challenge.

As the old paradigm that atomized human beings, isolated them, and set them against the universe and the community of living beings permeated through all our pores in our lives and created a collective subjectivity suited to its intuitions, so now the new paradigm must form new kinds of subjectivity and enter into all realms of life, society, the family, the media, and educational institutions in order to shape a new planetary man and woman, in cosmic solidarity and in tune with the overall direction of the evolutionary process.

First of all, we must bring about the great revolution in perspective that grounds the new cosmology; we cannot understand ourselves as separate from the Earth nor can we continue with the classic vision that regards the Earth as a lifeless planet, a clump of soil and water full of the hundred elements of which all beings are composed. We are much more than that. We are sons and daughters of Earth, we are the Earth itself become self-aware, the Earth journeying, as the great Argentine mestizo poet Atahualpa Yupanqui said, the thinking Earth, the loving Earth, and the Earth celebrating the mystery of the universe.

Hence, the Earth is not a planet on which life exists. As we noted in chapter 1, the mixture of elements, temperature, and chemical composition in the atmosphere and sea on Earth is such that only a living organism can do what it does. The Earth does not contain life. It *is* life, a living superorganism, Gaia.

The human species represents Gaia's ability to have a reflex awareness, a synthesizing mind, and a loving subjectivity. We humans, men and women, make it possible for Earth to appreciate its own lush beauty, contemplate its intricate complexity, and spiritually discover the Mystery that permeates it.

What human beings are in relation to the Earth, the Earth itself is in relation to the cosmos that we know. The cosmos is not an object in which we discover life; it is a living subject in a process of becoming. It has journeyed for fifteen billion years. It has doubled back upon itself and matured in such a way that in one of its corners, in the Milky Way, in the solar system, on planet Earth, there has emerged self-awareness, awareness of where it came from, where it is going, and whose symbol and image it is. When an ecological agronomist studies soil composition, the cosmos is studying itself. When an astronomer points a telescope toward the stars, the universe is gazing at itself.[4]

The change that such a comprehension should produce in people's minds and in institutions can only be compared to the change that took place in the sixteenth century when the Earth was proven to be round and to revolve around the sun. This is especially true of the fact of transformation; namely, that things are not fully formed, that new forms of self-realization are continually being born. Truth is achieved through an open approach rather than a code that is established and closed.

Second, time must be extended to global dimensions. Our age is not that of the duration since the day we were born—we are as old as the cosmos. We began to be born fifteen billion years ago, when all the energy and matter that go into the makeup of our body and psyche began to be organized. Now that that process has reached maturity, we have reached the moment of birth and we are born with an openness to further perfection in the future.

If we set the cosmic clock within the space of a solar year, as Carl Sagan has done,[5] we come up with the following picture: The big bang occurred on January 1. On May 1 the Milky Way took shape, and on September 9 the solar system. On September 14 Earth was formed, and on September 25 life began. The first hominids, ancestors to human beings, appeared on December 30. The first men and women emerged on December 31. The last ten seconds of December 31 would cover the history of *Homo sapiens (demens),* from whom we descend directly. The birth of Christ would have occurred at exactly 23 hours, 59 minutes and 56 seconds of the last day of the year. The modern world is said to have arisen in the 58th second of the last minute of the year. And we as individuals? In the last fraction of a second before midnight.

In other words, the universe and Earth have had reflex awareness of themselves for only twenty-four hours. If God should say to an angel, "Go looking through space and identify Peter or John or Mary in time," the angel would not succeed, because they are less than a bit of dust wandering through interstellar vacuum and they began to exist less than a second ago. But God could, because God listens to the heart of each son and daughter of God, for in them the universe is converging in self-awareness and celebration. It is not anthropocentric arrogance to say that each human being is a miracle of the universe. A pedagogy adequate to the new cosmology should bring us into dimensions that evoke in us the sacredness of the universe and the wonder of our own existence.

Third, the space where we are located must be understood comprehensively. Viewing the Earth from beyond the Earth, we discover that we are a link in a vast chain of heavenly beings. We are one galaxy, the Milky Way, out of one hundred billion galaxies. Twenty-eight thousand light years from its center, we belong to the solar system, which is one from among billions and billions of other stars, and we are on a planet, Earth, that is tiny but very well endowed with material useful for evolving ever more complex and conscious forms of life. On Earth we are on a continent that broke away around 210 million years ago, when Pangeia (the only continent on Earth) split apart and took on its present configuration about 150 million years ago. We are in this city, on this street, in this house, in this room, and at this table from which I relate to, and feel bound up with, the totality of all spaces in the universe.

Fourth, each of us urgently needs to realize how astonishing it is that we exist at all. From its very beginning the universe has been creating interiority and weaving the intricate web of relationships that constitutes it as a self-organizing reality moving forward. Just as the noosphere is the fruit of the biosphere, so the biosphere is the result of the atmosphere, and the atmosphere of the hydrosphere, and the hydrosphere of the geosphere, until we reach the sun, the galaxy, the supernovas, the primordial gas, the great explosion-expansion, and finally the original core of inconceivably condensed energy. Each human person is connected to this whole vast chain. The universe culminates in each individual in the form of consciousness, and capacity for understanding, solidarity, and free self-surrender in friendship and love. From this consciousness arises the feeling of self-esteem and discovery of the sacred as fascinating and tremendous that we experience as both very much within us and as something alien. All energies and morphogenetic fields have acted synergistically so that each one might be born and be that singular and unique person that he or she is: *Ecce mulier, ecce homo!*

Fifth, all human beings must discover themselves as members of the species *Homo sapiens (demens),* in communion and solidarity with all other species that make up the community of living things (*biocenose*). They are discovering themselves as members of the human family scattered over the four corners of the Earth. But the feeling of human family has still not fully taken shape. As one of the most eloquent articulators of global consciousness, Robert Muller, has written,

> With regard to the human cosmos, almost everything still remains to be done. Our planetary cathedral is still not occupied by a united, reverent, grateful, and fully developed family, but rather by rebellious groups of immature and unruly children.[6]

Sixth, we must always remain aware of our uniqueness as a species. We are condemned to be cultural beings. Lacking any specialized organ, we are forced to intervene in nature, to extend our arms, our hands, our eyes, and our ears through technical instruments and to create a culture for ourselves. The biological development of our brain, empowering our thought and our creative imagination, has produced in a moment what it would take evolution millions and millions of years to produce. We are copiloting the current phase of the evolutionary process in tandem with the guiding principles of the universe. This confers a great responsibility on us, for we can be the good angel who hears the message of nature and works with it and in harmony with it or we can be the destructive and exploiting Satan, who only hears his own exclusionary desire and subjects planet Earth to a murderous assault.

Seventh, and finally, it is crucially important that human beings become aware of our role within the overall direction of the universe that has been established in the course of fifteen billion years. Everything has moved in such a manner and in such complex and highly self-organized ways so as to give rise to the capacity to feel, see, hear, communicate, think self-consciously and love what is other. It is the universe and the Earth itself that through the human being feels itself, sees its ineffable beauty, hears its music, communicates its mystery, thinks self-consciously, becomes aware of its interiority, and passionately loves all. It is in order to create this possibility that human beings have emerged. Thus far we have not fulfilled our function very well. This is not so much a matter of being good or evil, but rather being immature and still unconscious of our true mission. As Miriam Therese MacGillis puts it in a powerful video "The Fate of the Earth," "It seems as though the Earth is leaving behind its juvenile fixation on itself and its powers and moving toward a new and more complete level of maturity, to the extent that you and I have made a qualitative leap, that is, through us the Earth has made this leap."

The whole pedagogical process should culminate in such consciousness-raising, which confers on the human being, man and woman, a noble universal significance. Such consciousness-raising enables people to see clearly that the supreme and global value is to protect planet Earth (and with it the universe) and to safeguard those conditions that the planet has labored to build up for fifteen billion years so that our life might maintain its inner tendency, which is self-actualization, reproduction, and progress, especially of human life.

THE PERMANENT MESSAGE OF ORIGINAL PEOPLES

All over the Earth there are still original peoples who live the dimension of the sacred and of connectedness with all things. Although they live in our age (synchrony) they are not at the same evolutionary level as we are (contemporaneity). Most of them are still at the neolithic village stage. But they are very important for the ecological crisis and for stimulating alternatives to the kind of relationship that we establish with nature. They show how we can be human, indeed profoundly human, without having to pass through the critical rationality of modernity or through the process of dominating the Earth as in the schemes of technology. And even while they take on the advantages of modernity in their own way, they know how to hold onto the feeling of the universe and the sense of the subjectivity of nature with which we establish relationships of reciprocity.

They are the assurance of a still possible human race, one that would be kinder and charged with sacramentality and with the reverence that we so much need. The well-known Brazilian champions of the indigenous, the Villas-Boas brothers, put it well when, after fifty years of work with native peoples in the Amazon forest, they said on a television program in 1989, "If we want to be rich, accumulate power, and rule the Earth, there is no point in asking the native peoples. But if we want to be happy, combine being human with being divine, integrate life and death, put the person in nature, connect work and leisure, harmonize relations between generations, then let us listen to the indigenous peoples. They have wise lessons to impart to us."

At a point where our paradigm of civilization is in crisis, we want to listen to the permanent message of the native people. Let us highlight the testimony of those who are on our continent, which is home to great cultures, including some of the most original, such as the Yanomamis.

First, I would emphasize *ancestral wisdom.* It is set down in the great stories and in the myths that remain focused on the mysteries of the universe and on the depth of the human psyche. Today we are able to develop interpretative methods that decipher for us the marvelous content of these lessons through linguistics, structuralism, and archetype psychology (J. Hillmann and his school). We note that on so many points they were better observers than we and expressed in their own way and more forcefully what our inner forces (which are also cosmic) are attempting to tell us about ourselves with regard to woman, man, child, sexuality, striving for happiness, and the mystery of God.

This is a wisdom built particularly on observation of the universe and listening to the Earth. For the Bolivian Aymaras, the sage is the one who learns to listen carefully, who discerns, who sees a long way, who looks at things on all sides, and who strives to gaze within. The elders, those who have accumulated the most experience, are the sages. When consulted by the community, they look attentively around them, contemplate the mountains, breathe the air deeply, stamp on the ground, and only then speak.[7]

This wisdom is displayed in the way they handle nature. To take one example, it is often imagined that the Amazon, which hosts the greatest biodiversity on the planet, is a virgin region uninhabited and untouched by human involvement. That is an illusion. For thousands of years this vast area has been inhabited by hundreds of tribes and profoundly worked by human beings. That involvement, however, takes the form of empowering nature and overcoming the limits of those ecosystems that contain the youngest and oldest lands on Earth but whose soils are acidic and poorly endowed with chemicals (75% of the territory). Research has shown that "the indigenous societies have modified the environment, encouraging biodiversity while promoting 'resource islands,' by creating circumstances favorable for making certain highly useful plant species dominant (*babaçu* palm, for example). At least 11.8% of the forests on dry land in the Brazilian Amazon may be regarded as human-shaped forests, especially those dominated by palms, bamboo groves, forests with a high density of cashews, enclosed forest islands, and others."[8] According to anthropologist William Balée, it was not so much that the native people adapted to the primary forest, but that they purposefully changed the habitat to encourage the growth of plant communities and their integration with animal communities and with the human being. "In some sense, the different profiles of these forests may be seen as archaeological artifacts in no way different from tools and shards of pottery, inasmuch as they open for us a window into the Amazon's past."[9]

The Tucano Indians of the Upper Rio Negro are familiar with no fewer than 140 species of manioc, while those of us who deal with industrialized farming manage just a half dozen. Who is the primitive in this instance? "These people are perfect environmental scientists," exclaimed Prince Charles with admiration in 1991 when he visited Brazil. He added, "Calling them primitive is perverse and paternalistic."[10] Shelton Davis, who has a deep understanding of indigenous problems in Brazil, says, "We regard the Indian as an inferior being with an inferior culture. But when you talk about living in the Amazon he is far superior because he harmonizes so perfectly with the whole ecological system. The tragedy is that the Indian is one of the major keys to the successful occupation of the Amazon, and as he disappears his vast wealth of knowledge is going with him."[11] Studies in indigenous communities in Brazil and Venezuela show that they know how to utilize ecologically 78% of the species of trees in their territories (keeping in mind the astonishing biodiversity of the area, around twelve hundred species in an area the size of a soccer field).[12] We find here an ability to act and an environmental wisdom far surpassing that of our most advanced ecological agricultural experimental research centers.[13] Here it is they who are our masters and teachers.

Because of the discrimination and arrogant ignorance of our administrators, who have not been willing to accept any knowledge from outside our scientific paradigm, particularly in Amazon projects like the Grande Carajás Project, this ecological knowledge has not been utilized, with the consequent enormous technical mistakes that are causing irreparable ecological damage to the region.[14]

Second, the *mystique of nature* must be given due importance. For original peoples the Earth is not a mere means of production but an extension of life and the body. It is Pacha Mama, the Great Mother who gives birth, feels, and envelops all. One example is the famous speech by Chief Seattle given in 1856 in the presence of Isaac Stevens, governor of Washington Territory, about the dignity of Earth.[15] Let us take note of an eloquent testimony by a Kuna chief from the Atlantic coast of Panama, Leonidas Valdez: "The earth is our mother and is also culture. The elements of our culture are born there . . . all the foods eaten in our traditional celebrations; the materials that our artisans use and that we use to build houses, all come from the hills. If we were to lose these lands, there would be neither culture nor soul."[16] That is why when they cut medicinal trees or any other trees to make an oar or build a house, they very reverently and respectfully celebrate rites for forgiveness.

An anonymous Indian who had already made knowledge of the Earth's chemistry part of his own mystique rightly said,

> The great resources and mines for gold, iron, copper, coal, and for elements like nitrogen, phosphorus, potassium and others are Mother Earth's internal organs; they are the pulse and heartbeat of our Mother who makes the trees and plants produce for the sake of food, clothing, housing and medicines for all the Earth's beings. Hence, Mother Earth's inner organs should not be abused and mistreated.[17]

Many indigenous people are aware that this stance toward nature has a high civilizing value for our contemporary situation. Guarani Indian Mario Jacinto of southern Brazil spoke for many when he demanded more land from the central government, "because Indians will show how to make nature be born anew, for nature is the most beautiful thing on the face of the earth."[18]

Third, the *issue of work* is linked to that of the Earth. Work for indigenous people never means merely production, as it does among us. It means the collaboration human beings give to Mother Earth in handling human needs. She is bountiful and sustains and nourishes all. But the human being helps her in her mission. Hence, indigenous people work enough to supply their human needs and enjoy life. Work is always a community activity and one of pleasure, the aim of which is not to produce profit but to live well.[19]

With forty-seven days of work a year, one Mayan Indian produced enough for five persons, thereby allowing time for community occupations, building temples, and pursuing the arts.[20] Even when they incorporate modern technologies they do not have to lose the profound sense of the Earth and of care for its balance. An Indian from Vale do Rio Doce, Ailton Krenak, the coordinator of the Union of Indigenous Nations and one of the most perceptive of Brazilian indigenous leaders, has said, "Yes, we have computers, but we are very careful in using them. If a tractor is used to prepare an area for growing crops and so enables people to have more time to dance, sing, have their celebrations, then it has a very important role—to add to the ability of those people to live better."[21] Technology is in no way being exaggerated here, but rather it is being used as a means at the service of the deepest sense of human life, namely, gratuity, the biblical sabbath, and celebration.

Fourth, *celebration and dance* are very meaningful for us. Original peoples are deeply mystical. They experience the Mystery of the world, of the God of a thousand names. Through celebration and dance they create the conditions for experiencing the divinity. It is for the sake of this experience that they communally take strong drink and ritual hallucinogens in their major celebrations and their all-night dancing.[22] The celebration is for the divinity, for the dead, to recall the founding myth, for the harvest feasts, for marriage, and for myriad other reasons. A great deal of time is devoted to celebration and dancing. Perhaps no people is so expressive in this regard as the Tarahumara (or Rarámuri-Pagótuame), who live in northwest Mexico. There are around fifty or sixty thousand Tarahumara, who are regarded as among the purest and least assimilated of the Mexican cultures. It is said that they live in order to dance and dance in order to live.[23] In Brazil, those known for their elaborate celebrations are the Xavantes and the Camaiuras,[24] and the Arawaté, who were contacted for the first time in 1976 in the Amazon portion of the Xingu River. They display a sense of celebration and graciousness that seem to be still at the dawning stage of humankind, especially their great celebration of *cauinagem* [based on *cauim*, a beverage of fermented manioc].[25] The celebration takes them to a world of utopia and transcendence that has become accessible through ceremony, beverage, rhythms, and ecstasy.

Celebration and dancing—practices of sheer gratuity and lightness—give bodily substance to humankind's original vocation. They exist in order to grasp the majesty of the universe, the beauty of Earth, and the vitality of all things. If everything exists in order to shine, human beings exist to celebrate and dance that shining. In responding to what is deepest within us we become humanized, integrated, and happy. The original peoples recall for us this perennial message.

Finally, the *experience of God* of the original peoples is a great lesson and a challenge to our secularizing and materialist culture.[26] It is not the result of complicated reasoning. God does not come out at the end of an anguished trajectory of seeking and does not occupy certain special spaces and times in life and the world. God fills all and pervades all. Human beings feel immersed in the world of the gods and of the ancestors who live with them in another dimension accessible through dreams, celebrations, and ritual drugs. The universe is transparent to the Divinity. Hence, for original cultures everything is a possible sacrament and a potential bearer of theophany. Being alive and vivifying, God fills the entire universe with life and each thing, which may seem lifeless but is not, speaks and radiates. The tree is not just a tree, closed in on itself. It is a being with many arms (branches) and thousands of tongues (leaves); it sleeps in winter, smiles in spring, is a bountiful mother in summer, and a harsh old woman in autumn. God is made present in all of these manifestations. The original peoples elaborate this vision not through reflection but through their overall experience. A representative of the Pueblos in North America said it well in 1984, "It is not a matter of saying that God is up there above, or that he is all around us, in me, in you, in the grass and in this book. It is rather a matter of feeling that He is everywhere. I experience him completely within me and outside of me. In him I feel at ease. Thank you."[27]

This is what is of permanent value in animism: everything begins and ends with life, because everything is enlivened by the God of life. Along this route all things are encompassed and alive.[28]

How shall we fail to feel affection with and kinship toward the whole universe and each thing, knowing that they are sacraments of God and that in them dwells a presence radiating beauty, majesty, and enthusiasm? The original peoples prove to us that this total experience is human and profoundly connects all with all, and is therefore radically ecological.

A NEW WORLD ECOLOGICAL ORDER AND SCENARIOS FOR REACHING IT

The crisis of the sustainability of life throughout the world has become so serious that we must make immediate decisions on actions to be taken. They cannot be taken in some arbitrary manner, but must be enacted within a radically new paradigm. Today we are called not to change the world but to preserve it—or must we perhaps change it in order to preserve it?

It is clear that time frames are becoming ever shorter. We are like a plane speeding down the runway and approaching the point of no return: it either takes off and goes on its way or it fails to take flight and smashes into the rocks at the end of the runway. Some people are already saying, "It's too late; the machinery of the means of production (destruction) is so well oiled that there's no stopping it; we are heading toward a natural collapse of the Earth-system." Others more optimistic are saying, "We can still change direction and trust in the capacity and sustainability and re-generation of Gaia." We face three possible scenarios.

• The current paradigm of a society plundering nature continues and social and ecological contradictions accordingly worsen; the rich and pow-erful will erect a wall of checkpoints and restrictions on their borders and will develop ever cleaner technologies to assure and raise their living con-ditions artificially, while abandoning the outcast and the impoverished to their fate, deprived of what is essential in the way of nourishment, energy, water, air, and shelter on an overpopulated planet, leading to a dangerous increase of regional and eventually global (i.e., North-South) conflicts.

• Human societies become aware of the growing Earth deficit reflected in the overall decline of the quality of life, and societal and ecological injustice, and they prove to have a minimum of solidarity and invent tech-nologies that are easier on the environment and forms of social and simple technological and economic development that are sustainable for all and for nature as well.

• People wisely and boldly move toward a new paradigm of benign relations with nature, of a new understanding of Earth as Gaia, and of human beings regarded as its sons and daughters organized in a sociocosmic democracy within a new pattern of development with rather than against nature, and so it will be possible to begin a new hope for planet Earth and a new world order.

The first scenario (conservative) represents what is happening in the 1990s. Globalized neoliberalism evinces very little sensitivity to the world-wide plight of the poor. While in the ascendancy, it has demonstrated its capacity for murder and ethnocide; now it can display its tendency to-ward ecocide.[29] But it is a solution that runs counter to the direction of the evolutionary process and the billions of years in search of connections and chains of solidarity. Sharper division, being closed in, and exclusion are being violently imposed. But how much injustice and inhumanity will the human spirit endure? There is a limit to everything, especially for this type of solution. To go along this route is to choose the fate of the dino-saurs.

The second scenario (reformist) still remains within the pattern of mo-dernity but seeks to minimize its unwanted effects. Hence, "eco-development" emerges, a kind of development that takes the ecological argument into account with the understanding that only a sound ecology can generate sound development. It accordingly introduces less polluting techniques, avoids filling foods with chemicals and soils with pesticides, and seeks greater social equity in the strong sense of a social ecology.

This is the setting in which people speak of sustainable development, which means: how much can we consume indefinitely without degrading the natural capital stock and the capital built up though human labor?

From an overall historic perspective both kinds of capital, natural and human, are complementary. Both have a particular scope and limiting factors that when not respected create ecological imbalance. Sustainability must assure that both kinds of capital are recovered. Otherwise, we commit a double ecological injustice: first, an injustice toward nature that has been organized over millennia to find its dynamic balance, which has now been broken; and second, an injustice toward future generations, which have the right to inherit a minimally healthy quality of life, a right now being denied them.[30] Experience thus far has shown that this scenario represents simply an ideal to be reached. As we have indicated earlier, it is a contradiction in terms. The prevailing type of development is not really compatible with ecological ideals, because it is based on the exploitation of nature and of human beings. That is why we continue to have clamorous breakdowns in ecodevelopment (actually, very often lurking behind them is ecocapitalism, which says, in the words of a large billboard that appeared on the outskirts of Mexico City: "Don't exploit man! Exploit nature!"); we safeguard development at the cost of ecology, especially in "developing" countries. The most depressing example is found in the huge industrial projects in the Brazilian Amazon (chapter 4), where the most advanced technologies are being applied intensively and indiscriminately with disastrous consequences in an ecological milieu that needs an entirely different approach. Growth is very high and the sustainability index is negative. That runs counter to ecology.[31]

Even so, we should emphasize that ecodevelopment represents an advance over unlimited growth heedless of the ecological costs. Even while remaining within the prevailing energy-consuming paradigm, there is much that can be done and achieved through ecodevelopment.[32]

We must insist, however, on the critique that we raised in chapter 2: we continue to be held hostage to the development pattern. Indeed this term *development* has been the focus of discussion for the last thirty years: development of the human being and all human beings in the 1960s, alternative development in the 1970s, ecodevelopment in the 1980s, and sustainable development in the 1990s. We must break with this paradigm and move toward the ecological age, when the sustainability of Earth and society will be pursued as a condition for being reconnected with all things among themselves.

Three prophets who received attention in the 1970s anticipated the more systematic elaboration of the currently prevailing ecological vision: Lewis Mumford, Ivan Illich, and E. F. Schumacher. Mumford presented a critique of the megamachine, which operates through the military-industrial-economic complex, and which he believed created capitalism, rather than the other way around. Thus it subjects national states to its interests and has also infected socialism.[33]

Ivan Illich goes further than Mumford and proposes "conviviality" as a constructive utopia. Such conviviality results when human beings, tools, and society are well combined. The victims of industrial society are the subjects who create a convivial society in which citizens control the use of tools (some tools are destructive no matter who uses them, such as the mafia, a cartel of oligopolies, a workers' collective that seeks only its corporate interests and not those of society) through democratic political process.[34] This utopia offers some encouragement as we search for a new paradigm.

E. F. Schumacher, an industrialist, is one of the first to carry out an ecological critique of political economy. He is especially critical of Fordism (the techniques applied by Henry Ford in his plants in the 1920s), which has spread around the world. It is based on the intensive exploitation of nature and of the labor force by applying mass production techniques. Schumacher became aware of the ecological devastation produced by such technology and of the illusionary nature of its assumption that natural resources are unlimited. He also criticizes the tendency toward complete centralization, the absolute uniformity of assembly-line production, and the tendency toward huge size in industrial installations.

To counter all this he proposed his alternative: "Small is beautiful." Smallness is the alternative, in smallness is found the human scale, smallness makes it possible to express uniqueness.[35] His proposal had an impact around the world, more because of the title, which became a cliche, than because of the specific suggestions that he made. Schumacher exemplifies contradictions due to his social location as an industrialist, since he criticizes only the Pharaonic mode of the paradigm, not the paradigm itself. He remains a prisoner of the industrial paradigm and simply applies it on a lesser scale. Issues do not change merely by changing size. What must be examined are relations of production (oppressive, in solidarity, etc.) and the overall perspective of the Earth-system. A small industry with pure technology could heavily exploit its employees, and hence it would still be anti-ecological because it would be disregarding social ecology. We must go further. Over the gate of the old paradigm is written the words that Dante placed at the entrance to hell: "Lasciate ogni speranza voi che entrate" ("Abandon hope, all you who enter here").

The third scenario (liberating) offers a genuine alternative. It involves a deep change in our civilization, assuming that we wish to survive together. And here we run up against what Machiavelli stated realistically in *The Prince:*

> Nothing is more difficult to handle, more doubtful of success, nor more dangerous to manage than to put oneself at the head of introducing new orders. For the introducer has all those who benefit from

the old order as enemies, and he has lukewarm defenders in all those who might benefit from the new orders.

The gravity of the situation means that we must not be timid. We must seek new paths, even it if means traveling over rocks; otherwise there is no salvation for the community of the planet.[36] Hence, over the entranceway to the new ecological paradigm are inscribed words that Dante no doubt could have placed at the entrance to purgatory, the antechamber to heaven, "Mai lasciate la speranza voi che entrate" ("Never abandon hope, you who enter here").

First, we must always keep before us the *global perspective.* There are no regional solutions, nor is there a Noah's ark to save some and leave the rest behind to perish. We have come to a such a point of interdependence that we are either all saved or all lost. "There is only one Earth, the preservation of a small planet" was the cry at the end of the United Nations Conference on the environment held in Stockholm in 1972. *Our Common Future* is the title of the concluding report of the 1987 UN World Commission on Environment and Development, also called the Brundtland Commission.[37] The Rio de Janeiro Declaration of the Global Forum concluded with this statement, "We understand that the salvation of the planet and its peoples, today and tomorrow, demands that a new project of civilization be prepared."[38] This project of civilization must be built synergistically by all. That will be the expression of planetary and earthly citizenship, and out of it will arise awareness of the rights of humankind and of *dignitas terrae* (dignity of the Earth).

The globalization of the ecological question accordingly demands that there be global bodies to deal with global interests. Hence it is crucial to support and refashion the existing global bodies, such as the United Nations and its eighteen specialized agencies and fourteen worldwide programs. It is true that the United Nations operates largely within the old paradigm out of which it arose, seeking to steady the balance of the few powerful countries that manage the planet. But within it are forces that grasp the urgency of the new paradigm and that give it shape through specific studies of the biosphere, natural resources, climate, species, hunger, food, illness, children's and human rights, providing documentation to aid in global decisions and serve regional governments.[39] The need for a central government is becoming more and more pressing—convergence toward a consensus in diversity—in order to manage matters having to do with all of humankind, such as issues of protecting the planet, food, hunger, illness, housing, the rights of peoples, peace, the common future, and so forth.

Second, we must move toward a *planetary ecological and social democracy.* The ecological crisis affects us all and hence it demands that all be involved in establishing of a new covenant with nature. The political arrangement that best embodies group participation is democracy. More than simply a way to organize common life in society, it is a universal value. Democracy can be lived wherever persons relate to one another—in the family, at school, in associations in civil society, in the churches, and in society.[40]

Every democracy is based on these basic points: *Participation* should be as broad as possible, because it leads to greater *equality* between citizens. Greater levels of equality should not cancel *differences* based on ethnicity, gender, culture, philosophy, and religion; we must value and accept such differences, which reveal the wealth of human unity. Given the interdependence of all with all, *solidarity* consolidates democracy, especially with regard to those who are less or have less. Finally, humans are beings of *communion*; through communion we open our subjectivity to others, we fashion values, and we celebrate the meaning of our life and of the whole universe. The very initial gesture of human culture may not have been the use of a tool to assure individual subsistence, as so many anthropologists insist, but the joint sharing of food by protohominids in a gesture of deep communion creating the original community.

The requirements of a social ecology must be embodied in such a social democracy.[41] It takes as its object human historical and social systems in their ongoing interaction with environmental systems. Human history is inconceivable without this mutual interaction. Like the human being, society with its institutions is also an expression of Earth and nature. Hence, social (in)justice cannot be separated from ecological (in)justice. Aggression unleashed against human beings due to the exploitation of their labor and of other living conditions to which they are subjected constitutes aggression against nature. As we indicated before, it is not whales or panda bears that suffer the greatest injustice in creation, but rather the poor of the world (for they are condemned to die before their time) and the peoples on their way to extinction, such as the Kayapos and Yanomamis in Brazil, among others. Hence the urgency of the option for the poor. From the standpoint of social ecology, this option also includes an option for the species most threatened with extermination (in the Amazon alone, fifty thousand species are threatened with extinction before the year 2000 under the destructive assault of huge technology projects), and indeed planet Earth itself.

It is because of this overlapping of human being and nature that we must include the ecological dimension in the notion of social and planetary democracy. In such ecological and social democracy, it is not just humans who are citizens but all beings that make up the social human world. Democracy accordingly issues in a biocracy and cosmocracy.

What would the human environment of a house or a city be without the landscape, without the blue sky by day and starry sky by night, without wind, clouds and rain, without lightning and thunder, without the earth under our feet, without the smell of the ground after rain, without dew, without plants and flowers, without animals and birds? Would we not be materially poorer and impoverished spiritually, since all these things dwell within us in the form of emotions, inspirational symbols, and archetypes? C. G. Jung, who understood the depth of such things, put it well:

> We all need food for the psyche; such food cannot be found in city dwellings, without a single patch of green or a tree in blossom; we need a relationship with nature. . . . We need to project ourselves in the things around us; what is mine is not confined to my body; it extends to all the things I do and to all the things around me; without these things I will not be myself, I would not be a human being; everything around me is part of me.[42]

Hence all beings in nature are citizens, have rights, and deserve respect and reverence.[43] We may accordingly conclude that there is a political need for an ecological education that will lead human beings to live together with their cosmic brothers and sisters in the same society. On the day when such a planetary ecological and social democracy prevails, the conditions for a covenant of brotherhood and sisterhood with nature will have been established. When such kinship with the elements and with animate and inanimate beings exists, human beings need fear no longer. They will be in tune with the entire universe. They will be able to enjoy universal communion with all beings as fellow citizens on the same planet and brothers and sisters in the same cosmic adventure under God's parental gaze. Is this not the utopia of a new world ecological order?[44]

Third, *the meaning of politics and economics* must be redefined in terms of this more advanced form of democracy. In the present paradigm crisis we must recover the original meaning of ideas, those original experiences underlying key words. Thus, politics has to do with human life in common (it is expressed most intensely in the city, the *polis*, from which "politics" is derived) insofar as it signifies the pursuit and realization of the common good. Today, the common good is not exclusively human; it is the common good of all nature. It includes the right to the future that all beings must have. More than a technique of power, it is a synergistic art of continually creating convergences in diversity, the art of making the impossible possible. It is the loving practice of creating conditions of life and dignity for all beings, reinforcing those factors that keep the evolutionary process open.

The same is true of economics.[45] In its origins it was not a technique for unlimited growth but for rational management of scarcity. Today scarcity affects the whole Earth, and hence economics must be an ecological economics. How can the economy be doing well if Earth is doing poorly? The purpose of ecological economics is to bring the economy of human beings into line with the economy of Earth, with a view to the sustainability and quality of life of the world, of persons, and of other beings in nature.[46] This means doing justice for the present generation and also for the one to come, so that it may inherit a sustainable society and nature. An ecological economy seeks to preserve the entire capital of nature, to create conditions so that it may evolve, since everything in the universe is within the evolutionary and cosmogenic principle, associated with the capital created by the work of human beings.[47] And when that intention is not achieved in an area, an effort is made to compensate for the balance that has been disturbed. Thus, just as the labor force is paid to sustain it, taxes should also be paid for the reproduction of nature.

Nature should be included in calculating the composition of capital and also in defining gross national product, which is so important for drawing conclusions on the well-being of a society and as the basis for investment policies. For example, maintaining a forest offers measurable economic benefits to people, such as pure air and water, soil conservation, better climate, supply of a landscape healthy for human balance, and recreation, and it serves as a habitat for other beings. However, such things are not factored in to conventional calculations of gross domestic product. The forest only enters if lumber is extracted, in other words, when it has been destroyed as a forest. An ecological economics computes all the benefits listed above and incorporates them into a comprehensive view.[48]

What we have said about ecological economics also must be said of eco-agriculture.[49] The aim is not to draw the maximum human advantage from the potentialities presented by the ecosystem but to create more life, greater soil fertility, and greater sustainability of the environment.[50] Assuring such quality also assures what it produces. The Earth is generous and pays back abundantly when it is handled in keeping with its own inner logic. That means, however, that fire should not be used for clearing fields, the intensive application of toxic agricultural chemicals is ill-advised, and using heavy equipment should be avoided. The Earth responds better when alien chemical additives are kept to a minimum; the chemicals that come from the metabolism of the regional subsystem itself should be given preference. It is crucial for eco-agriculture to observe the partnerships that nature itself makes, for example, plants that help one another toward an optimal level of life and production, their combination with a particular kind of microorganism, and their adaptation to a certain level of local humidity.

Nothing is more anti-ecological and unnatural than monoculture, for it disrupts the partnerships and solidarity that nature has established among all plants, with the types of soils, microorganisms, regional climate, and so forth. Agriculture practiced within and under the forest itself has been shown to be highly productive and sustainable, observing natural succession, the combinations of shade and light and linked partnerships.[51]

AN ETHICS OF UNLIMITED COMPASSION
AND SHARED RESPONSIBILITY

What we think, and especially what we feel, should aid us in achieving new attitudes. Hence, from politics we are driven back to ethics. Ethics presents demands that go beyond morality, and so we must distinguish ethics from morality. Morality shapes the imperatives required by a particular established order. Morality has to do with obedience and conformity with that order. What we must question, however, is not the harmony or lack of harmony with the established order (morality), but that very order and its nature. There can be a type of order and corresponding morality that is highly anti-ecological. Such is the case with conventional morality, which is utilitarian and anthropocentric; it makes the Earth a mere warehouse of resources for satisfying human desires with no sense of otherness and of the rights of other beings in nature. When an order is understood as established and static, it always becomes rigid. Morality becomes moralism, and people are suffocated by a castrating moral super-ego.

If, however, an order follows the rhythm of evolution then it is never understood as established once and for all. In keeping with the evolutionary process, the cosmogenic principle, and the principle of quantum uncertainty, it is dynamic and is enmeshed in a nonequilibrium order that is ever seeking new adaptations. This pursuit of harmony with the inner drive of things and the stance of openness and alertness to change are the bases for the distinction between ethics and morality.

What we need today is not a new morality but a new ethics; that is, attentiveness to change and the ability to adapt to what must be done at each moment—and today that means protecting the planet and all its systems, defending and promoting life, starting with those that are most threatened. Two principles embody this ethics: the responsibility principle, and the compassion principle.

Hans Jonas, the well-known philosopher of such an ecological ethics, has formulated the responsibility principle in this ethical and ecological imperative: "So act that the consequences of your action support the continuance of authentic human life on Earth"; put negatively, "So act that the consequences of your action will not be destructive of future conditions of life."[52]

The compassion principle is found in the great spiritual traditions of humankind, Western and Eastern, in original peoples and in modern peoples, and in the exemplary figures of the Buddha, Lao-tse, Chuang-tzu, Isaiah, Jesus Christ, St. Francis of Assisi, Schopenhauer, Albert Schweitzer, Gandhi, Chief Seattle, and Chico Mendes. They exemplify the ethic of universal compassion together with that of responsibility striving for solidarity and reverence among all beings and not simply human gain.

The guiding principle of compassion is, "Good is whatever preserves and promotes all beings in their dynamic equilibrium, especially living things, and among living things, the weakest and most threatened; evil is whatever harms and does away with beings or destroys the conditions for their reproduction and development." Or, as Albert Schweitzer put it concisely, "Ethics means unlimited responsibility for everything existing and alive."[53]

The supreme good lies in the integrity of the earthly and cosmic community, which at this phase of evolution is entrusted to human responsibility. Human beings live ethically when they maintain the dynamic equilibrium of all things and when, in order to preserve it, they prove capable of setting limits to their own desires. Human beings are not simply beings of desires; desire alone would make them anthropocentric and mimetic. They are also and fundamentally beings of solidarity and communion. When they become more so, they enter into harmony with the universal dynamism and carry out their cosmic mission as custodian, troubadour, and guardian angel for everything created, thereby realizing their ethical dimension.[54]

THE HEALING POWER OF INNER ECOLOGY

Politics and technology are subject to ethics, and ethics in turn requires a spirituality and a mystique. Otherwise ethics becomes a morality of the order thus far achieved and established, and easily slips into moralism. In speaking of spirituality and mysticism we are pointing toward overall visions that provide the basis for powerful convictions that give us the energy and inner enthusiasm to define a meaning for life and find a significance for the whole universe. Only a mystique and a spirituality can sustain hope beyond any crisis and even in the face of a possible collapse of the Earth-system.[55]

Earlier we saw that our relationship with the Earth, at least during the last four hundred years, has been based on false ethical premises and a deep spiritual vacuum: anthropocentrism, denial of the relative autonomy of beings, domination of the Earth, plunder of its resources, and disregard for the spiritual depth of the universe. Such premises have produced the current pathological stage of Earth, thereby affecting the human psyche, which likewise shows symptoms of illness.

Just as there is an outer ecology (ecosystems in balance or imbalance, atmosphere, hydrosphere, biosphere, and so forth) there is also an inner ecology (forms of solidarity and structures of connectedness together with the will to power and domination, aggressive instincts, and structures of exclusion that lead to plunder of nature and mistreatment of persons, animals, and plants). Both ecologies are very closely connected. As we have considered before, the universe possesses interiority. Far from being a random pile of objects composed of the hundred chemical elements, it is a communion of subjects interweaving ties of intimacy and organic connection to one another.[56]

When we start from Earth's inner ecology, all beings and the universe itself cease being neutral things, each going in its own direction. They speak, shine, evoke, delight, frighten, and share in the human drama. The Argentine tango expresses it well, "I'm not singing to the moon just because it shines. I sing to the moon because it knows of my long journey." The moon, the sun, the trees, the mountains, the forests, and the animals live in us as emotionally charged figures and symbols. The beneficial or traumatic experiences that human beings have had with these things have left deep marks in the psyche. They have proven to be archetypes that suggest possible behaviors, focal points of inner energy that guide us in the mutual relationships woven in our exchanges with the world.

Such archetypes are the basis for a true inner archeology. The deciphering of its code has been one of the great intellectual conquests of the twentieth century, with Freud, Jung, Adler, Lacan, Hillmann, and others. Deep down, according to Jung, glows the archetype of the Absolute. No one has developed this dimension better than Viktor Frankl, who calls it the spiritual unconscious.[57] This spiritual unconscious ultimately expresses the very spirituality of Earth and the universe. That is why attitudes more in tune with solidarity and the dynamic balance among all things are now coming to the fore.

It is this spiritual depth, for example, that makes us understand the exemplary ecological mindset of the Sioux Indians in the United States. In some of their ritual celebrations they like to use a particular type of bean that grows deep in the soil and is hard to gather. What do they do? They take advantage of the supplies that the prairie dogs in the area store up for winter consumption. Without this reserve the prairie dogs are in serious danger of dying of hunger. As they take these beans, the Sioux Indians are clearly aware that they are violating solidarity with their brother animal by robbing it, and so, before taking the stored-up beans, they offer a striking prayer:

> You, little prairie dog, who are sacred, have mercy on me and aid me, I fervently pray you. You are indeed little, but big enough to occupy your place in the world. You are indeed weak, but strong enough to do your work, because you are in touch with sacred powers. You are also wise, for the wisdom of sacred forces is always with you. May I also be wise in my heart. If sacred wisdom guides me, then this shadowy and confusing life will be transformed into permanent light.

As a sign of wisdom and solidarity, the Indians then leave behind portions of bacon and corn for the prairie dogs to feed on during the winter.[58] The Sioux feel spiritually united to the prairie dogs, and that leads them to maintain basic solidarity and to live in universal synergy.

This spiritual sense urges us to arise from the ashes of our collective unconscious and conscious. The ideological and political systems that dominate us are the result of the mechanistic spirit of modernity. In particular, the social system prevailing in the world today, neoliberalism in combination with the formal democracy that comes with it, creates collective subjectivities in keeping with the values and ideals suited to it. Because it is a system that rests on having and accumulating material goods, it powerfully stimulates the human being's need to have and subsist, and thwarts more basic needs such as the need to be and to grow.

Through the media the social system projects into us powerful symbols and messages indicating that life is meaningless if we do not have a certain number of material possessions and certain symbols of prestige and power. It encourages individualism and the competitive attitude, and it splits the psyche with categories of friend and enemy. It makes other people possible competitors and obstacles to our individual fulfillment. It denies, ignores, or expels another more basic need of the human being, that of being and working out our own uniqueness. Our need to be requires freedom and creativity, and perhaps the ability to stand up to conventions and the prevailing value system; it requires courage to open new personal (and hence fulfilling) paths. With the need to be as a starting point, we can integrate the need to have without succumbing to the fetish of being bewitched by it, and we can understand the meaning of money and material goods without making them an obsession, by consciously making them mediations for life and solidarity. Chief Seattle said aptly, "When the last tree has been cut down, when the last river has been poisoned, when the last fish has been caught, only then will we be aware that money cannot be eaten."[59]

Mental ecology, also called deep ecology,[60] seeks to awaken our ability to listen. The entire universe and each being, as tiny as it might be, are filled with history. They can tell their story and deliver their message that speaks of the grandeur and majesty of creation. The mission of the human being, man and woman, is to decipher this message and be able to celebrate it. Mental ecology or deep ecology seeks to nourish those psychic energies that enhance the covenant of kinship between the human being and the universe. It arouses the shaman hidden inside each person. Like any shaman, each individual can enter into dialogue with the energies at work in the building of the cosmos over fifteen billion years, energies that manifest themselves in us in the form of intuitions, dreams, and visions, and by enchantment over nature.

Without a spiritual revolution it will be impossible to launch a new paradigm of connectedness.[61] The new covenant finds its roots and the site where it is verified in the depth of the human mind. That is where the lost link that reconstitutes the chain of beings and the vast cosmic community begins to be refashioned. This link in the chain is anchored in the sacred and in God, alpha and omega of the principle of the self-organization of the universe. This is where all sense of connectedness is fostered and this is the permanent basis for the dignity of Earth.

CHAPTER 7

All in God, God in All

The Theosphere

Aristotle taught that *being* can be said in many ways. The same is true for *God.* God is said in a thousand ways and a thousand manners. How is God to be named in the new ecological paradigm? The answer will have to emerge in a natural way from within our overall holistic experience of the universe and of ourselves in it. The important thing is not the word. God's reality need not be brought in from outside, on the basis of an already-worked-out idea of God or from the spiritual or revealed treasury of some religious tradition. We must take all of that into account, because it is a manifestation of the religious consciousness of Earth itself, but it is important that we seek out what is unique about the current moment and that we point toward that experience of radicality, sacredness, enchantment, and mystery that is now part of the ecological experience. That is the point from which it makes sense to speak of God and of everything related to God, such as religion and the sacred.

Albert Einstein expressed it well:

> The most beautiful experience we can have is the mysterious. It is the fundamental emotion which stands at the cradle of true art and true science. Whoever does not know it and can no longer wonder, no longer marvel, is as good as dead, and his eyes are dimmed. It was the experience of mystery—even if mixed with fear—that engendered religion. . . . [I]n this sense and in this alone, I am a deeply religious man.[1]

What matters is not talking about God but about the mystery of the world.[2] God is the name we give to this mystery enveloping us on all sides and flowing over us in all realms. Mystery here does not mean an enigma that disappears upon being deciphered, nor does it point toward the limit

140

of our reason, which, upon proving incapable of penetrating into the dimensions of reality, surrenders and then calls whatever is incomprehensible a mystery. Mystery is not opposed to reason. It means what is unlimited in reason; that is, what may be known but forever remains unknown and that accordingly challenges knowledge to delve more deeply. Hence each paradigm will have its own experience of mystery and will draw on the category of *God* to name it.

The category *God* is not built once for all, for that would mean containing the mystery within the limits of our understanding and language. It is renewed in each root experience. God gains our reverence and our fascination; God comes forth whenever we shudder before the Holy of all things. The very Sanskrit origin of the word *God* is significant. The word comes from *di*, which means "to shine and illuminate." God is an experience of illumination, of discovery of that dimension that dispels the darkness of our life and shows us the way. From *di* we also get *dia,* "day." To wish someone a good day is to want them to have "a good God." Are there not countless people who have had such an experience of light and thereby experienced the meaning of God?

The ecological experience opens us to be thus shaken. Hence we note in advance that ecological reflection represents a break from the classical theistic framework. The latter tended to show God as a Being so absolute, self-sufficient, perfect, and transcendent that it was unaffected by the world. A worldless God easily paves the way for a Godless world. Tragically, that is what happened in the scientific and enlightened circles of modern society.[3]

AWARENESS OF GOD:
FIRST IN THE UNIVERSE, THEN IN THE HUMAN BEING

God is now emerging in the overall process of the evolving and expanding world. In keeping with the radical ecological character that we are maintaining throughout our observations, we must say that the feeling of God that is within us, and as it emerges in us (in other worlds it could be different), belonged first to the universe, emerged in our galaxy, took shape in our solar system, was embodied on planet Earth, and finally became conscious in the human being, man and woman. The primordial subject is the universe and the immediate subject expressing it is the human being, that portion of the universe in which universal consciousness becomes manifest. Because it is originally in the universe and on planet Earth it can then break into human consciousness, since that consciousness is fundamentally of the planet and the cosmos.

Billions of years passed before this latent consciousness could be made manifest. The species *Homo* is the organ that the entire universe employs to reveal what it holds from its beginning, the mystery of God acting within it.

We want to spell out the various routes in our cosmological story that beckon for God's advent in consciousness: quantum reality, the cosmic evolutionary process, the process and eschatological character of nature, the sacramentality of all things, and panentheism.

QUANTUM REALITY AND THE SUPREME AND TRANSCENDENT ENERGY: GOD

At the end of chapter 2, which dealt with the cosmological question, we asked who the universal observer was. Who caused the universal wave to collapse and thereby enabled the universe to cease being probability and become reality as we have it today? There had to be a universal observer who could interact with the probabilities and possibilities and could pull them from that situation and draw them to concrete realization. The religious and sapiential traditions of humankind give the name *God* to the principle that creates, sets in motion, and orders everything. Thus it was God who caused the universal wave to collapse; God is the Creator and the Organizer.

In the word *God* is contained the limitless aspect of our representation and the supreme utopia of pure energy, complexity, vital organization, order, symphonic harmony, passion, and supreme meaning with which the universe, all beings, cultures, and all individual persons are imbued. The word *God* has existential meaning only if it channels human sentiments toward these dimensions *in the manner* of the infinite and of supreme fulfillment. Without infinity and fulfillment we do not yet stand before ultimate reality, God.

How are we to explain the existence of being? The big-bang hypothesis assumes that the world has had a beginning and that it likewise will have an end. It also assumes an Agent who set everything in motion.

What was there before the inflationary universe, before the big bang? Nothing? But what is nothing? If nothing were some thing, it would no longer be nothing. Nothing can be said about nothing, assuming that we want to avoid contradiction. But if we postulate nothing, nonbeing, as prior to being as the presupposition of the big-bang hypothesis, we are led to a contradictory statement: nothing is the origin of being. That is plainly absurd, because from nothing there can come nothing. We are driven back to the conviction of the great religions and the mystical traditions of humankind: the universe comes from a Creator who said *fiat* and things came into being. That Creator existed before the big bang in a manner that we cannot conceive.

Arno Penzias, one of the discoverers of the still measurable echo of the big bang marking the beginning of time (for which he won the Nobel prize in physics), was asked on a radio program, "What was there before the big bang?" He answered, "We don't know; but we can reasonably say: there was nothing." Soon another listener called in, angry at his response, and accused Penzias of being an atheist. Penzias wisely replied, "Madame, I don't think you fully realize the implications of what I just said." He went on to explain the implications, which run counter to atheism, because they lead toward overcoming the historic hostility between modern science and religion. According to Penzias, the implications of the big bang are that only a Creator can draw something from nothing, since obviously from nothing, nothing comes. The nothing Penzias was talking about therefore did not include God. Before the big bang there was nothing of what exists today. Had there been anything, the question would then be: where did it come from? If there was nothing and suddenly beings began to appear, it is a sign that Someone created them from nothing. This Someone is what we call God. Furthermore, our curiosity does not stop at the nature of things but goes on to their significance, to the purpose that the Creator manifested in creating the universe and to our function within it.[4]

On the strictly scientific level we can stammer with reverence that prior to the big bang there was not simply nothing, because nothing is the negation of being. What there was was the Unknowable. Under the Unknowable can be many things, especially the existence of a Creator. We thereby recognize the limits of reason, and we fundamentally reject the simplistic rationalism that sets up the rational as ultimate reality so that whatever overflows its limits (as mystery) is declared to be irrational or nonexistent. That is the source of a certain type of superficial and arrogant atheism, for it confers on reason ultimate attributes proper to divinity.

Silence on the part of science—simply responding "nothing" or "the Unknowable"—does not seal the lips of the human being, nor does it make any potential human words illegitimate. The word of science or of discursive reason is not the only word. There is yet another word that comes from another field of human knowledge, from mysticism, spirituality, religions, and the realm of symbol. In those realms knowing does not mean drawing apart from reality to denude it in all its parts. Knowing is a way of loving, sharing, and communing. It is the discovery of the whole above and beyond the parts, of synthesis above and beyond analysis, of the other side of each question or each being. Knowing means discovering oneself within the whole, internalizing it, and plunging into it. Indeed, we only know well what we love. The mystics are proof of this. David Bohm, a well-known physicist who is sensitive to the mystical dimension, has said, "We could imagine the mystic as someone who is in contact with the astonishing depths of matter or of the subtle mind, regardless of what we call it."[5]

Science arose out of wonder in an effort to decipher the hidden code of all phenomena. Reverence leads to mysticism and the ethic of responsibility. Science seeks to explain the how of things. Mysticism surrenders to ecstasy over the fact that things exist, and it shows reverence to the One revealed in them and veiled behind them. It seeks to experience that fact and establish communion with it. What mathematics is for the scientists, meditation is for the mystic. What the physical laboratory is for the scientist, the spiritual laboratory is for the mystic. The physicist pursues matter to its ultimate possible division and breaks it down to its irreducible elementary substances. The mystic captures the energy concentrated on many levels up to its highest purity in God.[6]

Today more and more scientists, sages, and mystics are coming together around wonder and reverence toward the universe. Both science and mysticism arise out of the same root experience: the *mirandum*, fascination over beauty, harmony, and the mystery of reality. Both point in the same direction: toward the mystery in all things, considered rationally by science and experienced emotionally by mysticism as something beautiful, logical, and radiant. Everything converges on the name of that One who is nameless: God, Tao, Atman, Allah, Olorum, and so forth. Stephen Hawking put it well, "We continue to believe that the world must be logical and beautiful; we have simply put aside the word 'God.'" David Bohm says, "People intuit a kind of intelligence, which organized the universe in the past, and they have personalized it, calling it 'God.'"[7] The name, spoken or unspoken, matters little; God's reality is there.

God emerges from the very thrust of contemporary cosmology.[8] God arises from the chain of steps backward that research is forced to make: from matter we are driven back to the atom; from the atom to elementary particles; from elementary particles to the quantum vacuum. This is the final step for analytic reason. Everything goes out from there and everything returns there; it is the ocean of energy, the container of all possible contents. Perhaps its image emerges in the figure of the cosmic "great attractor," for there is a perception that the whole of the universe is being drawn toward a central point. Teilhard de Chardin saw in the omega point the great attractor, calling the universe to its supreme culmination in the theosphere.

But the quantum vacuum still belongs to the order of the universe. What happened before time? What was God doing before creating heaven and Earth, many have asked. "Preparing hell for whoever should irreverently seek to inquire into such mysteries," responded St. Augustine, who pondered the question of time and eternity extensively.[9] Before and after are temporal determinations, and time is a category of this world.[10] God did not create the world *in* time but *with* time. Before time there is eternity, just as before the creature there is the Creator. Even so, we may ask: what was there before the quantum vacuum? Timeless reality, in the absolute balance of its movement, all in perfect symmetry, endless limitless energy, power without limits and overflowing love, the Unknowable—what is hidden under the name God.

In a "moment" of God's fullness, God decides to create a mirror in which to view God's self, intending to create companions to share God's life and love for the great celebration of communion. Creating means going down or decaying, that is, allowing the emergence of something that is not God and does not have the characteristics of God's essence (absolute symmetry, life without entropy, coexistence of all contraries, infinity, infinite opening to new interactions). Something falls away from that original dynamic plenitude. Hence *decay* here is understood ontologically rather than ethically; it means the emergence of an otherness that comes from God without being God, but which depends on God, bears the marks of God, and points toward God.

God creates that tiny point, billions of times smaller than an atom, the quantum vacuum. A measureless energy flow is transferred from within it. All probabilities and possibilities are open there. A universal wave is in full force. The supreme Observer, in introducing these possibilities and probabilities in being, observes them (knows and loves them) and thereby brings it about that some of them take shape and are combined with others. The others collapse and return to the realm of probabilities.

Everything expands and explodes. The expanding universe emerges. Rather than a starting point, the big bang is a point of instability (chaos) that through relations and interactions (consciousness) makes possible the emergence of ever more interconnected holistic units and orders (cosmos). This is the expanding universe, a metaphor of God and image of God's exuberance in being, living, and celebrating.

If everything in the universe constitutes a network of relationships, if everything is in communion with all, and hence if images of God are presented as structured after the manner of communion, then it is an indication that this supreme Prototype is fundamentally and essentially communion, life in relationship, expanding energy, and supreme love.

Indeed, the mystical intuitions and the spiritual traditions of humankind attest to this line of thinking. The essence of the Jewish and Christian experience, for example, is organized along this line of a God in communion with God's creation, in covenant with all beings, especially with human beings, of a God who is cosmic, social, and personal, a God of human depth, of a life manifested in the three Living Ones, the Father, the Son, and the Holy Spirit—the Trinity, which is the Christian way of naming God.

GOD WITHIN THE COSMOGENIC PROCESS
OF THE UNIVERSE

The observations that we have drawn together in the first few chapters have brought us to see that cosmology is guided by a broadened theory of evolution. This is no longer the evolution of the species as understood by Darwin and Lamarck—indeed only the former proposed the evolution of species—but the evolution of the entire cosmos. Since its very first instant, the cosmos has been in an open evolutionary process. Nature has historicity. The theory of the flaming explosion (the "Flaring Forth" of Swimme and Berry, or Lemaître's big bang) means that the universe is moving in a direction set by the arrow of time. This is no longer Einstein's cosmological principle, which is static and established in a uniform manner on all sides, but a cosmogenic principle, that is, a principle that provides an account of the permanent genesis of the universe at all moments and everywhere.

It all seems to be set up so that out of the deep abyss of an ocean of originating energy there should emerge the elementary particles, beginning with the most primordial, the top quark, followed by organized matter, and then that complex matter that is life, and finally matter in which the vibrations are all in harmony making up the supreme holistic unity, human consciousness.

As the originators of the anthropic principle (Brandon Carter, Hubert Reeves, and others) say, had things not unfolded as they did (the expansion/explosion, primordial gasses, great red stars, supernovas, galaxies, stars, planets, and so forth) we would not be here to talk about them. In other words, in order for us to be here, it was necessary that all the cosmic factors over fifteen billion years should have been arranged and converged in such a manner, even going through detours and cataclysms, so as to make possible complexity, life, consciousness, communication, and the individual existence of each one of us. Had it been different, we would not exist, and we would not be here to ponder such things.[11]

Hence, everything is involved with everything. When I pick a pen off the ground, I enter into contact with the gravitational force that attracts all bodies in the universe. If, for example, as we said above, the density of the universe at the 10^{-35} second after the expansion/explosion had not remained at its proper critical level, the universe could never have been constituted. Either matter and antimatter would have canceled each other out, or there would not have been sufficient cohesion to form masses and hence matter.

There is a tiny range of measurements beyond which the stars would never have emerged nor life have exploded in the universe. This means that the universe is not blind but filled with purpose and intentionality. Even a well-known atheistic astrophysicist like Fred Hoyle recognizes that evolution can only be understood under the presumption that there is a supremely intelligent Agent.[12] God, the name of this supremely intelligent Agent and Organizer, is umbilically involved in the evolutionary and cosmogenic process. God is the initial mover, the power accompanying and continually energizing all, and the supreme attracting magnet of the entire universe. Thus the world is seen to be a system inherently open to God and in all its stages and developments transparent to God.

When they discover such interlinkages, scientists like Einstein, Bohm, Prigogine, Hawking, Swimme, Berry, and others are impelled to feelings of astonishment and reverence. There is an order implicit in all things that subsists beyond the dimension of chaos. That order is imbued with consciousness and spirit from its first moment. This implicit order points toward a supreme Order; consciousness and spirit point toward a supreme Consciousness and toward an unsurpassably intelligent Spirit.[13]

Process philosophers and theologians like Alfred North Whitehead (1861-1947) and his followers (Hartshorne, Ogden, Cobb, Griffin, Haught, and others) have made this evolutionary understanding the paradigmatic core of a whole new cosmology. Unlike classical cosmology, where God and world were set facing one another, here God is being set within the process of the world and the world is regarded as within God's process. They are perichoretically involved in one another; everything that happens in the world somehow affects God, and everything that happens in God somehow affects the world. The very fact that this reality proves to be ever mystery and continually open means that the perichoretic circularity is not complete. The Creator always involves the creature and vice versa, but each one retains its identity and difference. Difference is for the sake of union and communion. That is why we said that God and the world "somehow" affect one another. God is not identified *with* the cosmic process (one is not simply the other; otherness remains in relationship), but God is identified *in* the cosmic process (is embodied, is unveiled and makes known God's otherness in relation). Likewise we must say that the universe is not identified *with* God (one is not the other) but is identified *in* God (in God it gains its true being and meaning).

God and universe are not like a single circle that has just one center where they meet. They are related like an oval with two centers—God and world—but related and mutually implicated in one another. Because of God's character as mystery, seen that way by peoples and individual persons, God remains sovereign vis-à-vis the universe. God is immanent in the world, shares in its open process, reveals God's self in it and is enriched with it. God is also transparent in the world and through the world, and hence the world in its totality and its details constitutes a boundless divine sacrament. God is also transcendent vis-à-vis the world in God's character as absolute mystery beyond any imagination and cosmic grandeur. God is in the world and beyond it, continually creating it, permeating it, and drawing it toward ever more complex, participatory, and communing forms.[14]

What shall we call this God? Supreme expansion energy? Infinite passion for union? Deep mystery of interiority? All these names and a thousand others as well. We will each name it as we are stirred to reverence. Better, we must feel that we are organs through which the very universe and Earth experience the Energy, Passion, Spirit, and Mystery dwelling and acting within us: God.

GOD IN THE COSMIC DANCE OF CREATION

The observations made thus far concern not simply the universe and nature, but rather nature and the universe as creation, as expression of that which is inexpressible and that set everything in motion. But it is not enough to say that God set everything in motion by way of cosmogenesis. Let us go further: in assuming nature as creation we are implicitly assuming a design and a purpose placed there by the Creator. Then the basic question that lies at the root of any and every cosmology is, why do we and the universe exist? What does God want with all this that has been created? What is it that God wants, after all? Answering this question involves the reason, the heart, and loving intelligence. If we succeed, "then we would know the mind of God," says Stephen Hawking confidently.[15] Perhaps there is no merely functional reason or meaning. It is pure gratuity and divine self-outpouring, divine dance and theater of the Creator's glory, like a flower, which, according to the mystic Angelus Silesius, "flowers in order to flower, with no care for whether it is observed or not; it is simply a flower."

If creation is filled with purpose, how is that made manifest? Significant thinkers in contemporary cosmology tell us that order, harmony, and the arrow of time are revealed through the four basic interactions that govern the entire process of evolution and cosmogenesis: gravity, electromagnetism, and the strong and weak nuclear forces. What are these forces? Thus far there is no scientific theory that provides an adequate account of them. They make it possible to understand the processes of the universe, but they themselves resist being understood. Hence they have the nature of a principle. They are like the eye: it makes seeing possible, but it cannot see itself. Newton calls gravity the force that attracts and repels, whereas Einstein sees it as the curvature of space-time. These are descriptions, not definitions. No one knows what these interactions are in themselves and in their intricate connections.

From the standpoint we have assumed throughout this book we can say that they are the universe itself insofar as it is an organism that acts, creates, develops, becomes complex, and develops interiority. They do not point to anything beyond, above, in front of, or beneath themselves. They are the universe itself acting as universe insofar as they hold the whole and each of the parts inescapably united, interconnected, and interdependent. The manner in which it processes this phenomenon of connectedness is manifested in the form of four primordial interactions that always act together and inclusively. Gravity, which explains the falling of a rock thrown into the air, involves the simultaneous action of the electromagnetic force and the strong and weak nuclear interaction. They constitute a perfect perichoresis—mutual inter(retro)relationship. The universe as an active organism is the subject of everything that happens in the cosmos. From the outset it is organizing itself in an open process that comes down to us.[16]

From such an understanding we can conclude that creation is not something mechanical. It is not a machine set in motion in the beginning; rather, the world organism is always open to whatever is around it, in ongoing interplay in which potentialities not yet embodied are being realized. It is a true *creatio continua,* as was intuited by one dynamically oriented strand of Christian tradition, especially the orthodox.[17] Today we would say that creation as an interconnected whole is an open system.

Actually existing being is now seen to be the result of this open and cosmic process. Within this cosmogenic vision it is not so much a matter of *operare sequitur esse* (action follows being) as the opposite, *esse sequitur operare* (being follows operation). The process continues to constitute beings that are themselves open and process-oriented and hence ever producing and reproducing their existence in a dance of relationships, exchanges, communications, and unities. Indeed, God is involved in this cosmic dance, which is God's creation, as Jesus indicated in the gospel of John: "My Father works until today and I also work" (Jn 5:17).

This ongoing operation of creation as open process is characterized by what Swimme and Berry (like Teilhard de Chardin) call *differentiation* (or also diversity, complexity, variation, disparity, multiform nature, heterogeneity, and articulation), *autopoiesis* (or subjectivity, self-manifestation, identity, inner principle of being, voice, interiority), and *communion* (or interrelatedness, interdependence, mutuality, reciprocity, complementarity, interconnectivity, affiliation, kinship).[18] We prefer to speak of complexity, interiority, and connectedness, as we have been doing throughout our observations.

From its very beginning, evolutionary cosmogenesis has produced ever richer *complexities*, from the first two particles interacting one with another to the complexity of life, and especially human life, in its biological, sociological, and historic aspects, to the complexity of civilizations, dreams, ideas, religions, and human faces. (Nothing denies the meaning of the universe so much as homogeneity and the imposing of a single idea, a single conviction, a single way of living together, a single way of praying and speaking of God. Just as we respect biodiversity we must also accept "religiodiversity" and "ideodiversity.")

As complexity increases so likewise does *interiority*. Each being has its own uniqueness, its own entry on stage, and its own way of making its presence felt. It has not only an outside but an inside in the way it organizes itself and constitutes the texture of its relationships. Even the most primitive atom has its presence and its way of relating. This interiority gains clear expression, when, given its greater complexity, there emerges a central nervous system in animals and a brain in the human being. Greater spontaneity and freedom now blossom; planet Earth is surrendering to self-determining and imponderable forces.

Finally, there is a third principle at work, that of *connectedness*. One of the most important findings of modern physics and cosmology is the profound unity of the universe. All four interactions operate alike throughout cosmic space. Everything is interconnected. Through gravity one galaxy depends on another. Electromagnetic and nuclear equilibrium sustains the symphony of the universe, preventing chaotic events from destroying the harmonic whole. Indeed, they make possible new connections and the emergence of new things that have not been tested in the process of cosmogenesis. Such connectedness causes the interiority of beings to communicate with one another. Beings listen to one another's voice and can hear the story that each can tell in its process spanning billions of years. Listening to the voice of the other is not merely a metaphor; it points toward a reality. Thus the mountain hears the voice of the wind and the interaction is established between the two, the wind with the trees, the trees with the animals, the animals with the atmosphere, and the human being, holistically, with all these beings and events, and so forth. One reacts to the other and interacts in keeping the dynamic equilibrium established between them. A geographer examining a riverside cliff bank is able to read the meaning of each layer deposited, can read the story of the floods, droughts, and cataclysms that have occurred throughout the long history of the river. He or she reads the message announced by those signs. Killing a being or wiping out a species means closing a book, burning a library, and forever condemning to silence a message that comes from the entire cosmos, indeed from God.

Creation thus understood is a vast book written internally and externally that bears God's signature: "*Deo creato, made by God, egressus de coelis.*" It is up to human beings—it is part of their function in the cosmos—to know how to read the book of creation in order to be joyful and celebrate, to thank and praise the Creator. It contains God's ongoing revelation and is the most deep-rooted and continuous manifestation of the sacred. For fifteen billion years God's self-surrender to the creation and the manifestation of God's inner self has been taking place in proportion to the emergence of the self-organization, complexification, interiorization, and connectedness of beings.

The sacred texts and traditions that attest to revelations are only possible because the sacred and the revelations are first in the world. It is because they are there that they can be in the inspired books and in the rituals of religions. It is the same God who speaks in both places. That is why ultimately there cannot be contradiction between the book of the world and the book of the scriptures. Or rather, they are not simply historic constructs but mediations through which the cosmos itself and Earth make known the sacred, and the divine trembles within them and radiates outward.

Such a vision enables us to reclaim a theology of creation that the churches and religions need so badly. Almost all of them are held hostage to their founding texts; they draw inspiration from them and nowhere else. Few know how to connect the book of creation to the book of scriptures, in keeping with the ancient tradition that extends, in the case of Christianity, from Origin, and passes by way of Augustine and Bonaventure to modern ecotheology. A creation-centered theology requires the overhauling of all religious and ecclesial institutions. They must be at the service of the cosmic revelation, which applies to all; they must recover original grace above and beyond original sin; they must extend to the cosmos theological claims that have been applied only to human beings (theological anthropocentrism) but that are valid for the entire universe, such as grace, final destiny, divinization, resurrection, eternal life, and the reign of the Trinity.

Christ and the Spirit are cosmic realities that have been emerging slowly to the point where they take personal form in Jesus of Nazareth and in Mary,[19] as we shall see further on. Similarly, creation spirituality overcomes the dualism of God and world, person and nature, matter and spirit, and fashions an overall experience of being in the world as in our own house, and in the social and cosmic body that are the temple of the Divinity. Asceticism does not mean so much the pursuit of autonomy and freedom from the world as a sense of connectedness with the cosmic community and freedom for the world in the responsibility of caring for it, and celebrating the magnificence that it manifests, and knowing how to read the wise lessons that the cosmic magisterium communicates to us. If we make God disappear from the cosmos, we also make God disappear from human beings, because ultimately we are cosmic beings.

Such a creation-centered religious interpretation leads to a deep sense of the sacramentality of all things. God announces the divine presence in each being and in its history. The human being is that one capable of hearing the thundering of galaxies and supernovas, as well as picking up the song of the bird in the forest, or the soft breathing of a newborn child, and rising up to the *Spiritus Creator,* who fills all and to the mystery of God surrendering God's self to all beings. Everything is or can be sacramental.

We must keep in mind, however, that sacramentality must not aim simply at a vertical vision of God and the universe but must be directed at the horizontal–God as process of evolutionary cosmogenesis. No being is completed; all are open to new advances and hence to new revelations. This means not allowing sacramentality to become rigid, but rather keeping it in process and open to the newness of new kinds of manifestation of the mystery of God.

It is the eschatological perspective that opens us to the world as future and promise. Eschatology views the present on the basis of the future, the process underway on the basis of its joyful culmination. The eschatological vision relativizes all the steps; that is, it places them in relation to the end and thereby deabsolutizes them, and also prevents the present from being eternalized.

Our minds are thereby opened to the absolute newness of what has not been seen and tested. Each being has this openness to the eschatological, to a perfection that is still to come, because every being is in process and in permanent openness. Hence we must accept that the cosmos is grand but incomplete; its harmony is dazzling but not final. Its sacramentality is always fragmentary and hides the promise and the future that have not yet been fulfilled but that are anticipated in the drives inherent in each being and that on one delightful day will come to pass. Only at the end of the evolutionary process (neither in the beginning nor in the middle) will the inspired words of Genesis be true, "And God saw that all was good." Only at the end will there be Sabbath rest for all creation and indeed for God.

PANENTHEISM: GOD IN ALL AND ALL IN GOD

The ecological view of the cosmos emphasizes God's immanence. God is seen to be involved in all processes without being merged into them. Rather, God directs the arrow of time toward the emergence of orders that are ever more complex, dynamic (and hence drawing further away from equilibrium in the pursuit of new adaptations), and charged with purpose. God does not figure merely as Creator, but as Spirit of the world, as we will see in greater detail in the next chapter. The Creator as Spirit (*Spiritus Creator*) establishes a dwelling place in the cosmos, shares in its developments, suffers with massive extinctions, feels crucified with the impoverished of planet Earth (St. Paul's "ineffable groanings of the Spirit," Rom 8:26), and rejoices with advances toward more convergent and interrelated diversities, pointing toward a final omega point.

God is present in the cosmos and the cosmos is present in God. Theology in the early centuries expressed this mutual interpenetration with the concept of perichoresis.[20] Modern theology has coined another expression: *panentheism* (Greek: *pan*=all; *en*=in; *theós*=God); that is, God in all and all in God. This term was first proposed by Karl Christian Frederick Krause (1781-1832), who was fascinated by the divine splendor of the universe.[21]

Panentheism must be clearly distinguished from pantheism. Pantheism (Greek: *pan*=all; *theós*=God) claims that all is God and God is all. It holds that God and the world are identical; that the world is not God's creature, but the necessary mode of God's existing. Pantheism does not accept any difference. Everything is identical; all is God. The heavens are God, Earth is God, the rock is God, bacteria are God, the human being is God, each thing is God. This lack of difference easily leads to indifference. If everything is God and God is everything, then it does not matter whether I devote myself to street children murdered in Rio de Janeiro, or to carnival, or to soccer, or to the Kayapó Indians on their way to extinction, or to a serious effort to discover a cure for AIDS, or to collecting beer cans from around the world. That is obviously wrong. One thing is *not* another; there are differences in this world. Panentheism respects such differences, while pantheism denies them.

All is not God. But God is in all and all is in God, by reason of the creation by which God leaves God's mark and assurance of God's permanent presence in the creature (providence). The creature always depends on God and carries God within it. God and world are different. One is not the other. But they are not separated or closed. They are open to one another. They are always intertwined with one another. If they are different, it is so they can communicate and be united by communion and mutual presence.

This mutual presence means that simple transcendence and simple immanence are overcome. There emerges an intermediate category, transparency, which is precisely the presence of transcendence within immanence. When this happens reality becomes transparent. God and the world are therefore mutually transparent.[22] Like no one else in this century, Teilhard de Chardin lived a deep spirituality of *transparency*. As he said,

"The great mystery of Christianity is not exactly the appearance, but the transparence, of God in the universe. *Yes Lord, not only the ray that strikes the surface, but the ray that penetrates, not only your Epiphany, Jesus, but your diaphany.*"[23] He expressed it in this other prayer,

> Once again, Lord, I ask which is the most precious of those two beatitudes: that all things for me should be a contact with you? or that you should be so "universal" that I can undergo you and grasp you in every creature?[24]

The universe in cosmogenesis invites us to undergo the experience that underlies panentheism: at the slightest manifestation of being, at each moment, in every expression of life, intelligence and love, we are facing the Mystery of the universe-in-process. Persons sensitive to the Sacred and to the Mystery dare to name the Unnameable. They take God out of anonymity and give God a name, celebrate God with hymns and songs, invent symbols and rituals, and convert themselves into this Center that they feel to be outside of, within, and above them. They experience God. And they discover in God the source of supreme happiness and fulfillment. They feel at home, in the primordial womb, in the true Oikologia, God the ultimate and fulfilling Sphere of all beings and of the entire created universe, "in whom we live, we move, and have our being" (Act 17: 28): the theosphere. Can we take our discourse on God any further? It seems that we can. Some speak of God as Trinity. How is this manner of naming God to be understood?

GOD, INTERPLAY OF PERICHORETIC RELATIONSHIPS: THE BLESSED TRINITY

Ecological discourse offers us the possibility and plausibility of speaking of God as a trinity of Persons. That is the discourse of Christians, those who believe in the coexistence, simultaneity, and coeternity of the Father, the Son, and the Holy Spirit. But the trinitarian intuition is not nor could it be (by God's very nature) solely limited to Christianity. There is a trinitarian line passing through the great religious traditions of humankind.[25] Today such discourse may attain new insight through ecology.

Ecological discourse is structured around the web of relationships, interdependencies, and inclusions that sustain and constitute our universe. Together with unity (a single cosmos, a single planet Earth, a single human species, and so forth) diversity also flourishes (galaxy clusters, solar systems, biodiversity, and multiplicity of races, cultures, and individuals). This coexistence between unity and diversity opens an area where we may consider our understanding of divinity in terms of trinity and communion. The very fact of speaking of Trinity rather than simply of God entails going beyond a single-chord substantialist vision of divinity. The Trinity centers on a vision of relationships, reciprocities, and inter(retro)-communions. This is metaphysics of another kind, a processive and dynamic metaphysics rather than a static and ontic type.

Hence, when Christians speak of Trinity–Father, Son, and Holy Spirit–they are not adding numbers: 1+1+1=3. If it were a matter of numbers then God is one alone and not a trinity. With the Trinity Christians want to express the unique experience that God is communion and not solitude. John Paul II put it well during his first visit to Latin America on January 28, 1979, in Puebla, Mexico: "There is a profound and beautiful saying that our God, in his innermost mystery, is not aloneness but a family, since God embodies paternity, filiation, and the essence of the family that is love. In the divine family that love is the Holy Spirit."[26] God-Trinity is thus relatedness par excellence.

In the language of the medievals who elaborated trinitarian thought philosophically and theologically, the Persons are nothing but "subsistent relations"; in other words, an utter relationality of each one with regard to the others, so much so that they are reciprocally intertwined with and included in one another forever and at each moment, although one is not the other.[27]

Within this logic we must understand that the Father is unique and there is none like the Father; the Son is unique and there is none like the Son; the Holy Spirit is unique and there is none like the Holy Spirit. Each is unique, and as mathematicians know, what is unique is not a number but the absence of number. So are there then three Uniques, three gods? That would be the logical argument. However, trinitarian logic is otherwise. It is not substantialist but processive and relational. It says that the Unique ones relate among themselves so absolutely, they are intertwined so intimately, they love one another so radically, that they become one. This perichoretic communion is not the result of Persons who upon being in themselves and for themselves thereupon began to relate. Rather, it is simultaneous and original with the Persons. They are communion-Persons. So there is one God-communion-of-Persons. Putting it in another way, there is one God and "three" Persons, or one Nature and "three" Hypostases, or "three" Lovers and a single Love, or "three" Subjects and a single Substance, or "three" Unique ones and a single Communion.[28]

If there were only "one" divine figure, solitude would prevail and everything would be reduced to unity and unicity. If there were "two" figures, Father and Son, facing one another, it would be a narcissism of the "two." But there is a "third" figure, the Holy Spirit, who forces the other "two" to turn their gaze from themselves in another direction. We accordingly have the perfect dialectic, for everything circulates as among the father, the mother, and the child, making a single family. The important thing to see is not each person by itself and for itself but the circularity that inherently enwraps one in the other, the ongoing play of relationships. The very words *Father, Son,* and *Holy Spirit* suggest this relational circularity. The Father exists only as the Father of the Son. The Son is ever the Son of the Father. And the Holy Spirit is the breath (the root sense of Spirit is "breath") of the Father and the Son.

We avoid tritheism (three gods, which assumes an essentialist interpretation of the Trinity) by perichoresis, that is, by the communion and complete relationality among the divine Persons. They are what they are by their essential and intrinsic communion and inter(retro)relating. St. Augustine, the wonderful theologian of the Trinity, put it well: "Each of the Divine Persons is in each of the others, and all are in each one, and each one is in all, and all are in all and all are only one."[29]

A modern ecologist could hardly express better this interplay of relationships, inasmuch as it constitutes the basic logic of cosmogenesis. If God is communion and relationship, then the entire universe lives in relationship, and all is in communion with all at all points and at all moments, as we have repeatedly emphasized. For this is what quantum physicists, those working in the Earth sciences, including ecologists, continually repeat.

Thus the Trinity emerges as one of the most suitable representations of the mystery of the universe, as we interpret it today (web of relationships, arena of interdependencies, cosmic dance), mystery deciphered as God. This God is seen to be a Reality of relationship and communion, whose expression is the Trinity, one and unique Mystery offered as Father, Son, and Holy Spirit.

Although it comes from early Christianity and is witnessed in the most ancient religions, the doctrine of the Trinity likewise emerges as the most modern. It is perfectly in tune with our cosmology.[30] Moreover, it makes it possible to critique all closed systems in all fields because everything must be image and likeness of God-communion, an absolutely open and processive reality. At the same time, it emerges as promise for the future of the universe: to continue as a more organized open system plunged into the infinite openness of life and of the reign of the Trinity.

THE SILENCE OF THE BUDDHA
AND OF MEISTER ECKHART

Finally, we want to pose the question that matters to any truly radical theology and that constitutes one of the basic intuitions of Buddhism: the apophatic stance (silence before the supreme Reality). We may ask: Could it not be that even the Trinity is an expression of yet another truly ultimate reality? Of this ultimate Reality we cannot say anything, not even whether it is or is not. It is beyond determinations of existence and nonexistence, for it is in itself ineffable (ontically apophatic) not simply for us human beings. If we say that it is, it means that it is thinkable, communicable, and belongs to the order of manifestations. Then it is not the ultimate Reality but simply a manifestation of it. If we say that it is not, the problem would go away. But can we simply say that it is not? Is it not beyond our determinations of being or nonbeing? Actually we should say that it *is* but beyond being-and-not-being as opposition and affirmation or of negation of one and the other. It is, in a manner that is completely beyond the grasp of anyone whatsoever. If it could be grasped, again it would mean that it is not the ultimate Reality. Buddhism has posed this question, as have radical mystics like Meister Eckhart.[31]

This view of things provides a basis for understanding the silence of the mystics, and especially that of the Buddha. When the Buddha goes silent it is not for any personal reason, nor is it linked to the interlocutor or to human reason. He refuses to respond because of an exigency of ultimate Reality. The only worthy stance before it is noble silence. The Buddha accordingly took the resolution never to speak of it but rather to speak of the route leading to it.[32] Certainly the route that points most toward the ultimate Reality is the most holy Trinity, interplay of relationships and communion. For us Christians, the route is the historical Jesus in the living power of the Spirit. They, together with the Father who sends them into the world, are the economic Trinity, which is made manifest and which is a reflection of the immanent Trinity, absolute Mystery. In any case, without proceeding to discuss this radical theme (it should properly be treated in another context), the Trinity helps us to delve deeper into understanding our common home, planet Earth, the universe, and its future, because they are all woven of the most intricate and open relationships, in the likeness of the Trinity. The Blessed Trinity constitutes the common sphere of all beings and entities: the theosphere.

CHAPTER 8

"The Spirit Is Sleeping in the Rock"

It Dwells in the Cosmos

To understand the cosmos as cosmogenesis and to comprehend reality as energy fields and an intricate web of relationships situates us within that experience that prompts the emergence of the category of spirit in all human cultural traditions. *Spiritus* to Romans, *Pneuma* to Greeks, *Ruach* to Hebrews, *Mana* to Melanesians, *Axé* to Nagôs and Yorubas in Africa and their descendants in the Americas, *Wakan* to Dakota Indians, *Ki* to the peoples of North-East Asia, *Shi* to the Chinese—no matter what the names may be, we are always dealing with life, with the universe as an organism too vast to measure (the *membra sumus corporis magni* of the Stoics), with reality that is emerging, fluctuating, and open to surprise and novelty. The world is filled with the Spirit, which emerges in the spirit found in springs, mountains, trees, winds, persons, houses, cities, heaven, and Earth.

This experience of vital energy passing through all beings was formulated systematically in animism. The great scholar of animism E. B. Tylor[1] called it a true "well ordered and connected rational philosophy." Well-known phenomenologists of religion, including Gerardus van der Leeuw,[2] have held similar positions. Animism is not a set of particular beliefs but rather a unique way of interpreting the entire universe and each thing within it on the basis of the principle of all movement and all life: the *animus,* the spirit.

Animism constitutes the original human mindset, and it reaches down into the deepest layers of our psyche. In this sense we moderns are also animists to the extent that we experience the world emotionally within a unifying comprehensive dimension and to the extent that we feel part of a living whole in which we are enveloped. Everything sends us a message; everything speaks or can speak: trees, colors, wind, animals, roads, persons, and household things. All of them, by their very presence, are charged in a way that affects us and makes us interact. They have a "spirit," because they are located within the realm of life. It is because things speak and are charged with sacramentality that enthusiasm, poetry, painting, invention, and all the inspiration present in each type of knowledge up to the most formal knowledge of modern physics are all possible.

Shamanism arises out of this interpretation of reality. Shamans are not simply enthusiasts swept up by a spiritual force that makes them do extraordinary things. They are people who enter into contact with cosmic energies, know how to control within themselves the energy flow, and by their mere presence through gestures, dances, and rites put those energies at the disposal of human beings as they seek balance with nature and with themselves. All must awaken within themselves this shamanistic dimension as a moment of coming into harmony with the dynamic balance of things.

We want to delve more deeply into the category of "spirit" as it has been developed by our Jewish and Christian Western tradition. We could do so through other traditions, but the important thing is to see how it helps us to understand what contemporary cosmology has achieved and how it enriches us and embodies our experience of the spirit and of the *Spiritus Creator* presiding over the entire cosmogenic process.

FROM COSMOS TO SPIRIT

Although the reality of spirit certainly does not depend on an etymological derivation, words do express root experiences and etymologies do give us access to those experiences. The Hebrew word for spirit is the feminine *ruach*, which appears 389 times in the Hebrew scriptures. Recent studies have shown that in all Semitic languages (Syriac, Punic, Akkadian, Samaritan, Ugaritic, and Hebrew) the verbal root of *ruach* is *rwh*, whose original meaning is not "breath" or "wind," as usually given, but "the atmospheric space between heaven and earth," which can be calm or turbulent. By derivation it also means "unfolding and spreading," "expansion and extension of living space."[3] Properly speaking, *ruach* means the vital sphere where the human being, the animal, or any other living thing imbibes life.[4] Expressed in contemporary language, *ruach* is the energy-giving reality that fills the expanding cosmic spaces; near us is the vital atmosphere, the biosphere that envelops all living things. Since the biosphere does not exist by itself but is closely tied to the hydrosphere, the lithosphere, and the geosphere, we may conclude that the *ruach* fills the entire universe, as the scriptures say (Wis 1:7).

Life makes itself felt most palpably in breathing, and hence *ruach*-spirit often means vital breath. Such an attribution was not restricted to living beings. The Earth is also understood as a living being. Its breath is the wind, whether in the form of a soft breeze or a whirlwind. The wind is also called *ruach*-spirit.[5]

Ruach means originating cosmic power permeating all and giving it life. It is creative and imparts order. That is why *ruach*-spirit appears on page 1 of Genesis, which gives an account of the creation of the universe. The spirit hovered over the *tohuwabohu* (the Hebrew expression in Genesis 1:2 that expresses the original chaos of the waters), giving rise to the various beings in an orderly way.

The Hebrew expression of the movement of the spirit over the waters (*merahephet*, "hovered over the waters") refers to the way the water birds circle over the waters or break the egg—here the cosmic egg—from which all proceeds.[6] In matriarchal cultures the presence of the bird or dove indicated the activity of the Great Mother generating life. Interestingly, since *ruach* is feminine in Hebrew, it preserves a hint of a maternal function.[7]

Starting from this original meaning, *spirit* takes on various particular forms, all amply documented in scriptural texts[8]: first, in the cosmos as a whole, in its seminal energy, in its elementary components, for the cosmos is the spirit's creation; then in the physical world, for everything that moves is moved by the spirit; then in the living world, where plants and animals are permeated by the spirit and its energies; in human beings, since they are regarded especially as bearers of the spirit because they have interiority and a dynamism that makes them principles of creation and communication; in the prophets, in particular, who are men and women of spirit, as are charismatic leaders, poets, and mystics; finally in God, for God is revealed as the originating root energy, the true domain of life, the "*ruach*sphere" (Hebrew) or the "*pneumato*sphere" (Greek). This fact must be kept in mind: the spirit is present from the beginning of the universe, permeating it, emerging in a series of forms until it reaches its highest expression: the divine Spirit.

FROM SPIRIT TO HUMAN SPIRIT

The human spirit offers the basis for speaking of the divine Spirit. When we speak of spirit we do not intend to indicate one part of the human being as opposed to another, such as its material-bodily structure. Spirit defines the totality of human beings insofar as it expresses a way of being alive and aware, capable of a totality, of communication, intelligence, sensitivity, and freedom. This conscious vitality is basically made manifest in four connections:

• The human spirit is a *force for synthesizing and creating unity*. Conscious vitality is structured around a vital center, the conscious and unconscious self; it signifies the unity of all experience with which human beings come into contact, in communion with or rejecting the thing affecting them, both on the phenomenological level and on the level of depth and archetype. Living means being able to bring things together continually in a dynamic and open way, without ever coming to a complete unity closed in on itself. It is always an open, delicately balanced system, relating to self, the other, mystery, and the all.

• The human spirit is *a force for socialization and communication.* It always coexists as a node of relationships; the self is constituted on the basis of an interplay with others with which it engages in reciprocity and complementarity.

• The human spirit is a *power of meaning.* Everything that human beings confront has meaning for them. A fact is never merely a fact; it is something to be deciphered and interpreted. The human being is capable of symbolizing, adding something to what is given, and seeing it as bearer of a manifest or hidden meaning.

• The human spirit is a *power of transcendence.* Human beings can never be encapsulated in a formula or enclosed in a structure. They spill over and ever remain an open question above, alongside, within, and beyond themselves. This is their living transcendence, the reason human beings are perennial "protestants," never satisfied with their own given nature.

In saying "spirit," we seek to express this vital drive embodied in the human being. It is not, strictly speaking, something in the human being, but the proper and unique way of being of man and woman.[9]

This experience of the human spirit provides the basis for our understanding of the meaning of the divine Spirit, who extends the characteristics of the spirit in the form of infinity, eternity, and fulfillment.

FROM HUMAN SPIRIT TO DIVINE SPIRIT

To say that God is spirit is to seek to give expression to God in the framework of life, of irruption, communication, transcendence of whatever is given, overflowing abundance, passion, and fiery love. It means leaving behind a particular kind of metaphysics that takes direction from what is static, ever identified with itself, and from the ladder of being rising up to a top occupied by the *summum Ens, unmoved mover,* God. Spirit entails another way of access through energy, utterly open process, a way that knows no limits or barriers. The spirit-as-cosmic-force and vital energy blows where it wills and energizes the entire cosmogenesis. It is the *ubique diffusus, transfusus, circumfusus* of the church fathers, that is, that which fills all things and is spread throughout all spaces and times.[10]

There is no point in pitting one metaphysics against another, however. They are actually complementary, rather as the understanding of reality from the quantum perspective is complementary, namely, as material particle and as energy wave.[11] The Spirit is energy, life, ever self-actualizing process, communicating itself, and transcending itself. At the same time, without losing its process character, it is a substantial (not imaginary) reality of communion and love. Understanding God as spirit directs our experience down the path of what is vital, of interplay of relationships, and subjectivity. As we deepen these experiences we come up against the absolute Spirit, who enlivens the whole universe (*Spiritus vivificans* of the Christian creed)—what we call God.

God accordingly emerges as divine Spirit—in religious language the expression is Holy Spirit. The connotation of the word *holy* is ontological rather than ethical. Biblically speaking, it defines God's identity, that is, what sets God apart from everything else, that which is the Sacred par excellence, the One who dwells in light inaccessible and whom we may approach with reverence.[12] In human terms a number of experiences point toward the perception of the spirit in our midst.

First there is *ecstasy*. Ecstasy should not be understood as within the realm of the miraculous but as the experience of a certain wholly unique kind of presence that also takes place in the everyday. Ecstasy occurs whenever an extreme intensification of presence occurs. Presence is the radiation of that being that is completely open to the outside and to others. The Spirit is grasped in the existential ecstasy of the singularity of life, in the grandeur of the starry sky, in the impact of a charismatic person (full of the power of the spirit).

Another dimension that the Spirit reveals is *enthusiasm*. Etymologically, the term refers to "having a god within" (*en-theós-mos*). Actually, the experience of enthusiasm is to feel oneself possessed by an extraordinary energy that cuts huge obstacles down to size and that leads people to take on major initiatives. Enthusiasm displays the exuberance of life that is made manifest in the decision to work and create, to rejoice and dance. It changes the person into an *éntheos*, that is, someone inhabited by God.[13] The Greeks understandably associated enthusiasm with the god Dionysus, who is worshiped with songs, feasts, and a great deal of wine. The *charism* that we observe in some persons—that is, a special ability to speak, create, or relate to others and to God—reveals this same structure of enthusiasm. Nothing great and truly creative is ever achieved without the powerful influence of enthusiasm.

Another sign of the Spirit's presence is *inspiration*. As with enthusiasm, inspired persons feel possessed by a greater power; it is not they who are thinking and writing, painting or sculpting, but someone greater who is strongly impelling them to execute the work. Inspiration arises out of the experience of the everyday, as when we say that a person "shows spirit." This generally happens in a difficult situation, even one with no way out.

The right word must be found or the proper action must be performed. Suddenly, without knowing how and why, a person manages to express or do what must be done or said in a convincing way. He or she has shown the presence of spirit. The New Testament sees the presence of the Holy Spirit in such a constraining situation: "When they lead you away and hand you over, do not worry beforehand about what you are to say. For it will not be you who are speaking, but the holy Spirit" (Mk 13:11; Mt 10:19ff.; Lk 12:11ff).[14] A number of religious traditions, such as the Jewish and Christian, understand their sacred writings as inspired by the divine Spirit.

Another sign of the presence of the Spirit is *communication.* To communicate means to go out from ourselves to break the closed circle of our own identity, and to surrender to the other. Communication is a process of self-transcendence. The Spirit is this communication and establishment of relationships in all directions. "In the beginning was the relation" (Martin Buber); that is, in the beginning was the Spirit relating outward and drawing all things from nothing.[15]

Finally, the Spirit is announced by the presence of *reasonability and order* in the universe. This was what fascinated Newton and Einstein. Even after the new cosmology, which utilizes chaos theory and Heisenberg's uncertainty principle, by the power of the Spirit chaos is seen to be always generative and indetermination has produced the most varied kinds of being and life. The arrow of time, which is deduced from the cosmogenic process, points toward an intention that is being achieved in process over the course of millions and billions of years. Does not reason demand acceptance of a supreme Rationality, an infinite Spirit?

FROM THE DIVINE SPIRIT TO THE THIRD PERSON OF THE CHRISTIAN TRINITY

How was the step made from the Holy Spirit to the third Person of the Christian Trinity? This is not the place to attempt to ground the uniqueness of the Christian way of naming God as Trinity of Father, Son, and Holy Spirit. The considerations in the previous chapter will suffice. The Christian community needed generations to come to a clear realization that the Spirit spoken of in the scriptures and that piety adored as God must be regarded as within the realm of the mystery of the Trinity.

The great issue for the early church was Jesus Christ and the deciphering of the mystery surrounding his practice, his messianic claim, his passion, and especially the event of the resurrection. After three generations of community meditation brought together in the texts that now make up the Christian scriptures, they concluded that Jesus was, in their term, the

Son of God. Against the well-known theologian, Arius of Alexandria, who out of respect for the transcendental mystery of God denied the divinity of the man Jesus of Nazareth, the Council of Nicea in 325 defined: "We believe in one God, Father almighty . . . and in one Lord Jesus Christ, Son of God, begotten by the Father . . . not made, of the same substance as the Father." This formulation runs a risk of staying in a kind of binarism (Father-Son); to maintain trinitarian faith, Nicea adds, "and we believe in the Holy Spirit," with no explanation.

Subsequent theological reflections would deepen the content of this dry and plain profession of faith. Who—or what—is the Spirit? Is it God, and thereby the Uncreated Creator?* Is it a creature of God, cosmic drive, pointing toward One prior and greater? For an entire generation great minds, including some of the greatest in Christian intellectual history, of the stature of St. Basil, his brother Gregory of Nyssa, and Gregory Nazianzen, engaged in highly sophisticated discussions endeavoring to see in what sense the Spirit was a Person and what its place was in the trinitarian mystery. How is the Spirit situated alongside the Father and the Son? Their quest culminated in the Council of Nicea-Constantinople in 381, with the statement: "We believe in the Holy Spirit, Lord and giver of life, who proceeds from the Father, who together with the Father and Son is worshiped and glorified and who spoke through the prophets."

That formulation makes it plain that the Holy Spirit has the same substance as the Father, for it proceeds from him; however, the Spirit is also God and hence deserves to be adored and glorified. To strengthen this convergence in faith, Pope Damasus (366-84) called a Council in Rome in 382 and ordered the publication of a series of canons on the Blessed Trinity and the incarnation.[16] There it is stated textually, "Any one who does not say that the Holy Spirit, like the Son, is really and truly from the Father, of the divine substance, and true God, is heretical" (*DS* 168). Then even more clearly, "Any one who does not say that there is only one godhead, one might, one majesty, one power, one glory, one lordship, one kingdom, one will and one truth of the Father and of the Son and of the Holy Spirit, is heretical" (*DS* 172).

The collective mind of Christianity thereby became set: the way to name God is trinitarian; God is not the solitude of one but the communion of the divine Three, connected perichoretically so as to constitute a single God-love, a sole Divinity-communion and a sole Mystery-relationship.

When, however, the attempt was made to explore intellectually the relationship between the divine Three and the order of attribution (the three are equally God, but that does not make it correct to say that the Father is

---

* Boff uses male pronouns (*ele* = he) for the Holy Spirit. The (not fully satisfactory) translation option here is to use neuter language (it)—*translator*.

the Son or the Holy Spirit and vice versa; there is an order of attribution starting with the Father, passing through the Son, and culminating in the Spirit, who is the breath–spirit–of the Two), there began a debate that remains unfinished even today. With regard to the Holy Spirit: Does it proceed from the Father alone or also from the Son? If like the Son, the Spirit proceeds from the Father alone, are there two Sons? Or does it proceed from the Father *through* the Son? This is the famous issue of the *Filioque* ("and also from the Son"), which led to the break between the two sister churches, Orthodox and Roman Catholic, when Photius was patriarch in Constantinople.

The councils of Lyons (1274) and Florence (1438) formalized the Western position: the Holy Spirit proceeds jointly from the Father and the Son, thereby assuring the full consubstantiality of the three divine Persons and overcoming the suspicion that the Holy Spirit might be a divine creature or the presence of God's power in history and not a unique Person together with the Father and Son.

This discussion, however, entailed some theological disadvantages. Saying that the Spirit proceeds from the Father and the Son places it somehow in a double dependence. It always comes later and in the third place; its order in the trinitarian process is defined with regard to the two other Persons who are *prius natura* to it. That is why many theologians, including this author, hold for a perpetual divine perichoresis and maintain the simultaneity of the divine Persons, who are equally eternal and infinite. They do not proceed from one another as in a kind of theogony, as if the metaphysical principle of causality were valid for God and thus were above God. The language of procession is analogical, and it is a metaphorical and symbolic way of showing the inclusion of the Three and the eternal communion by which the divine Three are always one through the other, for the other, with the other, and in the other (perichoresis or circumsession). The relations are of participation and reciprocal relation rather than hypostatic derivation. They are more by way of correlation and communion than production and procession. The Persons are not produced and do not proceed from one another but from the intratrinitarian and interpersonal revelation. One Person is the condition of the revelation of the Other in an infinite dynamism, like mirrors triply reflecting one another without end. Hence there is not only a *Filioque* but a *Spirituque* and *Patreque*.[17]

This discussion has kept reflection on the Spirit hostage to the problems unresolved in the argument between the two sister churches, thereby failing to do justice to the vast work of the Holy Spirit in the cosmos, in human history, and in the life stories of people in all cultures. Greek theology tended toward monarchianism (the monarchy of the Father in the order of intratrinitarian relations; according to this theology it is the Father who upholds the divine substance and communicates it differently to the Son and to the Holy Spirit) and Latin theology has tended toward Christomonism (Christ is all, centralization in Christ, yesterday, today, and forever, as though there were no Father and Spirit). Both theologies are lacking in the Spirit, and hence they are ultimately linear, authoritarian, and hostile to freedom. The charismatics and prophets and reformers who invoke the Holy Spirit typically have been summarily forced to submit to criteria that are monarchical (the patriarch who represents the Father decides) or Christomonic (the hierarchy represents Christ and so decides) and have been condemned. The rejection of Joachim of Fiore, Martin Luther, and the liberation theology movement today all attest to the amnesia regarding the Holy Spirit within the churches. When the poor cry for life and justice and are not heard by the churches as happens in so many places in the Third and Fourth Worlds then this amnesia becomes blasphemy against the Holy Spirit, for according to the ancient tradition expressed in the liturgical hymn of the mass of Pentecost, the Spirit is the *pater pauperum* and the *consolator optime*, the father of the poor and true consoler. The church may be persecuted and calumniated by the powerful of this world–but it cannot be abandoned and cursed by the poor. If it loses the poor, it loses the Father of the Poor, the Spirit, and betrays Christ, who became poor when he passed through this world and died naked on the cross.

Since the 1970s, however, we are witnessing an advent of the Spirit in the churches and in the awareness of humankind. Groups claiming the Spirit are springing up on all sides.[18] The many ambiguities and even contradictions of these groups notwithstanding, something unites them all: they are pursuing a living encounter with God more than taking hold of a teaching on God. They seek not a new religion but a new spirituality, one that places at its center the Spirit who comes from God, permeates the cosmos, bursts into life, emerges very obviously in people's awareness, and is celebrated by communities of faith. This spirituality may give rise to a new religion, whose mission is to reconnect all human experiences, thereby imparting a new meaning and direction to civilization.

THE SPIRIT IN CREATION AND CREATION IN THE SPIRIT

Inasmuch as the Spirit is God with the Father and the Son, to what extent does it enter into the mystery of creation? By way of perichoresis (the essential interrelatedness of the Divine Persons) creation has a trinitarian character. In the act of creation the three Persons act together, but each one does so personally with the properties of its own Hypostasis (Person). The Father creates *through* the Son *in* the Holy Spirit.

By reason of co-creation all things possess a mysterious depth coming from the mystery of the Father (where the Trinity reveals its unfathomability). But there is a dimension of light and intelligibility, for creation is projected by the Son, which is where the trinitarian mystery reveals its light and its wisdom. Finally, there is a perspective of communion and love, for it is loved in the Holy Spirit which is where love and communion are revealed.

By the joining of the three Persons in creating (perichoresis), everything comes interwoven with relationships, interdependencies, and webs of intercommunion. The cosmos is shown to be an interplay of relationships, because it is created in the likeness and image of the God-Trinity.

Saying that creation is projected and created in the Spirit means that creation reveals the unique features of the Person of the Holy Spirit. Let us look at some of these features. The first is the initiation of newness and the renewal of all things. Thus the Spirit is present in the initial creation (Gn 1:2). It creates, orders, and causes each being to emerge in its time and circumstance. It is acting and intensely present in the creation of the definitive being, who is first in the course of the cosmogenic process and has now arrived, Jesus of Nazareth. The gospels attribute the incarnation of the Son to the Spirit: "It is through the Holy Spirit that this child has been conceived in her" (Mt 1:20). St. Luke says that the Spirit established a dwelling over her, which is tantamount to saying that she was raised to the divine height; and so the one born of her is holy and Son of God (cf. Lk 1:35). It is the Spirit who raises Jesus from among the dead, beginning a totally full kind of life, one no longer subject to entropy and already displaying divine characteristics (cf. Rom 1:4; 1 Tm 3:16). It is the Spirit that gives rise to the church, the community that bears the legacy of Jesus forward in history (Act 2:32). It is the Spirit as enthusiasm and life who becomes present in each human being.

Second, the Spirit is creator of differences and complexities. The multiplicity of beings, biodiversity, the diversity of the constructive energies in the universe point to the diversified activity of the Spirit, who values difference. In the human community the Spirit grants the diversity of talents and is present in the Christian community through many charisms, as St. Paul attests (1 Cor 12:7-11).

A third characteristic is that the Spirit is the principle of communion. There is a diversity of energies, particles, beings, and forms of life and intelligence. But there is a single cosmos. "There are different kinds of spiritual gifts but the same Spirit," reflects St. Paul (1 Cor 12:4). Diversity and difference allow community and unity, the fruit of the openness and self-giving of all to all. What is valid for the community of faith is valid for the cosmic, planetary, and human community: "To each individual the manifestation of the Spirit is given for some benefit" (1 Cor 12:7), which is never merely human, but is all-encompassing and cosmic. Although the Spirit is the principle of differentiation, it is also a factor of communion: "Whether Jews or Greeks, slaves or free persons, we were all given to drink of one Spirit" (1 Cor 12:13) so as to be "one body." To put it in cosmic language: whether primordial energies, whether elementary particles, whether galaxies and galaxy clusters, whether billions of stars with their planets, whether organic and inorganic beings, whether intelligent and extremely complex beings, all come from the same Spirit, who permeates all of them, fills them with movement and radiance, and loads them with promises to be fulfilled in the future. Just as at Pentecost all heard the same liberating message in their different languages (Acts 2:11), so the diversity of energies and of beings points toward the same creative source, the *Spiritus Creator* and the *Dominus vivificans*–the Spirit in the relationship of relationships.[19]

For Christians, there is nothing new in speaking about the incarnation of the Word. The eternal Son became an earthly son of the human family whose forebears the evangelists take the trouble to list (see Mt 1:1-17; Lk 3:23-37). Through the Son the entire universe is somehow taken up into the mystery of the Trinity itself. But we are not used to hearing of the dwelling of the Spirit. Just as the Son "becomes flesh" (*sarx egéneto,* Jn 1:14), so the Holy Spirit "pitches its tent" among us (cf. Lk 1:35) and "sets its dwelling" in the universe. It is also sent by the Father as the Son is sent. If we stop to think about it, it is the Spirit who is sent first. The one who is last in the order of trinitarian speech is first in the order of creation. It hovered over the waters. It first descends over Mary. With her *fiat* it begins to shape the holy humanity of the Son of God out of the female and motherly reality of the Virgin-betrothed of Nazareth.

To say that the Spirit pitches its tent and dwells in creation means recognizing that it is present to the utmost with its unique personality not in a temporary fashion, as in the life of a prophet or an inspired charismatic figure, but in a continual and permanent way. The Spirit has taken on the universe and made it its dwelling place since the initial zero point. The profession of faith in "the Spirit and giver of life" (*Dominus vivificans*) presupposes that the spirit has communicated itself personally to the universe. It has surrendered unreservedly and has thoroughly gone out of itself and into its creation. Because the Spirit is within, it can emerge in a variety of ways in accordance with the various stages of the cosmogenic process.

The Spirit's presence is made known through the vitality of all things: everything is shot through, as we have observed previously, with the reality of life, starting with the most elementary energies and particles. It is proclaimed by the differences in beings and expressions of complexity, of subjectivity, of interiority, and the capacity of communion of each being, especially the more complex. The Spirit shapes its temple in the human spirit.[20] Diversity notwithstanding, the universe remains one and constitutes an organic, dynamic, and harmonious whole. The Spirit is seen to be the driving force of the cosmogenic process, an arrow of time, charged with purpose and as convergence in diversity. In the course of achieving convergences and ever higher levels of complexity-interiority-transcendence, the Spirit shares in the ups and downs of creation; it does not stand off at a neutral distance. By the fact of having assumed it from the outset and of dwelling in it permanently, the Spirit rejoices with creation, suffers with it, groans along with the other creatures awaiting redemption and liberation.[21] Because it loves creation and has pitched its tent in it, the Spirit can be "quenched" and "grieved" by its drama (cf. 1 Thes 5:19; Eph 4:30). The tent (*shekina*) of the Temple of Israel has journeyed with the people, has gone with them into exile, and so the Spirit goes into exile to be identified with its ailing creation, which is rising step by step to its eschatological culmination.[22]

From the East comes a short poem that translates this pan-en-spiritualism: "The Spirit (God) is sleeping in the rock, dreams in the flower, awakens in the animal, and knows that it is awake in the human being."[23] The Spirit permeates all and is manifested as energy/explosion, matter in motion, interiorization, and the coiling of the universe in upon itself, as awakening of consciousness, desire, tension, sigh of freedom, and as power of communication and communion.

Such a vision offers us a cosmic and ecological mystique. We find ourselves plunged into a field of absolute Energy—the *Spiritus Creator*— who is manifested in the energies of the universe and in our own vital and spiritual energy. With and in the Spirit we make up a whole. The spirituality that arises from this conviction sees itself as linked to natural and cosmic processes. To allow ourselves to be imbued and charged with them is to live according to the Spirit in a spontaneous and natural manner.

THE SPIRIT AND THE FEMALE: DIVINIZATION OF WOMAN

We said above that *spirit* is feminine in Hebrew and Syriac, and its attributes show that it is always linked to life processes, to the gestation, protection, and expansion of life, matters that are more female than male. Wisdom, beloved as a woman (Sir 14:22ff.), is presented as wife and mother (Sir 14:26f.; 15:2f.), and also identified with the Spirit (Wis 9:17), a practice common among theologians of the early church. In the *Odes of Solomon*, written at the beginning of Syrian Christianity, the dove at Jesus' baptism is compared to the mother of Christ who gives milk with the breasts of God.[24] Macarius, a Syrian theologian (d. 334), says:

> The Spirit is our Mother, because the Paraclete, the Consoler, is ready to console us like a mother with her child, and because the faithful are reborn of the Spirit, and hence are children of the mysterious Mother, the Spirit.[25]

It should be said that from a strictly theological standpoint, God is beyond sexual features (these are modes of beings of creatures). Gregory Nazianzen (329-89), whom the Orthodox church calls "the theologian," stresses that God is neither male nor female (cf. Oratio 31: PG 36, 140-46), but that nevertheless the value of the feminine and the masculine find in the attributes of the Divine Persons their basis and archetype. That is why the human being as man and woman is presented as image and likeness of God (Gn 1:26), the God who for Christians is always the Trinity.

Setting that matter aside, we may ask: if, like the Son, the Spirit has been sent, what was the receiving subject? Our reply is that the Spirit dwells in the cosmos and animates the entire cosmogenic process. Certainly it is intensified in the human spirit, but where has it emerged in a sacramental and paradigmatic way to the point that we can say, Here the Spirit as Divine Person is fully present in complete self-communication? With regard to the Son, Christian faith has answered immediately: in Jesus of Nazareth. He is the incarnate Son. Or Jesus is the *assumptus homo,* the man completely assumed within the mystery of God the Son.

Can we say the same of the Spirit? And if we can, who would be the privileged and anticipated receiver? We answer: Mary of Nazareth. We have already taken up this question in detail in two earlier publications[26] and we do not intend to go extensively into it here. We will note the basic thesis: "The Virgin Mary, Mother of God and of all men and women, realizes the feminine absolutely and eschatologically, inasmuch as the Holy Spirit has made her his temple, sanctuary, and tabernacle in so real and genuine a way that she is to be regarded as hypostatically united to the Third Person of the Blessed Trinity."[27]

Here are the basic lines of the argument. In the gospels of Matthew and Luke there is a close connection between Mary and the Holy Spirit. The highly instructive Lucan text says, "The holy Spirit will come upon you, and the power of the Most High will overshadow you. Therefore, the child to be born will be called holy, the Son of God" (Lk 1:35). There is a direct relationship between the Spirit and the woman. She is not mediated Christologically. She is strictly pneumatological. From the text itself we can infer a proper (and not just appropriated) mission of the Spirit to Mary. For the first time the scripture says that the Spirit has descended directly upon a woman. At Vatican II the council fathers are on the mark when they say that Mary was "fashioned by the Holy Spirit into a kind of new substance and new creature" (*Dogmatic Constitution on the Church*, no. 56). The relationship is so close that it involves the mystery of creation, the creation that is work of the Spirit par excellence. It is most fitting that Jesus, the new Adam (1 Cor 15:45), should have the last Eve as mother. Only God can beget God. If God wants to beget God outside God, a creature will have to be raised to God's height. She will be hypostatically united to God, and the one to be born of her, as the Lucan text says, will be Son of God (Lk 1:35). That is what happened with Miriam of Nazareth.

The expression "the power of the most high will overshadow you" (in Greek *episkiásei*, which comes from *epi*, "over," and *skené* "tent," "shall pitch his tent over you") reminds us of the Old Testament theology of the tent, God's temple with human beings, expressing the ongoing and permanent presence of Yahweh among us (Ex 40:34-36; cf. also 25:8; 26). St. John, in the prologue to his gospel, in order to parallel "the Word was made flesh" uses the same expression of the Word who "pitched his tent among us" (Greek *eskénosen*, Jn 1:14).

By reason of this unique relationship to the Spirit, the angel greets Mary as "full of grace" (*kecharitoméne*, Lk 1:28). In many places in the Bible grace is synonymous with the Holy Spirit.[28] The Third Person of the Trinity descends personally over Mary. The same Spirit that fills the cosmos, that was acting at the beginning of the life of plants and animals, that gives enthusiasm to charismatic leaders and inspired prophets and sacred writers, this Spirit, who is the power of the impossible (cf. Lk 1:37), is intimately bound up with Mary. It assumes her as the place where it is present and active in the world in the fullest way possible, to the point where it can go no further. For this is a complete surrender of itself, its complete emergence on the personal level, within creation. With her *fiat* Mary is hypostatically assumed by the Holy Spirit. Thus as the Word "wordified" Jesus, in the language of many Greek fathers, so the Spirit "spiritualized" or "pneumatified" Mary. This event inaugurates the era of the Spirit, as that moment in history in which the full parousia and epiphany of the Spirit takes place.[29]

We thus come to a theological balance. Not only was the male in the form of the man-Jesus assumed by God through the Son and thus divinized, but likewise the female in the form of the woman Mary was assumed by God through the Spirit and also divinized. Male and female, jointly the creational image of God in the universe (cf. Gn 1:26) come to their supreme destiny, that of being subjects to whom God communicates God's self totally and through which human history begins definitively to belong to God's history. They are created subjects, open to God's full self-communication through the Son (Jesus) and in the Spirit (Mary). Each in his or her own way is assumed by the Divinity. They have been made by God for "verbification" and "spiritualization."

St. Irenaeus, who is so rich in metaphors, says that the Father reaches us with his two hands, the Son and the Spirit, and protects us and draws us close to him and divinizes us.[30]

At one moment of the history of humankind and the universe, a woman is at the center of everything. In her dwells the Spirit. Out of her this Spirit produces the holy humanity of Jesus, the man assumed by the Word. At one moment the two divine Persons are in her, the Spirit and the Word, communicating themselves, anticipating the blessed end of the entire creation and opening the perspective of what is to happen with each human person, each in his or her own way, time, and measure: beings able to receive God and hence, while preserving the differences between creature and Creator, capable of unity with God, that is, of being one with God the Trinity.

Jesus and Mary represent all humankind, and they anticipate the blessed destiny of all, men and women. Whether it is Mary or Jesus, as these particular historic beings, is not the crucial point. They could have had other names and could have been in another people and another culture. There is something of the fortuitous nature of history here that is only understandable within the hiddenness of Mystery. The important thing is to be able to celebrate that the male and female have been made bearers of God, revelatory of God from within the cosmic process, and that they have been assumed by God. Thus creation has arrived at the seventh day of creation and at its ultimate Sabbath (Gn 2:2-3), at least in these two who represent it. Everything is at rest, because everything has attained its supreme dynamic equilibrium. It is a time for celebration; it is the moment for celebrating the firstfruits of the new heaven, the new earth, and the new humankind.

THE SPIRIT AND THE FUTURE OF THE COSMOS AND HUMANKIND

Ecological and cosmogenic awareness has awakened us to the fact that both the cosmos and humankind are in a vast unfinished birth process. It is in the future, rather than in the past or the present, that the realization of our true essence is to be found. Neither the cosmos nor we ourselves are what we shall be called to be. The categories of cosmogenesis, future, hope, project, new heaven and new Earth, express the sense of this vast process that is under way. This ascent takes place always within the arc of the dialectic of chaos and cosmos, of order, crisis, and new order reaching ever more complex and higher levels of the radiance of energy and being.

Throughout the biblical and theological tradition, the Holy Spirit is always situated in relation to the future. It is presented as the principle of new Earth and new cosmos. When the Spirit is poured out over our reality,

> Then will the desert become an orchard,
> and the orchard be regarded as a forest.
> Right will dwell in the desert
> and justice abide in the orchard.
> Justice will bring about peace;
> right will produce calm and security. (Is 32:15-17)

In the biblical understanding, history will have a happy ending when the Spirit is poured out over all flesh and over the whole universe (Jl 2:28-32; Acts 2:16-19). The new man and new woman will emerge by the power of the Spirit, who will reconnect us to the new Adam, Jesus Christ (1 Cor 12:13) and the new Eve, Mary (cf. Gn 3:15; Jn 19:27). The new birth is attributed to the Spirit (Jn 3:3-8). All are promised a "spiritual body" (1 Cor 15:44); that is, a real life in the cosmos that takes on the features of the Spirit that have been manifested in the risen body of Jesus—fullness of life, total communication, and transfiguration of material reality. At the end of history there will be a "pneumatification" of all creation, full of dynamism, of life, and of communication of all with all and with God. God dwells fully and definitively in creation, and hence it will not cease to be an open system. On the contrary, that is when it attains complete openness. Rather than plunging into God's life, it will mean plunging into God's living, which is a process of infinite self-fulfillment with neither loss nor entropy, a process that began at the beginning of the universe. Thus the culmination of the cosmogenic history will be the end of prehistory. The eternal history of the unbounded unfolding and of the inexhaustible appropriation of the Reign of the Trinity will begin.[31]

The Spirit uniting everything inside and outside the Trinity will orchestrate the universal symphony. Ecology will be complete, for all will be in their true *oikos* in an infinite bond of sympathy, in their maternal and paternal home where the Spirit has ever been dwelling, now fully illuminated and transfigured by the Spirit's utter self-communication.

CHAPTER 9

"Split a Piece of Wood . . . and I Am There"

The Cosmic Christ

Just as the Spirit gradually emerged within creation—to the point of coming to dwell in a woman—so also the Word gradually ascended the ladder of energies and beings to the point of taking on a specific face in a Jew, Jesus of Nazareth, who was then called the Christ, God's Anointed. Just as the spiritual principle was at work in creation, so was the Christic principle. The aim of this chapter is to show the cosmic relevance of Jesus Christ and how the story of the universe should be interwoven with the story of Christ.

At the outset we must broaden our horizons beyond the Mediterranean, the region that witnessed the birth and activity of the historical Jesus. We must go beyond the Christian confessions, for they do not have a monopoly on the meaning of Christ, although they have a high value, for they are communities that preserve his memory and strive to pattern their lives in the light of Christ's person and message. We must transcend the anthropocentrism that is common in Christologies, for Christ has divinized and liberated not only human beings but all beings in the universe.

FROM COSMOGENESIS TO CHRISTOGENESIS

It is interesting that in their collective awareness of the meaning of Christ the earliest Christian communities were already placing him in a universal and even cosmic domain. In Matthew's account the roots of Jesus reach back to Abraham, a noble ancestor, father of the Hebrew people (Mt 1:1-17). Luke views the entire history of humankind beginning with Adam as involved in the life of Jesus (Lk 3:23-38). John projects the origins of Jesus the Christ back into the very mystery of God: "In the beginning was the Word . . . the Word was God . . . and the Word was made flesh" (Jn 1:1-14). In the year 50 when Paul writes the first letter to the Corinthians, even before the gospels, he attests to the belief that Jesus Christ has to do with the mystery of creation:

> Yet for us there is one God, the Father,
> from whom all things are and for whom we exist,
> and one Lord, Jesus Christ,
> through whom all things are and through whom
>   we exist. (1 Cor 8:6)

Christ is seen as the Wisdom that was with God before the creation of the world and through which all things have been made (cf. Prv. 8). He is the divine milieu in which all that exists, subsists, and abides (cf. Col 1:17).

How did these people whose tradition was the strict monotheism of the Hebrew scriptures arrive at such bold statements? How could they claim things so decisive and final about a man, Jesus, "that we have seen with our eyes . . . and that our hands have touched" (1 Jn 1:1)? Scholars of Christian origins generally believe that what explosively impelled reflection on the transcendent meaning of Jesus was the resurrection event.[1]

The oldest texts attest that Jesus was not simply brought back to life in some kind of reanimation of the body like Lazarus. The grave is open and empty, but this merely serves as a sign and a question mark–it proves little. It is the appearances, seen by some of his followers and by the original community, that cause an impact. They are not the sort of visions that might be subjective in origin but apparitions; that is, external events having an impact on them. They come to this conclusion: Jesus, the One with whom we traveled, who had raised our hopes but who died miserably on the cross, is alive. "The Lord has truly been raised and has appeared to Simon!" (Lk 24:34). This is the earliest creed of the church. But Jesus is alive in a completely unique way, "according to the Spirit," that is, like God's life.

To translate this experience they first employ the apocalyptic terminology that speaks of elevation and glorification, and then they use the eschatological framework expressed by resurrection terminology. The latter ultimately prevailed.[2] What is important is not the means of expression (elevation or resurrection) but the source reality that they want to communicate: the new life of Jesus.

By resurrection, they intended to express that the earthly life of Jesus was transfigured and brought into God's mode of being. We would say that resurrection entails such an intensity of life that death no longer exists, nor is any entropy at work. Jesus has been transported, as it were, to the end of history and whatever was latent in the billions of years of cosmogenesis and anthropogenesis has been made open. Stated more technically, Jesus' fate has been "eschatologized." This event of infinite consolation and boundless hope has been read as the beginning of the new age, the in-breaking of the new humankind (the new Adam in 1 Corinthians) and the embodiment in the life of Jesus of the utopia of the Reign of God.

On the basis of the resurrection event, faith communities extended the meaning of Jesus to all realms of salvation history including the history of the world. The one who displays history's happy ending—resurrection—must have been at work at its very beginning.

This background of faith in the resurrection has been the basis for elaborating the other theological categories that have sought, and still seek, to decipher the mystery of Jesus, living, dead, risen, and believed in as universal savior by the Christian communities that come together around his name, categories such as Christ, Son of God, incarnate Word, saving value of the cross and resurrection, and so forth.[3]

These statements were understood within a static and extrinsically oriented cosmology, in which the Word (the Son) comes from outside and assumes the reality of Jesus which is already finished and ready made. Thus the incarnation expresses the shared life, without confusion, admixture, or separation, of the entire humanity of Jesus with his entire divinity. How this shared life in one and the same Jesus is possible constitutes the never-ending *crux theologorum* (cross of the theologians), but this is not the only approach to understanding the profession of faith. Another is opening it up with the new ecological paradigm of connectedness.

We earlier insisted that one of the surest empirical findings of modern cosmology is the realization that cosmos is cosmogenesis and that anthropology is anthropogenesis. Everything is in a process of genesis and gestation; nothing is utterly finished, and anything is open to further acquisitions. The *given* is never given but appears as *made* out of the potentialities in reality, which are not exhausted in a particular given but are ever active—fashioning, refashioning, and completing each given. The four axial interactions of the universe are active in all beings from the most basic energies and the tiniest particles to the human brain and the complex relationships of a society. God the Trinity permeates this whole and continues to emerge from within it. As we observed previously, the theological meaning of creation is to enable God the Trinity to emerge from and to surrender God's own self to one different who may accept and establish community with God. When at a certain stage of the evolutionary process a new level of interiority and consciousness breaks forth, it is the whole universe that is thereby expressing itself. It is also God communicating and surrendering part of God's own mystery.

This logic also applies to the phenomenon of Jesus Christ. Christology becomes Christogenesis. First, the fact that all beings are seen to be simultaneously in the form of energy wave and material particle helps us to glimpse the simultaneity of the humanity and divinity in one and the same Jesus. He is a version of the structure of the universe. Moreover, if he established such intimacy with God, so as to call God Abba, Father of kindness and goodness, and hence to feel and consequently call himself Son, it means that the entire universe, through Jesus, takes a leap forward and upward and offers the human mind a datum that it bore within itself but that had not yet emerged to this extent: that God is Father and that we are all sons and daughters. Hence, we can rightly say that we are sons and daughters in the Son, and that he is the "firstborn among many brothers" (Rom 8:29). Moreover, it is indeed God who communicates Godself as Father and as Son and does so in the light and enthusiasm of the Spirit.

When Christians give the title Christ to Jesus they intend to say: in this specific man, with whose humble origins in the town of Nazareth we are familiar, the son of Joseph the carpenter, husband of Mary (Mt 1:18; Lk 1:27), the mystery of God has been made supremely manifest. He is the *ecce homo* (Behold the man), he in whom this self-revelation of God has been given.

He is the "anointed," the one "predestined" to fulfill such an in-breaking. This is the meaning of the title *Christ* in Greek and *Messiah* in Hebrew. It is not a noun but a modifying adjective. In itself *Christ* is not a word that should damage ecumenism between religions.[4] Instead of *Christ* one could use some other term, such as *sophia-wisdom, Krishna, karma,* or *karisma.* All are terms that have a cosmic dimension. We retain the term as found in Western Jewish and Christian traditions, but it is not restricted to that culture, as C. G. Jung has shown in his work, when he locates the *Christ* in the realm of the archetype of the collective unconscious.[5]

If the *Christ* has taken shape and consciousness in Jesus, it must be that it already existed in the cosmogenic and anthropogenic process. In nature there is a "Christic" element, as Teilhard de Chardin called it.[6] It has an objective character, linked to the structuring of the universe itself, whether or not we are aware of it. Teilhard calls this "pan-Christism."[7]

This Christic element is part of evolution until it breaks forth in consciousness and is internalized and assumed by persons of faith. It then becomes Christological and Christic as contained in consciousness. The bearers of this awareness are cognitive vanguards of an objective process that is taking place within the cosmogenic process. Referring to the community of faith in Rome, when he was there in 1948, Teilhard insisted, "At this moment in history there is no doubt that one of the poles pass through Rome, the prime pole of ascent of what . . . I call 'hominisation.'"[8]

FROM CHRISTOGENESIS TO THE CHRIST OF FAITH

The Christic becomes the Christological by reason of the incarnation of the Son. This incarnation should be understood as the crystallization of the Christic, as its personalization and not as a random deed, resulting from an *ad extra* intervention by God. The incarnation is already present at the beginning of the universe. The Son who was always within, accompanying the evolutionary process—*Christus evolutor*—comes into bloom. A maieutic process is taking place, as is true of revelation in general—but not in any old way or at any moment. It blossoms when the conditions for such an event are cosmogenically in place. Teilhard de Chardin, who pondered a great deal about this question, said it in a kind of creed on October 28, 1934: "I believe that the universe is an evolution. I believe that evolution proceeds towards spirit. I believe that spirit is fully realized in a form of personality. I believe that the supremely personal is the Universal Christ.[9] In 1950 in *The Heart of Matter* Teilhard relates the insight that was his lifelong pursuit: the cosmic, the human, and the Christic, but ever in cosmogenic terms, cosmogenesis–biogenesis–noogenesis–Christogenesis.[10]

The emergence of the Christological presupposes a whole labor of the cosmos in terms of creating a consciousness, and indeed consciousness attaining levels of universalization, internalization, and achievement of higher synthesis. The result would be an advance of all and for all when the Christological emerges through the incarnation of the Son. Evolution needs to reach a certain convergence, to attain an omega point. Only then does the discourse on the incarnation make sense as Christians understand it, and only then does it allow for moving from the Christic to the Christological. This is the entry point of Christian faith, the spearhead of cosmic consciousness. Faith sees in the omega point of evolution the Christ of faith, he who is believed and announced as head of the cosmos and of the church, the meeting point of all beings.[11] If what faith proclaims is not sheer ideology or insubstantial fantasy, then it must somehow be displayed in the evolutionary process of the universe. Incarnation is this display, for it represents the point toward which all ascending lines of evolution are going. It is convergence of all fibers of the real, the point for establishing a new stage of cosmogenesis–Christogenesis–like hydrogenesis, biogenesis, and noogenesis, which in their own time begin a new phase of the evolutionary process. Hence Teilhard confesses, "Doubtless I should never have ventured to . . . formulate the hypothesis rationally if, in my consciousness as a believer, I had not found not only its speculative model but also its living reality."[12] This is how the step is taken from Christogenesis to the Christ of faith.

FROM THE CHRIST OF FAITH
TO THE HISTORICAL JESUS

The Christ of faith rests on the historical Jesus, of whom it is an interpretation. This historical Jesus is linked to the history of the universe. He is made up of the same cosmogenic principles of which we spoke in the earlier chapters. The elements with which all beings and bodies are composed go into him as well. Today we know that with the exception of helium and hydrogen, which are original and cannot be reduced to simpler elements, all the elements in the cosmos were formed inside the giant stars through the process known as nucleosynthesis.

In our solar system, the Earth, each being contains material recycled from those ancient stars. Jesus' body therefore had the same ancestral origin and even materials from the cosmic dust that may be older than our solar and planetary system. The iron that ran in his veins, the phosphorus and calcium that strengthened his bones, the sodium and potassium that allowed signals to travel through his nerves, the oxygen making up his body, and the carbon, all this had the effect of making his incarnation truly cosmic.[13] The Son was clothed in this entire reality when he emerged from cosmogenesis.

Cosmogenesis has subjectivity and interiority. It accompanies the evolution of matter. Thus, the subjectivity of Jesus is inhabited by the more primitive movements of consciousness, by the more archaic dreams, by the more basic passions, by the deeper archetypes, by the more ancient images and ideas.[14] The Christological council of Chalcedon (450) dogmatically reaffirmed that Jesus in his humanity is consubstantial with us, in body and soul. In terms of our cosmology this means that Jesus is a product of the initial great explosion and inflation, that his roots are in the Milky Way, his homeland is the solar system, and his house is planet Earth. He took part in the emergence of life and the formation of consciousness. Like any human being, he is a child of the universe and of Earth. He belongs to a human family. And the human being is that one by whom the cosmos itself comes to its own self-awareness and the discovery of the Sacred, the biological site where divinity breaks into matter.[15] This fact makes us understand very specifically the traditional theological statement that "incarnatio est elevatio totius universi ad divinam personam" ("the incarnation is the raising of the entire universe toward the divine person")[16] Furthermore, the incarnation has touched not just the *assumptus homo* Jesus, but all humans. The humanity that we all share has always belonged to God and was the receiving subject of God's self-communication. With Jesus it has reached a peak. And all are called to be assumed in their way and their manner by the Word, and will also be verbified.[17] The incarnation is accordingly seen to be a process still on its way. The Word continues to emerge from the matter of the world and from the human mass to verbify the whole universe and bring it into the Reign of the Trinity.

The incarnation roots Jesus in the cosmos—but it also limits him to the constraints of space-time. Incarnation is always limitation and kenosis. Jesus is a Jew, not a Roman; a man, not a woman. He was born in the age of *Homo sapiens* rather than that of *Australopithecus*, under Tiberius Augustus, and he died under Pontius Pilate. For the *Christus evolutor*, taking part in evolution entails taking part in the vicissitudes of evolution. The cosmogenic process presents cruel facts like those we mentioned earlier: the mass extinctions of most species, the great human cataclysms of wars, and the genocide of whole peoples, such as happened in the Americas with the European invasion in the sixteenth century. Evolution presupposes selection, and selection means that those less able to adapt are made its victims.

THE PASSION OF THE WORLD
AND THE COSMIC CHRIST

The cosmic Christ is also crucified from the beginning of the world. He suffers with all who suffer and die. Christian mystics like the great Julian of Norwich (1342-1413) have perceived the connection between Christ's cosmic passion and the passion of the world. In one of her visions she says: "Then I saw that, as I understand it, there was a great union between Christ and us: for when he was suffering, we were suffering as well. And all creatures who could suffer were suffering with Him."[18] In the seventeenth century William Bowling was even more specific when he said, "Christ poured out his blood as much for cattle and horses as for men."[19]

Christ's cosmic solidarity descends into the hell of the contradictory condition of evolution. In Jesus he suffers the full force of human and cosmic evil. To say, as the creed does, that he descended into hell is to express the cruel reality of human death, solitude, and helplessness (cf. Heb 5:2, 7-9).

This reality of an evil linked to the idea of evolution raises questions about the meaning of history. More complex forms of life and higher levels of unity and interiority leave behind billions of living beings who have been defeated and have not risen. It is not difficult to see the meaning of the arrow of time from the standpoint of the general cosmogenic advances and successes. This is a view of the whole, but such a meaning becomes obscure as applied to the specific individuals who suffer, die, and are forgotten. Taken by themselves, outside the overall process, such facts leave us perplexed and tormented by their absurdity. No interpretation sheds light on them or resurrects them so as to return them to the system of life. No interpretation has the power to undo such facts.

In a similar context Paul vents his anguish, crying out and asking, "Miserable one that I am, who will deliver me from this mortal body?" and he replies, like one emerging from suffocation, "Thanks be to God through Jesus Christ our Lord" (Rom 7:24-25). How can Christ redeem if he himself is a victim of the evil of evolution and also needs redemption?

This is where the category of resurrection enters in, as we indicated at the outset, as that reality that has launched the process of uncovering the cosmic, historical, and anthropological meaning of Christ. But resurrection can only offer illumination when it is understood against the background of Christ's cross and passion. If resurrection were not the resurrection of the Crucified One and with him of all those crucified in cosmogenic history (human beings and all others), it would be one more myth of the vitalistic exaltation of life and not an answer to the dramatic results evolution leaves in its wake.

Teilhard writes, "We are often too inclined to regard the Resurrection as an isolated event in time, with an apologetical significance, as some small individual triumph over the tomb won in turn by Christ. It is something quite other and much greater than that. It is a tremendous cosmic event. . . . After being baptised into the world, he has risen up from it. After sinking down to the depths of the earth, he has reached up to the heavens. 'Descendit et ascendit up impleret omnia' [He descended and went up to bring all to fulfillment] (Eph 4: 10)."[20] Through the resurrection Christ leaves behind the limits of space-time imposed by incarnation. His limits are now the same as the dimensions of the cosmos; he is truly the cosmic and universal Christ.

RESURRECTION: REVOLUTIONIZING EVOLUTION

The resurrection shows that death and entropy do not have the last word. Life comes back transfigured and at an incomparably higher level (of ubiquity, full communion, and communication, because the body has assumed the qualities of the Spirit, the "spiritual body" of 1 Cor 15:45). It is not, however, the life of a Caesar who, besides dominating the present, wants to conquer the future, but that of one crucified. In other words, the fulfillment of life is achieved in someone who comes from the midst of evolution's victims, those left out and left behind. He represents them. The resurrection of the victim displays the eschatological dimension of the cosmos. What is intended by the expression *eschatological* is that the happy ending, the revelation of the end of the cosmogenic process, is anticipated in time. The future is brought into the present. As Moltmann says perceptively, "In the risen one evolution becomes revolution in the original meaning of the word."[21]

Moreover, resurrection makes plain the possibility of a complete reconciliation, one that includes the past and the victims. It is not just the future that is assured; the past is also rescued. Ultimately, no one is left behind. God does not have a trash container for everything that apparently did not work. What God has loved has also been made eternal. All beings will be rescued and will come to sit at the banquet table of natural and divine life. Hence it is significant that the resurrection has taken place in the Crucified One, who is regarded as the refuse of humankind, an earthworm, and cursed by God (texts from Isaiah 53:2-12 applied to the Crucified One in the Christian scriptures and liturgy). He demonstrates what is promised to all beings, particularly those who have shared in the passion of Jesus.

The cosmic Christ accordingly emerges as the moving force of evolution; he is its liberator, and the one who brings it to fulfillment. These three steps may not be dissociated without risk of disfigurement: either we glorify the universe because it is pregnant with Christ; or we destroy any meaning because there is too much violence and the victims are forgotten; or the splendor of cosmic fulfillment through the resurrection makes us forget that resurrection is always resurrection from the dead and fullness out of a process that is open, incomplete, and undefined. Cosmic Christology seeks to provide an integrating and balanced vision.

This cosmic vision enables us—at last—to understand a series of statements in the Christian scriptures without which this reflection on the cosmic Christ might seem to be mythical or the expression of exaggerated religious arrogance. They display the dimensions of the Pantocrator, the Christ extending from within the cosmos to its limits and beyond them, for it encompasses God's self.

There is a series of texts that connect the Kyrios, the risen Christ directly to the mystery of creation (Jn 1:3; Heb 1:2, Col 1:15-20; Eph 1:3-14; Rv 1:8, 21:6). The most explicit is the hymn in Colossians, probably a hymn of Hellenistic heretics that Paul or one of his disciples has taken and transformed into New Testament orthodoxy:

> For in him were created all things in heaven and
>   on earth,
> the visible and the invisible, . . .
> all things were created through him and for him.
> He is before all things,
> and in him all things hold together. (Col 1:16-17)

The Stoics used such terminology to express the interpenetration of God with the world. Here the epistle applies it to Christ.[22] In a kind of summary Paul simply says, "Christ is all in all" *(pánta en pásin o Christos)* (Col 3:11). It would be impossible to take this perichoresis between the risen Christ and creation any further.[23]

Elsewhere the expression of cosmic fulfillment, *pleroma* (plenitude: Col 1:19; 2:9; Eph 1:22; Eph 4:10), is applied to him. Pleroma is the universe insofar as it is saturated with the Spirit and hence full of vitality. The risen One fills the universe with his new life.[24] He is called head of the cosmos and of the church (Eph 1:10; Col 2:12). In Jewish tradition this expression *head* also has a unique cosmic connotation.[25] A noteworthy passage is the one from the epistle to the Ephesians that speaks of *anakephalaiosis*: "to sum up all things in Christ" (1:10). The cosmos and each thing, according to this epistle, only find cohesion and meaning by being ordered to Christ, who recapitulates all. Without Christ, things would make up a torso without the most expressive part, the head.[26]

The text that best expresses this cosmic Christology is found in saying 77 of the Coptic gospel of Thomas, where the cosmic ubiquity of Christ attains its full force: "I am the light that is over all things. I am all: from me all came forth, and to me all attained. Split a piece of wood; I am there. Lift up the stone, and you will find me there."[27] This is pan-Christism, resulting from a comprehensive interpretation of the mystery of Christ. He was the preexisting Word, he became the incarnate Word, and finally he has become the transfigured Word. The cosmic and universal Christ encompasses all these phases of the manifestation of the Word in creation. When we embrace the world, delve into matter, feel the force and energy field, or perform the most humble and heavy tasks, like splitting wood and lifting stones, we are in contact with the risen and cosmic Christ. Space here opens up for an ineffable experience of communion with the total Christ.

For Christians, it is in the eucharist that this Christic cosmology takes on sacramental form and becomes most intense. As Teilhard de Chardin saw very well, the eucharist prolongs in some fashion the incarnation and maintains Christ's connection to the elements of the cosmos in an ongoing manner. The bread and wine are rooted in the matter of the entire universe. The host is not simply the piece of bread on the altar. The whole universe becomes host in order to be the cosmic body of Christ. In this regard, it is well to recall Teilhard's meditation on "The Priest," which he wrote at the front in World War I:

Since today, Lord, I, your Priest have neither bread nor wine nor altar, I will extend my hands over the whole of the universe and I will grasp this immensity as the matter of my sacrifice. Is not the infinite circle of things one final Host that it is your will to transmute? The seething cauldron in which the activities of every living and cosmic substance are bubbling, is it not the painful chalice that you wish to sanctify? . . . May creation repeat to itself again today, and tomorrow, and always as long as the transformation is not entirely completed, the divine saying: "*hoc est corpus meum*, this is my body."

Pondering the eucharist, Leibniz (1646-1716) also developed a cosmic vision of Christ. For him, the eucharistic Christ is the basis or *vinculum substantiale* (substantial bond) connecting all beings in the universe, above and beyond the preestablished harmony that he regards as in effect between all the monads and that make it a uni-verse.[28] Maurice Blondel (1861-1949) reassumed Leibniz's intuition and arrived at a magnificent pan-Christic vision[29] in critical dialogue with Teilhard de Chardin.[30]

THE ULTIMATE FOUNDATION OF COSMIC CHRISTOLOGY

What are the ultimate roots of cosmic Christology? For Christian thought, such a radicalization of the question takes us to within the mystery of the Trinity, because that is where the origin and destiny of all things is to be found. The Trinity is communion of life among the Divine Persons and an interplay of perichoretic relations of love grounding the unity and unicity of God (chapter 7). As it already appears in the Platonic dialogues and in the ongoing reflection of Christian theology, it is the nature of love to be *diffusivum sui*, that is, to communicate and spread in all directions.

In the very act in which God communicates and expresses Godself within the interplay of the immanent Trinity–it is the Son in the power of the Spirit–God also expresses all the possible imitations that are not God but will be creatures of God. The cosmogenesis, biogenesis, and anthropogenesis are present in this internal and eternal divine plan, including that conscious and free being who can receive the Son in itself to the maximum degree, becoming the incarnate Son and, as such, loving God in a supreme and divine manner. The medieval Franciscan Duns Scotus (1264-1308), who delved most deeply into the primacy of Christ in the order of creation, says that God willed "that non-highest nature that could have the highest glory" to return the highest glory and the highest love.[31] For that reason God proposed to unite it to the Divine Person of the Son. Thus he could be God outside of God and could love and glorify God as only a man-God could do.

Such a trinitarian plan did not remain solely within the immanent Trinity. It was put into effect in the economic Trinity, giving of itself in history. Thus creation has emerged in the specific way in which it has come to us in the form of cosmogenesis, biogenesis, anthropogenesis, and Christogenesis. And within Christogenesis, Jesus was that one intended to receive the Son maximally within all human reality, and with him all other humans, each in his or her way and moment, for all have been projected in the Son, for the Son, and with the Son to be receptacles of the Son. St. Justin (100-165) says that all beings have been created in the Logos (Son) and that in the incarnation this Logos became the Anointed, the Christ, and that through him, all things have been anointed and "Christofied."[32] The cosmic root of Christ is found at the heart of the inner life of the Trinity. All things are marked by the Son, just as they are permeated by the Spirit.

From this standpoint it is clear that the incarnation of the Son was not due to human sin. Such a view is anthropocentric and reduces the meaning of the coming of the Son to the last few seconds of the history of the cosmos, those containing human history and Christian faith. This would make sin too central, and it would deprive the cosmogenesis prior to anthropogenesis of any Christic thrust. Through the cosmo- and verbocentric view, the incarnation belongs to the mystery of creation, which is Christic by its very nature. The Son would have been incarnated regardless of sin, because creation was projected in, for, and through the Son, a position vigorously upheld by the Scotist tradition.[33] The creation cries out for Christ as it cries out for its own fulfillment, which only the Son can give to his brothers and sisters. The incarnation, which encompasses the entire universe, touching all beings and becoming promise in each human being, signifies the supreme glorification of God. It was for this feast and celebration that the universe has been called into existence. In wanting to go out from Godself in order to be completely outside and fully communicate Godself to what is other, God creates what is different. This created difference finds its reason for being in the fact that it is a receptacle of Divinity. In becoming united to what is different, God shares in our cosmogenic history and allows our history to share in the divine history.

Sin has not destroyed the original plan of the Trinity but rather has given it the unique way it comes into being, in the form of the Suffering Servant and the Crucified One who shares in the passion of the world.[34] This is the prevalent view today, as can be established from the official documents of the church's teaching authority.[35]

Given the Christic nature of the universe, Christians may not be indifferent, profane, or pessimistic with regard to the future of our planet and the cosmos. The Spirit enlivens them from within and the Word is the driving force of evolution and its great attractor. Both endure the passion and "vanity" (cf. Rom 8:20) that make it necessary for the cosmogenic process to go through a paschal experience (of death and resurrection). All of this will one day end, however. It is the necessary passage toward the great transformation. *Et tunc erit finis: omnia in omnibus Christus,* "And then it will be the end: Christ all in all things" (Col 3:11).

CHAPTER 10

Eco-Spirituality

Feeling, Loving, and Thinking as Earth

Spirituality has been entailed in everything we have been saying, especially in the theological meditations in the chapters on God in cosmogenesis, the cosmic Christ, and the Spirit in matter. However, we realize that we have a long way to go in working out a spirituality that will be able to connect all our experiences and help us establish a new covenant with the created and the Creator. This spirituality will not be the fruit of the musings or wonderful discoveries of an individual thinker but the result of the spirit of a whole age or even several generations. Spirituality by its very nature means that we must be humble and unpretentious when we speak about it and want to help it emerge.

THE NEED FOR SPIRITUAL REVOLUTIONS

In 1969, while the worldwide youth "revolution" of 1968 was still in full swing, physicist Werner Heisenberg (who formulated the uncertainty principle) made some observations that provide a fruitful starting point for our topic. His conference to the Association of German Scientists was titled "Changes in the Thought Structure Produced by Scientific Progress." Actually, he originally intended to call it "How to Carry Out a Revolution," reflecting the fashion at that moment in history.[1]

Heisenberg shows how a revolution takes place in the physical sciences. It is not because some scientists want it, or because a charismatic leader inspires researchers, or out of a sense of seizing the moment. A revolution explodes inexorably in response to new phenomena that can no longer be understood or made to fit within the understanding current at that moment in science. Max Planck, one of the formulators of quantum physics, an

187

avowed conservative, formulated his hypothesis of quanta of energy only when he could no longer interpret the new electromagnetic phenomena related to the so called "dark bodies" in terms of the principles of classical physics. Similarly, Albert Einstein did not come to the theory of relativity because he wanted to. In studying the movement of bodies in relation to the ether (an assumption of Newtonian physics, the stable element among all interstellar spaces), he concluded that the categories of space and time could no longer be absolute but had to be relative to the velocity of masses. Everything would be relative to a point from which the velocities would be calculated. Everything is accordingly relative in the sense of being related to the point that we define as the reference point. However conservative scientists might be (and such was Einstein's tendency), they are forced to give up certain structures for understanding and to erect new ones. These must take new phenomena into account or else such phenomena remain as unresolved problems.

As much as possible, insisted Heisenberg, we must avoid unnecessary innovations,[2] but when there arises a phenomenon that is not explained by the traditional understanding, a revolution becomes necessary. "The change in mental structure is made necessary by the phenomena, by nature itself, and never by human authority."[3]

Heisenberg suggests that it is possible to extrapolate from the field of the sciences to other fields of human history. Here again one can find the same logic of the need for a paradigm change. Luther, for example, did not want to found a new church or divide the body of the church. Like others in previous centuries, he recognized that the ecclesiastical institution needed reforming. He recognized that granting indulgences for money was an abuse of the good will of the faithful, and he was impelled to do something to correct such a sacrilege. The inexorable effect was the unleashing of the Reformation, whose demands that the Roman Catholic Church change its centralized style of power remain to this day. That is why the Protestant principle—evangelical, liberating, community-oriented, and rescuing the subjectivity of the people of God—is said to be ever valid.

A revolution is successful only when it is the response to an urgent need for changes; unless those changes are made, problems will continue, crises will deepen, and people will lose hope and meaning in their lives. Revolution represents what ought to be—and what ought to be has a power of its own. It disregards authorities who either confirm it or refuse it; it pays little attention to conservatives or novelty seekers. Changes, as small as they might be, go on, tearing up old foundations and laying down new ones, provided they respond to real and still unresolved problems. They do not invalidate everything built up previously. They assume what has gone before and open the way for grasping the new, which accordingly requires a new theory, a new language, and sometimes a new paradigm.

What happened with the new physics has also taken place in biology, communications, psychology, and cosmology. Is not the same thing happening with spirituality? The observations made throughout this book indicate that a new spirituality, one adequate to the ecological revolution, is urgently needed. It is not a matter of speaking of spirituality as a deduction drawn from certain doctrines, a deduction that we might or might not draw. The point is to grasp spirituality as an overall experience of the connectedness of all searching, of encounters, of experiences of meaning— as that thread stringing all the pearls so as to form a necklace. It is needed in order to respond to an urgent demand that is not being met adequately. That is why it is like an inexorable revolution.

The conventional spirituality of the churches and of most historic religions is tied to models of life and interpretations of the world (world views) that no longer suit contemporary sensitivity. They often leave the universe, nature, and daily life outside the realm of spiritual experience. The prevailing version of Christianity is anthropocentric. Everything is centered on human beings: salvation is for them; they alone have a future. When have we heard of the incarnation of the Word and the spiritualization of the Spirit transfiguring the stars, raising mountains, including plants, involving animals? When have we heard of the resurrection of flora with its plants, flowers, and grasses, and of the fauna with its vertebrate and invertebrate animals and microorganisms, and of the entire cosmos with its galaxies, star systems, and planets? We miss a great deal of the sacramental character of matter and the transparency of all things, because we know little of things or because we disregard the importance of knowing things in order to know God. Thomas Aquinas, who in addition to being a theologian was a learned man, wrote this wonderful observation: "Knowing the nature of things helps destroy errors about God. . . . They are wrong who say: the idea that one has of creatures is not important for faith, provided one thinks correctly about God. An error about creatures results in a false idea of God."[4]

It is important that we know our cosmology as well as possible in order to better savor God's grandeur and glory. We need to create the conditions so that spirituality can emerge as something so deeply inside us that we need not even think about it, but we simply live the presence of God in everything and of everything in God.

Instead of theorizing about such a spirituality, in the next chapter we present a historic figure who lived an incomparable ecological experience and who was able to discover traces of God in every manifestation of the universe: St. Francis of Assisi. This seminal example may pluck within us those secret strings that can yet be tuned and made to harmonize with the symphony of all things. Before doing so, however, we want to delve more deeply into some requirements of an eco-spirituality that is not content merely to speak about but strives to live *on the basis of* a new identification with Earth and the cosmos, which are indwelt and assumed by God.

SPIRITUALITY AND COSMOGENESIS

Spirituality comes from spirit. We want to examine spirituality along three different lines. They represent articulations of the single reality of the spirit: spirituality bound up with the experience of the spirit, spirituality in its religious manifestation, and spirituality as an expression of the spirit of the age.

Spirituality and the Experience of the Spirit

Let us take up the first point. We have already examined the category of spirit in some detail. It has to do with a root experience that is present in the derivation of the word *spirit*. Spirit means everything that breathes, that inhales and exhales; everything living is spirit or bearer of spirit. That means God above all, then human beings and animals, then vegetation, and finally Earth itself with everything that it holds. The Earth is seen as full of spirit, for the wind surrounding it is Earth's breath. It is experienced as Gaia, living superorganism, the great and bountiful Mother (Pacha Mama, Nurse, etc.) who gives life to all creatures and expresses her inherent vitality in all beings. As we observed in chapter 7, the very experience of spirit/life points toward an even more original experience, the cosmic energy of which all imbibe and thereby exist and live. This cosmic energy is seen as mystery pointing toward God.

This integrating vision is far from the modern understanding of spirit, which understands it merely as the unique way of being man or woman, whose essence is defined as freedom. Spirit in the person is indeed that, but not that alone, for it cannot be disconnected from spirit in nature, spirit in the body, and spirit in the cosmos. Human beings are not the only bearers of spirit, nor can they remain isolated from the cosmogenic process within which spirit has been constituting itself and gaining growing visibility. Hence the importance of starting with the all-encompassing idea of spirit in its cosmic dimension and from there its manifestation in the human being.[5]

By spirit we understand that capacity of primordial energies and of matter itself for interaction and self-organization, for becoming established in open systems, for communicating and forming the extremely complex web of inter(retro)relationships that sustain the entire universe. This dynamism reveals the presence of spirit, vivifying the universe. It is not simply inert but is charged with energies interacting with everything that exists.[6]

The human spirit is this same dynamism become conscious, aware that it is connected to an animate body and through it to all bodies and energies in the universe. The spirit in the body means life, communication, enthusiasm, and radiance; it also means creation and transcendence beyond itself, creating community with what is most distant and most different, and even with the absolute Otherness, God. The human spirit is most open and universal in what exists, a node of relationships and connections in all directions and dimensions. Conscious, free, and creative life sums up all this wealth.

The Christian scriptures rightly say that "God is spirit" (Jn 4:2) and that "the spirit is life" (Rom 8:10). This reality reflects an unending dynamism.[7] Thus understood, spirituality means a person's entire orientation, which is centered on life-reality (not on the will to power, or accumulation, or in pleasure) taken in its fullest and most comprehensive meaning possible. To enhance the dignity of all life and protect and promote it, starting with the lives of original peoples and of those who are most threatened, as the liberation church seeks to do with its liberation theology, is an expression of spirituality;[8] another expression of spirituality is the effort to keep all systems open (the pedagogy of a school, a neighborhood organization, or a Christian base community) and to energize any kind of relating and communion, where communication and communion processes and communities arise.

If spirit is life, then the opposite of spirit is not matter but death, and the realm of death includes all the processes that lead to breakdown and prepare the way for death, such as oppression, injustice, and neglect of living conditions, which cause illness and dehumanized human relations, as well as the destruction of the landscape and the loss of the physical and chemical balance of the soil and atmosphere.

Spirituality accordingly entails a true basic life-direction that confronts the logic of death as it exists in the current process of accumulation and total market, which are maximum organized expressions of the assault against nature and community around the planet. They are exclusionary and produce countless victims. Today, this spirituality is discovering the ecological dimensions of our responsibility for peace, justice, and the integrity of everything created. Opting for life means opting for planet Earth as an assaulted and wounded organic whole (geocide), so that it may continue to exist in a such a way as to preserve the independent worth and relatedness of all beings on it. This is a first rudimentary notion of spirituality. This project is open to the future and is pregnant with the hope that life will ultimately be the final word that God pronounces over creation, beyond all chaos, beyond all mass extinctions, beyond the death of his own Son on the cross and the stifling of his spirit in the "spirit of swine" in his sons and daughters.

Life has a subjective aspect as well. The greater the complexity of beings, the more they are bearers of life. The more alive they are, the greater their interiority and subjectivity. This is especially true of human beings, who are spiritual beings by the very fact of being human. They have depth, a depth that is lost in mass and consumer culture.[9] They have a center around which their entire dynamic self is organized. They put spirit into things and into practices when those practices arise from within, from convictions and inner maturity. The inner microcosm of the human being is as complex as the macrocosm, and in it reside ancestral energies, deep archetypes, passions that can be as fierce as typhoons and earthquakes, tendencies of affection and solidarity that wipe away every tear and dispel every perplexity. Within them lie the *profunda Dei* [depths of God] (1 Cor 2:10), and out of them may arise angels or devils. To communicate with this inner world, to integrate it out of a personal core, to channel its manifold energies, especially the structure of the libido and the archetypes of masculine and feminine, into a coherent and free life project that reveals the person, means engaging in the process of individuation. Taking on the individuation and personalization process means building spirituality. This spirituality is part of human self-building, even if it is not guided by specifically religious reference points, which are actually part of the path of human beings toward conquering ourselves and our own hearts.

Obviously religious people know that their inner core is not marked solely by the preceding universal history, but that we are indwelt by God and God's grace. In the expression of Meister Eckhart, God the Father is continually begetting God the Son in the love of God the Holy Spirit in the depth of the human heart, making each person a son and daughter in the Son and spiritual and inspired in the Spirit. If the Trinity can be encountered sacramentally somewhere in the universe, that place is surely the human spirit. Therefore, loving a person, and loving that person as he or she is, entails loving the Mystery that he or she bears: God the Trinity. We must love all as though we were witnessing the birth of God-communion within them. Communicating with our own interiority, heeding the calls arising in our inner core, means listening to God and hearing God's Word.

Spirituality in Its Religious Manifestation

Second, spirituality has to do with religions. Religions are the cultural expression of the encounter with the divine Mystery. The response to this encounter is given in faith. Faith is the posture of accepting God. It means being able to say "Yes, amen" to that reality experienced as absolute Meaning, complete gratification, and ineffable plenitude (this is the etymological meaning of "believing" in Hebrew, the word for which is *amin,* from which the expression *amen* is taken). When it is translated in specific terms, this faith experience takes on cultural forms. Religion arises as a set of faith expressions in the realms of understanding (creeds and doctrines) and practices (ethics), in symbolic or ritual expressions (liturgy), or in the esthetic dimension (sacred art, churches, monuments, music, and so on).

Religions operate with ultimate concepts and project supreme values; in them the great yearnings of the heart are fashioned. They serve for designing the overall utopias that provide a sense of eternity to the transitory pilgrimage of human beings through this world. Religion is preeminently the universe of ultimate meaning in history and the cosmos.

More than an ethics, a ritual, or a body of doctrines, religion means a stance whereby human beings connect all realms of reality, the conscious with the unconscious, the male with the female, society with the individual, God with the world. Out of religion flows an experience of wholeness that is not the sum of human experiences but something original, dynamic, holistic, and the source of deep conviction. Through connectedness the religious person succeeds in seeing God in all things and seeing all things in God.

If we understand metaphysics to mean the unified and classified representation of reality by stitching all the parts into an organic whole, then we must say that religions may represent the most ancient metaphysics in history, and certainly the most popular and most long-lasting metaphysics of all in people's minds. It is generally religion that enables people to have an undivided and non-chaotic experience of reality, which is so often contradictory and even malevolent. By using religious categories even people untrained in schools and little connected with the wider society interpret the mysteries of life, death, the meaning of history, the significance of human and natural dramas, and what we can hope for in life beyond life.

Inasmuch as religion has arisen out of spirituality and the experience of the faith encounter with divinity, its function is to continually renourish this spirituality and encounter. It cannot replace the striving of the human being for ultimate Reality and encountering that Reality. Religion cannot enclose religious persons in dogmas and cultural representations. It must serve as an organized place where people may be initiated, accompanied, and aided in having the experience of God. Spirituality in the realm of religion then means internalizing and translating into personal integrated experience the religious content as established in doctrines and creeds. It is not thinking about God but speaking to God. Spirituality is less about religious ideas than convictions, and less about theological reasoning than the emotions of true "pietas." Spirituality is about feeling God in an all-encompassing experience, and not so much about thinking of God.

Spirituality is the area not controlled by the institution or by the religious community. Spirituality constitutes the space of inner freedom, of the most personal experience of the Sacred, of lovingly naming God, of complaining *coram Deo* (before God) about existential absurdities, of building the universe of ultimate meanings as each individual represents them in accordance with his or her inner and inaccessible code.

Spirituality is the field of creativity par excellence. That is why institutionalized religions have always feared spiritual people and mystics. Such people do not invoke religious authority to legitimize their convictions but appeal rather to God's own authority as immediately experienced. They do not speak out of hearsay, but like Job they testify, "Now my eye has seen you" (Jb 42:5), and so they speak on the basis of personal, irreplaceable experience with the authority that such expression always possesses.

Every religion also has something to say about nature as a dimension of the whole. It projects a cosmology or world view, as Durkheim explained very well,[10] not in the sense of doing science but of showing the connectedness of everything with the Divinity. Hence there is always a religious ecology. It is not necessarily aimed at conservation or integration, however, but may foster an aggressive stance that destabilizes ecosystems, as, for example, in one particular understanding of the Jewish and Christian doctrine of the human being as lord and king over creation. But it may also, as in the case of St. Francis, internalize the Christian truth that we are all sons and daughters of the same eternal Parent and on that basis emotionally experience the bond of radical kinship that unites all beings from the ant on the roadside to the most distant star, from the tiniest elementary particle to the largest galaxy or quasar in the universe. The result is an attitude of deep reverence for each being in creation, an attitude that is absolutely necessary today if we want to ensure the preservation and integrity of all that is created.

Spirituality as an Expression of the Spirit of the Age

Third, spirituality is linked to the spirit of the age. This is pre-eminently an overall representation rather than a defined and narrow concept. By the *spirit of the age* we mean the powerful motivations, the spiritual and moral forces moving a generation, the utopias that energize practices, the sensitivities characterizing the way reality is approached, the generative and prevailing ideas that confer meaning on the whole. The spirit of the age also includes contradictory manifestations, group pathologies, and whatever might be regarded as counter-values that also have a bearing on human practices. The spirit of the age is produced by complex processes that sink roots into the collective unconscious, the cultural visions of a people, in their historic experiences, in their own idea of themselves, in their self-esteem or deprecation of themselves or of aspects of their situation, in their modes of production and social organization, in the type of prevailing rationality and the kind of science that becomes dominant, in their philosophy of life, in their religious expressions and their charismatic leaders, and in the various realms of human, cultural, artistic, political, scientific, and religious expression. The spirit of the age is the common atmosphere where all breathe more or less the same convictions, dream more or less the same dreams, practice more or less the same rationality, and develop more or less the same feelings. In short, the spirit of the age is the world view proper to each age.

From this standpoint, spirituality means the set of values, projections, generative ideas, and models that give life personal and social meaning and that unify the sum of experiences that people undergo. It means the way we make the group world view our own. Spirituality by its very nature entails subjectivity. That is why it cannot be fully described or controlled. It is in spirituality that individuals may preserve their idiosyncrasies and stake out their differences. Even though the spirit of the age is something objective (for it has to do with the particular age) and can be described, there really is such a thing as a collective spirituality. Spirituality likewise has to do with the subjective way the spirit of the age is assimilated and made personal, whether by accepting or rejecting it, or by selectively fashioning a synthesis and syncretistically drawing on elements of other world views.

The main function of the spirit of the age, of the world view and its corresponding spirituality, is to unify our vision of reality by coherently connecting all our experiences, knowledge, and practices. The spirit of the age represents a boundless need of human beings for an overall vision and a grasp of a whole. Things are not just thrown in somewhere, in the midst of an arbitrary juxtaposition of conjunctures and happenings, but everything must make sense, even if that sense is not always manifest. It must nevertheless exist as a given or as something to be built collectively. The basis on which spirituality lives is the conviction that there is a whole, and that it is much more than the sum of its parts; that we are set within this whole; and that the parts are in the whole and the whole in the parts (hologram). Although it appears with elements of fragmentation and chaos, the whole always tends to be generative and harmonious, for it is ordered with a drive in that direction.

In this sense each generation has its own spirituality—and so does ours. Given the acceleration of history and of the global interchange of cultures and human experiences through the means of communication, there is an overwhelming variety of spiritualities—indeed, even a conflict of spiritualities. Let us see how a spirituality for the spirit of an age that has taken on ecological concern would look.

AN ECOLOGICALLY SUSTAINABLE SPIRITUALITY

Modern cosmology based on Copernicus, Kepler, Newton, Descartes, Galileo, and Bacon is characteristically rationalist and dualist. Everything is basically either matter or spirit. The universe, in Newton's metaphor, is a huge machine operating mathematically, and is therefore a closed system. God is its great architect. Even though the founders of scientific thought held to that belief, it was later abandoned; the operation of the universe, according to the spokespersons of modernity, can be explained without the God-hypothesis (Laplace). The world as a collection of beings, however, remains an open question: is it eternal, is it created, or is it an expanding system? Behind these questions, the previously abandoned questions about God and the origin of the universe once more raise their heads.

According to this world view, human beings stand at the center. They are challenged to be lords of the universe, to scrutinize the laws of matter, and to subject matter to their interests and turn nature into a vast inexhaustible storehouse of resources for achieving their plans and desires. Subjective reason is no longer guided or even limited by objective reason. It imposes its own logic (the will to power) on the logic of reality. The face of the planet has certainly been transformed, but it has also been subjected to a dangerous process of imbalance to the point where the whole ecosphere is threatened. An ecological cataclysm with irreversible consequences and an apocalypse within history for the biosphere is not beyond the realm of possibility. We cannot continue with this paradigm of modernity, which understands human activity as transformation of nature for the sake of unlimited linear progress without any consideration for the internal logic of nature. What is required today is not to change but to conserve the world. To conserve the world, however, we must change the paradigm and shift our collective mind toward other less destructive objectives.

Modern spirituality understands the human being as the world-creating agent, the lesser god who must represent the greater God. The stance is that lordlike stance of Adam, who in naming things (Gn 2:20) takes possession of them and subjects them to his intentions. Everything centers on human beings. They are understood as torn away from cosmic forces, from the energies surrounding them on all sides; indeed they have broken the covenant with nature and placed it, in Francis Bacon's metaphor, on the Procrustean bed to torture it until it yields up its secrets. In this interpretive framework, human beings are alone in a lifeless world made up of the basic chemical elements on the periodic chart. They do not feel part of a larger whole, with which they are in communion, nor do they become aware of the planetary communion within which they are placed.

God is represented as the absolute Subject who creates subjects so that they may also be creators, like miniature gods. Human practices are an extension of the creative and organizing activity of God down through the ages toward the supreme realization of all that is created. This conception, which is correct, was made absolute and thereby became harmful because it did not connect with the other conception that makes human beings like gardeners who must take care of the inheritance that they have received in a feeling of deep cosmic community with all other beings, which are also created by God and arise from the same common soil.

Such reductionism follows a linear logic. Going ever upward, human beings believe that they can attain by themselves the higher stages of evolution until they break into the omega point of perfection, leaving behind the other beings in the universe. This spirituality, which at one time drove the spirit of progress and of intervention into nature, has shown that it is powerless vis-à-vis nature, societies, and human persons. It urgently needs to be constrained and overcome; it does not help us avoid the abyss but actually encourages us to march toward it. It has not even proven itself capable of bringing human beings back into the community of living beings and of returning Earth to them as their common homeland.

We need a new spirituality. It cannot arise out of the exalted minds of a few enlightened ones, like Athena, who was born fully armed out of Jupiter's head. It will be the fruit of the new sensitivity that underlies the new cosmology, which is slowly but steadily gaining acceptance everywhere.

We do not intend to repeat what we have already written about the new cosmology, which represents the great story of our age. Let us simply recall once more the two metaphors that best express it, game and dance.

A game, such as soccer, is a combination of all the players, their interdependencies, the harmonizing of offense and defense, and the clarity of the tactics. At the same time, in playing the game each player must be creative about how best to set up a shot at the goal. The logic of the game is not linear but complex and open; it is always being worked out at each moment.

The universe may be seen as a vast game: it has an order by which the arrow of time is present, but chaos is also pervasive, thereby allowing for the creativity that gives rise to a new and higher order. Operating in it is a most intricate web of relationships by which each kind of energy and each type of being become partners in the success of the whole, which is then truly a uni-verse, the diversity that becomes one. As in any game, human beings do not feel passive, mere spectators in a world outside them in which they have no part; they are an essential part of the game.

The universe is also like a dance.[11] In dancing, the important ones are the dancers. Their movements are jointly harmonized to the rhythm of the music. There is creativity in their steps and in the arrangement of the entire choreography. It is not at all rigid but loose and open to many variations. Yet the dance is not a confusion of sounds and steps, bodies and movements; it is cosmic harmony. It is in dance more than in any other art that spirit takes on body and body gains spirit. "We have in dance, in nascent form, the properly human and divine power to confront chaos, and to overcome and transcend it."[12] In Asian and African traditions dance is the liveliest and most concrete symbolic representation of the world. The dance of Shiva Nataraja in Hinduism seeks to represent the mystery of the universe, which is a dance among creation, preservation, destruction, rest, and redemption. Shiva's right hand holds firm the drum that produces the musical sound, that creates the harmony of the world; his left hand holds the burning flame with which things are selected and destroyed. The dance connects the two hands; that is, the two elements that give the cosmos movement and harmony and the circle of life and death that marks all processes.

A whole vein of thought in the early church is familiar with the heavenly dance as a metaphor of God's creation. St. Gregory of Nyssa writes: "Once there was a time when the whole of rational creation formed a single dancing chorus looking upwards to the one leader of this dance. And the harmony of that motion which was imparted to them by reason of his law found its way into their dancing."[13] Christians, however, give the metaphor a liberating meaning: the ultimate dance is not between life and death but between the life and glory of God in the Reign of the Trinity, where the true heavenly dance of the three Divine Persons with all creation takes place forever.

The image of God as Supreme Energy–Spirit–is thus seen to be the one most suited for expressing our cosmology as game and dance. The Spirit is the dynamic principle of the self-organization of the universe. The Spirit is life and giver of life. The Spirit is freedom and creativity. The Spirit inaugurates the new and begets all kinds of diversity and at the same time their unity. This Spirit "breathes where it wills" (Jn 3:8). Attention and openness are needed for grasping the smallest signs of its presence; therefore, it calls for leaving security behind, overcoming rigid identities defined once and for all, so that we may accept the processes that enrich these identities and ever keep them alive and current.

This Spirit leads us to find its presence both on Mount Gerizim (symbolizing the religions of the world) and in Jerusalem (the Jewish and Christian traditions, which regard themselves as bearing a special revelation). "The hour is coming, and is now here," says Jesus, "when true worshipers will worship the Father in Spirit and truth. . . . God is Spirit, and those who worship him must worship in Spirit and truth" (Jn 4:23-24). These words are now more prophetic than ever. With conscious cosmogenesis and the planetization of human consciousness underway, a spirituality must be able to identify and savor the action of the Spirit everywhere, in all cultures and peoples, in all movements and projects that evidence and promote life and the truth of life, which is communion and communication.[14]

But we should experience the Spirit primarily in our own spirit, discovering inside ourselves energies bubbling, the desire for life and communication, impulses upward and forward and the capacity for creation.[15] We behave not as a spectator or manager of this vital energy but as a celebrant. Through our own vitality, we feel that we are sharing in the universal Energy. We link up with everything. We don't need to be afraid! Our uniqueness will not be destroyed; rather, we will feel a spark of the universal fire that burns in us and in the whole cosmos.

"Be one with the all," says the Taoist tradition unceasingly. The *Upanishads* of India teach us, "You are that." And the *that,* wherever the hand points, is the universe, it is the chain of life, it is the beings being born, living and communicating. We are all drinking from the same spring, which gives us existence and life. But we are *that* to the extent that we leave behind, with no barriers or prejudice, all the things that enter into us, and we ourselves lovingly penetrate into things and listen to the messages that they have to share with us.[16]

We Christians use the category of the Reign of God, a central theme in Jesus' preaching, to symbolize the gradual realization of God's project for all creation. It is already there, but not yet fully implemented. It is being achieved in us and beyond us. We all share in building it, as did Jesus: "My Father is at work until now, and I am at work" (Jn 5:17). It means experiencing that all our activity–from cleaning house, to factory work, to caring for our children's education–is to aid in the leavening of the Reign and feeling that each of us is involved in bringing it about. "Street sweeper out sweeping the street, you are sweeping the Reign of God," said a poetic mystic. Knowing is not enough; we must experience it, let ourselves be swept away and enveloped by this fascinating truth.

One of the main thrusts of this spirituality is living with simplicity, the most human of the virtues because it must be present in all the others. Simplicity will guarantee the sustainability of our planet, rich as it is in bountiful energies and resources but also ever limited. Simplicity requires standing up to the culture and the system, which are consumeristic and wasteful. Simplicity prompts us to live in keeping with our basic needs. If all observed this prescription, the Earth would be enough for all with generosity and even with modest abundance. Simplicity has always produced spiritual excellence and great inner freedom. Henry David Thoreau, who lived for two years in his cabin in the forest by Walden Pond, purposefully limiting himself to only what he needed for living, constantly recommends "simplicity, simplicity, simplicity."[17] He observes that simplicity has always been a characteristic of all sages and all saints in all cultures.[18]

An ecologically sustainable lifestyle is based on cooperative relationships in all activities and at all times, for it is one of the laws ruling the universe itself that sustain the chain of interdependencies of all beings. Such a lifestyle also involves a respectful use of all that we need and a willingness to recycle it when it has fulfilled its purpose, for that is also the way of nature, which utilizes everything and wastes nothing.

Enchantment with nature opens us to our specific mission in the universe, that of being priests celebrating and giving thanks for the grandeur, majesty, rationality, and beauty of the cosmos and everything in it. Everything can be transformed into material for prayer to the Creator. We find splendid examples in the testimonies of the astronauts who have contemplated the Earth from above.[19] James Irwin said,

> The Earth reminds me of a Christmas tree suspended against the black depths of the universe. The further away we go, the smaller it gets, until finally it is reduced to the most beautiful imaginable little ball. That living object, so beautiful and so warm, looks frail and delicate. Contemplating it changes a person, because you begin to appreciate God's creation and discover God's love.[20]

And Gene Cernan observed:

> When I was the last man to walk on the moon in December 1972, I stood in the blue darkness and looked in awe at the earth from the lunar surface. What I saw was almost too beautiful to grasp. There was too much logic, too much purpose—it was just too beautiful to have happened by accident. It doesn't matter how you choose to worship God. . . . He has to exist to have created what I was privileged to see.[21]

Human beings are spontaneously moved to reverence and thanksgiving. That is why they exist in the universe.

Finally, another astronaut, Joseph P. Allen, observes with fine intuition, "With all the arguments, pro and con, for going to the moon, no one suggested that we should do it to look at the Earth. But that may in fact be the most important reason."[22]

When they see Earth from beyond it, human beings come to understand that they and Earth are a unit and that this unit belongs to a larger unit around the sun, which is part of a larger unity, the galaxy, and that pushes us back to the whole universe—and the universe itself points us toward God. "You don't see the barriers of color and religion and politics that divide this world," says Gene Cernan. Everything is united on the single planet, Earth.

"On the first and second day, we picked out our own country; on the third and fourth day our continent; by the fifth day we were simply aware of the Earth as a whole," observed astronaut Salman al-Saud.[23] In eco-spiritual terms, all that they observed has meaning as temple of the Spirit belonging to the reality assumed by the Word. Living in the totality of being, with trembling feeling, in intelligence reaching out unendingly, in the heart that is flooded with emotion and tenderness—this is what it means to have an eco-spiritual experience.

Like all spiritual paths, eco-spirituality lives in faith, hope, and love. In eco-spiritual terms, faith makes us understand that our work of caring for and preserving our beautiful planet is absorbed into the work of the Creator, who at each moment is sustaining and maintaining all beings in being. It is the part that we offer as collaboration to the *Spiritus Creator* for what, according to St. Paul, really counts, that is, "the new creation" (Gal 6:15).

In terms of eco-spirituality, hope assures us that despite the threats of destruction that the human species's destructive machine has mounted and uses against Gaia, a good and kind future is assured because this cosmos and this Earth belong to the Spirit and the Word. Something of our universe and of our male and female humanity has already become eternal, has already passed the threshold of absolute dynamic perfection, is already in the heart of the Trinity through Miriam and Jesus of Nazareth and through all the just ones who have captivated us. God will not finish the job on the ruins of Earth and the cosmos.

In terms of eco-spirituality, love leads us to identify ever more with the Earth, for love is the great unifying and integrating power of universe. For centuries we have thought *about* the Earth. We were the subject of thought, and the Earth was its object and content. After all that we have learned of the new cosmology, we must think ourselves *as* Earth, feel ourselves *as* Earth, love ourselves *as* Earth. Earth is the great living subject feeling, loving, thinking, and through us knowing that it thinks, loves, and feels. Love leads us to identify with Earth in such a way that we no longer need to become aware of these things, for they have become second nature. Then we can be mountain, sea, air, road, tree, animal. We can be one with Christ, with the Spirit, and ultimately with God.[24]

A modern spiritual legend expresses our observations here. An old and holy monk was once visited in a dream by the risen Christ, who invited him to take a walk in the garden. The monk enthusiastically agreed but was curious. After walking for a long time up and down the garden paths, as monks do after meals, he asked, "Lord, when you walked along the roads of Palestine, you once said that you would return one day with all your pomp and all your glory. This coming of yours is taking such a long time. When are you actually going to return, Lord?" After a period of silence that seemed like an eternity, the Lord responded, "My brother, when my presence in the universe and nature is so obvious, when my presence under your skin and in your heart is so real as my presence here and now, when this consciousness has become body and blood in you to the point where you no longer think about this, when you are so imbued with this truth that you no longer need to ask with curiosity as you asked, then, my dear brother, I will have returned with all my pomp and with all my glory."

Let us now look at the spiritual path of a person in whom this legend became history: the patron saint of ecology, the universal brother, the brother of the wolf, of thieves, of the Sun and Moon, the Fratello and Poverello, Francis of Assisi.

CHAPTER 11

All the Cardinal Ecological Virtues

St. Francis of Assisi

Thus far we have devoted considerable discussion to the underlying assumptions of modern Western society that have brought about the ecological crisis that today spans the globe. We have offered a critique of the anthropocentrism that has been partly responsible for the way nature has been seen as deprived of its autonomy and as existing merely to serve human beings reigning as monarchs over the universe. Such a posture certainly aided the development of science and Western technology, because it desacralized the world and delivered it up for human creativity and interests, which almost never serve to bring about a just relationship with nature. Even so, the Jewish and Christian spiritual traditions bear within themselves an antidote that can be brought up to date and that will serve as a protection for creation and for overcoming the plundering methods that continually fuel the ecological crisis. This is not so much a new doctrine but rather a new alternative attitude, one of deep reverence and kinship toward the universe and of compassion and affection toward all members of the cosmic and planetary community. We have in mind the figure of St. Francis of Assisi.

As far back as 1967 American historian Lynn White, Jr., who in his much discussed article entitled "The Historical Roots of Our Ecological Crisis"[1] made the Jewish and Christian traditions the primary culprits for the current ecological impasse, went on to find in the cosmic piety of St. Francis of Assisi an alternative paradigm for that impasse. White also suggested that St. Francis be officially declared, "patron saint of ecologists."[2] On November 29, 1979, Pope John Paul II did declare him "patron saint of ecologists" with "all the liturgical honors and privileges" entailed in that proclamation.[3] Thus, as we saw the presence and operation of the modern paradigm, which is a spirit of domination over nature in the Amazon megaprojects, we are going to observe in St. Francis the living embodiment of another paradigm, one of a spirit that acts in kinship, one that is filled with compassion and respect before each representative of the cosmic and planetary community. We will delve into St. Francis's spirituality in some detail because it will serve as a counterpoint to the spirit that is wreaking havoc in the Amazon and on our planet.

THE SECRET TRUTH OF RELIGIOUS POLYTHEISM

A new paradigm is validated only when it becomes living truth in the life stories of those who begin to usher in a new consciousness and a new alternative practice, as happened with St. Francis. A civilization needs such exemplary figures, who serve as mirrors in which the dreams fostering the practices and values that nourish great motivations are persuasively portrayed. They give meaning for people to live, suffer, struggle, and hope.

St. Francis is a name that Christianity will always pronounce with sweetness, and one of the people of whom the West will always be proud. One of his modern biographers has observed, "His qualities arouse sympathy, his flaws, if any, enchant the spirit, his holiness has nothing esoteric, effeminate, or fearful about it, his teaching pours out such freshness, so much poetry and serenity that even the most jaded spirits can find in him reasons for living life and believing in the divine goodness."[4] He lived a new relationship with nature in a way that was so moving that he became an archetype of ecological concern for the collective unconscious of humankind. Although he lived eight hundred years ago, he seems new. We feel old when we compare ourselves to him.

The kinship that St. Francis lived with all the cosmic elements is of fundamental importance for human and Christian spirituality. It involves the recovery of the aspect of truth in paganism, with its rich pantheon of divinities inhabiting all the spaces in nature. Christianity, with its proper and sharp distinction between Creator and creature, had descended, for reasons that are not always discernible, into an unhappy separation between God and nature. All value was on the side of God or of God's representative in the world, the human being. Nature was deprived of its symbolic and sacramental character. It was viewed as a place of testing and temptation or as a purely natural place, and its magic and enchantment vanished.

To cure humankind of its polytheism, early Christianity subjected the faithful to a violent and harsh medication. With the existence of the gods denied, many doors of the soul were closed and many wellsprings of meaning in the depths of the psyche (which, as is well known, is polycentric)[5] dried up. Gods and goddesses cannot be interpreted solely in the language of essences. Even today they represent powerful cosmic, natural, and human energies that are at work in people's subjectivity and in the hidden meaning of things. These energies exert a fascination and power over spirits. They are valuable creative forces that emerge as soon as human beings free themselves from being centered on the self—the monotheistic myth of the hero—and begin to experience the world as alive and their own life as filled with dynamic centers.[6]

Human beings should deal with those energies, be guided by them, integrate them into a project of freedom, and thus come into harmony with the life of the entire universe. A rigid monotheism is not salutary for the soul—as if all spiritual riches could be reduced to a single principle. We have already pondered how the root Christian experience is trinitarian and opens out to a plurality of Persons, leaving behind the classic monotheism of religions and philosophies and drawing on the potential wealth of pagan polytheism. This is not a matter of defending a religious polytheism but of appreciating how it enters psychologically into the several energy centers of the psyche.[7]

However we might wish to interpret it, we have to acknowledge that in this regard the pagans had something remarkable—they saw the presence of gods and goddesses in all things: Pan and Silvos in plants; Gaia, Demeter, and Hestia in the Earth; Apollo and Phoebus in the sun; and so forth. G. K. Chesterton rightly noted that for its first thousand years Christianity employed a strategy of all-out combat or flight to deal with this excess of the divine and the sacred. With humor and obvious exaggeration, he says that Christianity took refuge in the desert so as not to see nature and thus think about divinities. It hid in caves in order not to see the sky and be reminded of stories of gods and goddesses. It shut itself in monasteries in order to find God in the sacred texts, in long hours of celebration and Gregorian chant, and in the winding paths of deep contemplation instead of catching God in life, underneath the everyday, in the sweaty face and warm hands of people.[8]

St. Francis brought this whole age of purgation to an end. Eyes recovered their innocence. Now one could contemplate God and the splendor of God's grace and glory in the extensive wealth of creation, which is the great sacrament of God and Christ. Intuitively and without any previous theological training, Francis reclaimed the truth of paganism: this world is not mute, not lifeless, not empty; it speaks and is full of movement, love, purpose, and beckonings from the Divinity. It can be the place for encountering God and God's spirit, through the world itself, its energies, its profusion of sound, color, and movement. The Sacred dwells in it; it is God's extended Body. Paganism gave expression to this experience in polytheistic frameworks, but that does not invalidate the psychological and spiritual wealth that make it possible to fill human attitudes with the sacred and prevent life from being smothered in immanence or delivered to lonely despair. The world is always enveloped in a kind of divine milieu, in which one breathes, feels, thinks, and experiences the Divine and its power.

How did Francis come to transfigure the universe and discover cosmic kinship? What was his path toward the sacred heart of matter?

THE DEATH OF HEROIC MYTH
AND THE TRIUMPH OF FOOLISHNESS

The life story of Francis helps us understand how he was able to bring together outer and inner ecology, the Most High in heaven and God's presence on Earth in all creatures. Let us look at the outlines of his life.

Francis was born in 1181 in Assisi, a small but very delightful and inspiring Umbrian city. The son of a wealthy textile merchant, Pietro Bernardone, who brought his products in from a number of European markets, particularly France (hence the name Francis), he was a typical representative of the emerging class, the commercial and financial bourgeoisie. Francis was the head of a group of young libertines who devoted themselves wholeheartedly to the *cantillenae amatoriae,* gambling, and sumptuous banquets.[9] Restless and very sensitive, he was a sounding board for the ambitions in the minds of young people at that time. Francis tried each of them: the bourgeois endeavor of becoming wealthy, the feudal endeavor of being a noble gentleman, the religious endeavor of being a monk. Each of these endeavors presented its particular utopia, its ideal of perfection and heroism. Francis tried them all. He wanted to be wealthy like his father; he experimented with being a knight in the wars; and for a short time he tried to be a Benedictine monk. But he drew back from each of them, because none spoke to his own depths and aroused enthusiasm in him. He fell into an existential crisis that everyone in the city could see. He did penance, like so many people in his time.[10] He lived in the nearby forests and in caves, devoted to prayer and searching. At last he found his own path.

The Legend of Perugia, one of the most reliable accounts,[11] relates an episode from his adult life that reveals Francis's original intuition. The friars around him, including some scholars, are gathered to discuss the direction of the community. They take as their reference point the rules of St. Augustine, St. Benedict, and St. Bernard, each of which is attested by experience. They go to Cardinal Hugolino (subsequently Pope Gregory IX) to persuade Francis to draw inspiration from such examples in order to have a well-ordered religious life. After listening to everything, Francis takes the cardinal by the hand and leads him before the assembly. He offers these memorable words, which are a key to understanding what he intends to do with his life: "My brothers, God called me to walk in the way of humility and showed me the way of simplicity. I do not want to hear any mention of the rule of St. Augustine, of St. Bernard, or of St. Benedict. The Lord has told me that he wanted to make a new fool of me in the world, and God does not want to lead us by any other knowledge than that."[12] The ancient heroes die, and creativity and newness rise up.

This is St. Francis's new path: beyond existing systems; beyond the emerging bourgeois system; beyond the declining feudal system; beyond the prevailing religious monastic system. He is a fool (*passus*) only to the systems that he is leaving behind. He follows his own route and that makes him, as his biographer Thomas of Celano put it, "homo alterius saeculi," a man of a new age, a new paradigm (2 Celano, 82). His endeavor is the *vita evangelica*, "living according to the form of the holy Gospel," as he sums it up in his testament.[13] The rule that he left reads, "The rule and life of the friars minor is this: to observe the holy Gospel of Our Lord Jesus Christ." The next words are an addition, demanded by those in Rome striving to exert control over religious: "living in obedience, without property, and in chastity."[14] Francis also calls his option "the way of simplicity" because he takes the gospels just as he finds them and lives them without commentary.

But Francis does not yet have the specific context in which he will give shape to his proposed endeavor. It comes about as follows: One day, after much fasting and prayer, his soul is enlightened. His friends perceive the changes and ask him, and he speaks the language of one in love: "I am thinking about taking a wife, an incomparable princess" (2 Celano, 7)– Lady Poverty. He has become converted to the poor. He switches his social location; he gives up his class by birth and opts for the poorest of the poor, lepers. He has not set up a leper hospital or work of charity, but he goes to live in their midst, takes care of them, caresses them, and eats out of the same cup as they (cf. 1 Celano, 17; 2 Celano 9). It is out of this option for the poor that he discovers the pure gospel as good news, and the Poor Man par excellence, Jesus Crucified.

He begins by materially repairing small churches and chapels that are in ruins. He later realizes that the spiritual edifice of the church must be rebuilt on the basis of simplicity, poverty, and the gospel. He takes on the evangelical and apostolic life: he travels along roads with small groups of followers, preaching the content of the gospel to those that they find in villages, public squares, and fields, in the everyday language. A new style of church arises, not the imperial and feudal church of popes and bishops or even that of the stability of place of the monasteries (*stabilitas loci*, typical of monastic life) but that of the *perigrinatio evangelii* (gospel pilgrimage), which is born down below, in the midst of the people and the poor, connecting faith and life, contemplation and action, work and celebration.

This rooting of the gospel in the people led to a reinvention of religious symbols: celebrating mass outside churches, reciting the canonical hours outdoors in nature, holding continual adoration of the eucharist in churches, representing the birth of Christ with the crib, inventing the stations of the cross, and reading of the scriptures by the people. All this was introduced by the Franciscan movement of poverty. It must be kept in mind that St. Francis was not a cleric but a layman, who, on his own, with no institutional mandate, shook the foundations of christendom and put a new face on Christianity.

In 1209 he obtained approval of his new way from the pope in Rome; it was given final confirmation in 1223. Thus was born the First Order of Franciscans. Multitudes of men and women followed it, like Clare of Assisi, his friend and confidant, who together with him founded the Second Order of Franciscans, the Poor Clares. Laymen living out their own professions became fascinated with his style of life and wanted to be associated, and thus there arose the Third Order of St. Francis. When he died in 1226 there were more than twenty thousand Franciscans almost everywhere in Europe.

RECLAIMING THE RIGHTS OF THE HEART AND THE EROTIC

What is this fascination that St. Francis exercised over his own age and that has come down to our own time? There are no doubt many reasons for it, but the main one is that he reclaimed the rights of the heart, the centrality of feeling, and the importance of gentleness in human and cosmic relations. He created a synthesis that Christianity had lost: the encounter with God, with Christ and with the Spirit in nature, and accordingly the discovery of the vast cosmic kinship and the preservation of innocence—childlike clearsightedness at an adult age—that brings freshness, purity, and enchantment back to the afflictions of life on this Earth.[15] Philosopher Louis Lavelle accurately observes that "perhaps there has not been any mind so open, any sensitivity more spontaneous and more brightly touched by nature, other beings, and God, any soul more constantly inspired than that of St. Francis of Assisi."[16]

Francis was the ever-joyful brother, as he was called by his fellow friars. This marks a departure from a harsh Christianity of desert penitents, the hieratic and formal Christianity of papal palaces and clerical curias, and the structured Christianity of bookish theological culture. What emerges is a Christianity of blood and song, passion and dance, heart and poetry. Francis shows the same affection toward the Sultan Kamil, whom he embraces in Damieta on the Nile delta, as to the leper shouting by the steps in Spoleto, or to the wolf threatening the inhabitants of the city of Gubbio. He wins people over with affection and charm. Here we find the incomparable relevance of Francis's manner for ecology and for our time, which is lacking in any magical, shamanic, or unifying spirit.

St. Francis freed the springs of the heart and the impulses of Eros. Eros is a moving force and the dynamic core of human existence, the capacity for enthusiasm and appreciation of beauty and for enjoying the marvels of the universe. The most powerful expression of Eros is human desire, as has been shown by Freud, who stands within the Western tradition coming down from Plato and Aristotle. St. Francis was a person possessed by desire, so much so that St. Bonaventure was to apply to him what the scriptures said of Daniel, that he was a creature of desire.[17] Desire led him to identify himself with the poor, with the crucified Christ, and with all beings in nature.

All of life is Eros, but its symbolic expression is the heart. Through the heart we approach things with sympathy and feeling; we attempt to live with, feel with, share with, and commune with them. That is how community with the thing known lovingly arises. It is not by accident that in the writings of St. Francis the word *heart* appears forty-two times as opposed to one time for the word *intelligence*; *love* twenty-three times versus the twelve times for *truth*; *mercy* twenty-six times versus once for *intellect*; *doing* appears 170 times while *understanding* appears only five. Everything in him is surrounded with cordiality (which comes from the Latin *cor*, "heart") and sympathy. Max Scheler, who has studied the essence and forms of sympathy most thoroughly, sees in St. Francis one of the brightest flashes of sympathy that has ever appeared in history:

> Never in the history of the West has there emerged a figure with such powers of sympathy and universal emotion as we find in St. Francis. Never again can the unity and wholeness of all the elements be preserved as in St. Francis in the realm of religion, the erotic, activity in society, art, and knowledge. Rather, the strong characteristic embodied by St. Francis has been diluted in a growing multiplicity of figures also marked by emotion and the heart, in a number of movements, which however are set up in a unilateral manner.[18]

Dante rightly called him the Sun of Assisi (Paradiso, cant. XI, 50).

Urbanity, affection, and gentleness are trademarks of Francis's activity, which was as inclusive as possible. They are shown in his relationships with God and Christ, where the accent falls on the crib, the cross, the eucharist; Clare, the woman in his life and his companion in spiritual experience[19]; his brothers, whom he advised to be mothers to one another; himself, whom he referred to as the Poverello (poor little man) or Fratello (little brother, affectionately); and everything in nature, which he called brothers and sisters. This spiritual pattern was the key to his kind and gentle way of relating. The ecological ideal is achieved in the kind of attitude lived in so thorough and exemplary a manner by St. Francis.

We want to highlight here Francis's relationship with creation, for that is where he is most forcefully relevant to ecology.[20]

KINSHIP WITH THE LEAST AND COSMIC DEMOCRACY

All the biographies of St. Francis written in the years after his death in 1226 (biographies by Thomas of Celano and St. Bonaventure, and *The Legend of the Three Companions, The Legend of Perugia, The Mirror of Perfection,* and others) unanimously testify to "the friendly union that Francis established with all things" (I Bonaventure VIII, 1). The first biographer, Thomas of Celano (1229) writes:

> Indeed he was very often filled with a wonderful and ineffable joy from his consideration while he looked upon the sun, while he beheld the moon, and while he gazed upon the stars and the firmament. . . . How great a gladness do you think the beauty of the flowers brought to his mind when he saw the shape of their beauty and perceived the odor of their sweetness? When he found an abundance of flowers, he preached to them and invited them to praise the Lord as though they were endowed with reason. In the same way he exhorted with the sincerest purity cornfields and vineyards, stones and forests and all the beautiful things of the fields, fountains of water and the green things of the gardens, earth and fire, air and wind, to love God and serve him willingly. Finally, he called all creatures brother, and in a most extraordinary manner, a manner never experienced by others, he discerned the hidden things of nature with his sensitive heart, as one who had already escaped into the freedom of the glory of the sons of God. (1 Celano, 81-82)

The universe of St. Francis is magic and shot through with "most tender affection and devotion toward all things" (2 Celano, 134, 165).[21] The author of *The Mirror of Perfection* comments that he "had an especial and profound love for God's creatures" (113). Consequently, he walked over rocks with reverence in attention to the One who called himself a rock; he took snails off the roads so that they would not be trampled by people; he gave honey and wine to bees in the winter to keep them from dying of cold and hunger (2 Celano, 165). One day he sought to persuade the emperor to issue a decree that on Christmas people should generously feed the birds, the ox, the ass, and the poor out of respect for the Son of God who on that day became our older brother (*The Mirror of Perfection*, 114). Kinship is more than human; it is cosmic. That is why "he was filled with compassion . . . even toward dumb animals, reptiles, birds, and other creatures, sensible and insensible" (1 Celano, 77).[22]

Near Francis's cell there was a cricket chirping sweetly in a fig tree. At times he would

> kindly call it to himself, saying: "My sister cricket, come to me." As though endowed with reason, it immediately got up on his hand. And Francis said to it: "Sing, my sister cricket, and praise your Creator with a joyful song." Obeying without delay, it began to sing, and it did not cease to sing until the man of God, mingling his own praises with its songs, commanded it to go back to its usual haunt. (2 Celano, 171)

He "had an especial and profound love for God's creatures" (*The Mirror of Perfection*, 113); they understood him and established with him a relationship of understanding and kinship (1 Celano, 59), for "even irrational creatures recognized his affection for them and felt his tender love for them" (*The Mirror of Perfection*, 59).

What we observe here is another way of being in the world, one quite different from that of the modernity that we have criticized. The latter stands *above* things in order to possess and dominate them, whereas that of St. Francis is together *with* them, to love them and live with them as brothers and sisters at home. Even with regard to anxieties and pains "he did not regard them as pains but as sisters" (2 Celano, 165). Death itself is greeted as a sister who leads us to life ("Canticle to Brother Sun"). The Franciscan universe is never dead, nor are things simply placed within reach of the possessive human grasp or tossed one alongside another, without interconnections between them. Everything makes up a grand symphony—and God is the conductor. All things are alive and personal; through intuition Francis discovered what we now know empirically, that all living things are brothers and sisters because they have the same genetic code. Francis experienced this consanguinity in a mystical way. We all live together under the same parental roof. Because we are brothers and sisters we love one another; violence among family members is never justified.[23]

In keeping with these beliefs Francis forbade the brothers to cut trees down at the root, thereby leaving hope that they might grow back. He ordered the gardeners to leave a piece of land free and uncultivated so that all the herbs could grow there (even harmful ones) "so that . . . they might announce the beauty of the Father of all things" (2 Celano, 165). He also asked that the friars set aside a place in their vegetable gardens for aromatic herbs "so that they would bring those who look upon them to the memory of the Eternal Sweetness" (2 Celano, 165).

Taking such a stance allows for a life in common with all kinds of diversities. It is in tune with the dialogical and perichoretic logic governing the associations and inter(retro)relationships objectively existing in nature, even among the most frail creatures. Cosmic democracy becomes human and spiritual democracy, assuring that there is a place for the poor and the outcast. St. Francis had a foretaste of such harmony and experienced it. Ecology—the science of living well in our shared planetary home—becomes "eco-sophy"—the wisdom of living well among all beings.

Curiously, the contemporaries of St. Francis grasped the newness of this way of being immediately.[24] His biographers never tire of saying that "he seemed to be a man from another world" . . . "the new evangelist of the final age" . . . "new light from heaven" . . . "a dawn extending over the darkness" . . . "the new man that heaven has given the world."[25]. Historian J. Lortz calls him "the incomparable saint,"[26] the essayist Adolf Holl calls him "the last Christian,"[27] and many others view him as number one after the unique One (Jesus Christ). They all highlight his significance, which goes beyond the religious space of Christianity and the cultural space of the West. It is a lightning flash of what is simply human, the emergence of something out of the ordinary that was in the code of our universe and in the human phylum.

ST. FRANCIS, NOT A ROMANTIC

What is the source of such great gentleness and reverence, which could save our Earth? Many answer, the romanticism of St. Francis; they hold that he was the great romantic prior to romanticism itself. But some claim that there is little tradition behind the ecological image of St. Francis, that it is a projection of nineteenth-century romanticism (Chateaubriand, Sebastier, Renan) and has the same questionable assumptions, represented by liberal theology and by feeling, which is overemphasized in reaction to the rigidity of institutions and formalized approaches to spirituality. This interpretation has irreparably impaired all current biographies of the Poverello.[28] The image of Francis based on feeling, union with nature, and the presence of dramatic and poetic actions in the life of the little brother is deemed to be romantic.[29]

We disagree with that interpretation. The witness of biographies from his own time and representation in art over the centuries (starting with Fra Angelico and Giotto and even folk art, where Francis is always presented with the birds, preaching to the fish, and with the wolf of Gubbio, where nature is the setting) all provide a secure basis for regarding him as the patron saint of ecology as we understand it today. Actually, the interpretation in terms of romanticism remains on the surface and does not reach the deeper layers of Francis's experience. St. Francis is not a premature romantic. He is an ontological poet and a mystic who arrived at the transfiguration of the universe and the discovery of relatedness with all creatures by way of a spiritual journey; it was arduous and full of purifications, until his eyes were opened.

Romanticism is a product of modern subjectivity. The feelings of the self are projected onto the world. For the modern romantic, nature sends consciousness back to itself, to its feelings, but not in order to listen to the message that comes from nature, a message that sends one back to something beyond the subjectivity of conscience, to the mystery of the world and its foundation, the mystery of the Creator. In romanticism the self remains in its own universe, which is rich and many-sided in emotion but remains enclosed in its own stirrings. In St. Francis's archaic (close to the *arché*, "originating principle") way of being, the self is called to rise above itself, to open the closed circle, and to become kin with things, so as to sing jointly the hymn of praise to the Creator. This attitude comes forth only when we give up possessing things, or rather, when we do as Francis did with the cricket, when we create community with it, join in the song, and sing with it the praises of our great heavenly Father. We want to delve more deeply into what constitutes the wellsprings of such a mode of being.

THE MARRIAGE OF EROS AND AGAPE

There are three main explanations for how St. Francis arrived at sympathy and synergy with all things. The first is that he was a marvelous *poet*–not a romantic poet, but an ontological poet, a poet of essence, one capable of grasping the sacramental message echoing from all things. In youth he was influenced by the erotic movement in Provence.[30] He liked to sing love songs to beautiful ladies and, surprisingly, did so even at the time of his death (*The Legend of Perugia*, 64; *The Mirror of Perfection*, 121). He regarded himself as God's troubadour.

Eros—desire, fascination, and enchantment at the wonder of the universe and the things in it—lies at the root of the experience of Francis. This is, however, an Eros purified of all easy seduction, of the ambiguities of courtly flattery of a charming woman. It is enlivened by Agape, which is the quintessence of love, the love sung in Paul's epistle (1 Cor 13:1-2), and hence freely given love, freed of possessiveness and open to the Absolute. Agape does not copy Eros, nor does it simply sublimate it, but it extends its original impulse in order to reach the foundation and what fascinates in all love, which is God as grace and graciousness communicating God's self in and through all things.

Conversion did not kill the poet in Francis but energized him, because Eros and Agape were united in marriage. Thus, for example, his love for Clare retained all the intensity of love, but was free of the ties of libido. The effect is that libido is radicalized so as to make visible the Mystery that fascinates them both: God's presence in the world, and especially his crucified appearance in the poor and lepers. Through this happy marriage of Eros and Agape, St. Francis was able to personalize all his relations, because he saw them as sacraments of the Divine Presence: the lark is Sister Lark, the sun is Brother Sun and Master Sun, the Earth is Sister and Mother Earth, robbers are Brother Robbers to one who runs after them to give them the rest of what they had not succeeded in taking.[31] When he sings he becomes one with the song that all things and the universe itself sing to God, and hence he is set apart from the modern romantic poets, as we noted above.

There is a second root that explains more deeply this way of being in kinship with things at home: the *religious experience* of the common origin of all things. In his biography of Francis, St. Bonaventure says, "The realization that everything comes from the same source filled Francis with greater affection than ever and he called even the most insignificant creatures his brothers and sisters, because he knew they had the same origin as himself" (*Major Life*, VIII, 6). Common origin means not only God, but the heart of the Father, through the intelligence of the Son, in the enthusiasm of the Spirit. Such faith convictions were not only dogmatic claims but stirrings of the heart. If we have the same common origin—the Father's heart, which is like that of a Mother—then we are all sons and daughters. If we are sons and daughters, then we are all—the farthest galaxy, the most undetectable virus, the most massive dinosaurs, the hummingbirds, the Yanomamis, and the heads of state who decide the affairs of the Earth—brothers and sisters. We are all brothers and sisters, and we are all under the same rainbow of God's grace and under the same parental roof. St. Francis's saying "Deus meus et omnia" should be translated, not as it is generally rendered, "My God and my all," but along the lines of its cosmic spirit, "My God and all things."

An old legend that became a song that is popular in Umbria to this day gives a good idea of this inclusivity of St. Francis's ecological love. One day Francis said to the Lord, weeping,

> I love the sun and the stars,
> I love Clare and her sisters,
> I love the human hearts
> And all beautiful things,

Lord, forgive me
For I should love only you.
The Lord smiled and replied:
I love the sun and the stars,
I love Clare and her sisters,
I love the human hearts
And all beautiful things,
My dear Francis
You need not weep
For I also love all this.[32]

Francis shows no fear of our cosmic roots. He does not define human beings in terms of what distinguishes us from others but by what we have in common and what makes us kin with others. We are not so much rational animals as simply human beings, sons and daughters of the Earth, from which all come and toward which all are going. When he sings he sings *with* creatures, as he says marvelously in his canticle to all creatures. He does not sing *through* creatures. That would mean using them and turning a deaf ear to the hymn that they all sing to God. "Our sisters the birds are praising their Creator. We will go in among them and sing God's praise, changing the divine office" (*Major Life*, VIII, 9).

There is yet a third reason for being kin with all things, radical poverty. Poverty as St. Francis understands it, does not lie solely in not having things, for human beings always have our body, our mind, our clothing, our being in the world. Essential poverty is a way of being by which man and woman let things be; they cease dominating them, bringing them into subordination, and making them the object of human will. We give up being over them, and rather place ourselves at their feet. Such an attitude requires a deep asceticism and a renunciation of the instinct to possess and satisfy desire. Essential poverty consists of the unique journey of St. Francis lived physically where the poor are. There he simply tried to be, with the poor, free of everything. Meister Eckhart would call this *Abgeschidenheit,* a word difficult to translate, because it points toward being in utter availability, total abnegation, being completely centered on the other rather than oneself, freedom from and for.[33]

Possession creates obstacles to communication between persons and with nature, for by possession we are saying, "This is mine," and "That is yours," and so we are divided. Possession represents human "interests"–*inter-esses*–that is, what is placed between persons and nature. The more radical poverty is, the closer human beings come to raw reality, and the more it enables them to have an overall experience, and communion without distance, in respect and reverence for otherness and difference. Universal kinship results from this practice of essential poverty. We feel truly brother and sister because we can experience things with no concern for possession, profit, or efficiency. Poverty becomes a synonym for essential humility, which is not one virtue among others but an attitude by which we stand on the ground alongside things. From this position we can be reconciled with all things and begin a truly cosmic democracy.

St. Bonaventure goes so far as to say that through the unity that he had established with all things Francis was "enabled . . . to return to the state of primeval innocence" (VIII, 1). After a long apprenticeship of searching for essential poverty, there emerged in his heart the lost paradise, the earthly paradise that must be built through the history of humility, solidarity, and heartfelt love for all and all things. St. Francis has shown that it is possible and the path toward attaining it.

FUSION OF OUTER AND INNER ECOLOGY

The most complete expression of St. Francis's ecological way of being is found in the "Canticle to Brother Sun," which is one of the jewels of Western poetry and of nature mysticism. In it we find a happy fusion of outer and inner ecology. We have already indicated these two directions of ecological thought. Outer ecology is that symphony which we work out in harmony with nature and its rhythms, with the cosmic process of order-disorder-interaction-new order that is taking place in each being, the effect of which is to preserve the legacy of nature and our own happiness. This is only achieved if there is a corresponding inner ecology. The world and its creatures are within the human being in the form of the archetypes, symbols, and images that inhabit our interiority and with which we must dialogue and that we must integrate. If violence persists in the relationships of human beings with nature, it is because aggressive impulses emerge from within human beings. These impulses indicate the lack of an inner ecology and a failure to integrate the three main directions of ecology as formulated by F. Guattari: environmental ecology, social ecology, and mental ecology.

The "Canticle to Brother Sun" reveals the extraordinary spiritual accomplishment of St. Francis: complete reconciliation with heaven and heart, with life and death, with the universe and God. We must know how to interpret the hymn, however. We must get beyond the mere literary level of words—*earth, sun, moon, wind, air,* and so forth—and move down to the level of archetypes, where such things are charged with libido and meaning.

Perhaps the setting of the canticle reveals its significance for ecology and inner integration. *The Legend of Perugia* preserves the account in its most detailed form (N. 43, *The Mirror of Perfection,* 100). It was about twenty years after his conversion and two years after he received the stigmata on

Mount Alverno. Francis was consumed with a burning love for all creatures, a seraphic love, which in the words of St. Bonaventure, who knew a
great deal about mysticism, "is a death without death" (*Major Life*, XIV, 1-
2). He was also ill and beset with all kinds of inner sufferings over the
future of his movement, which was, against his will, becoming more and
more institutionalized.[34] It was autumn 1225 in San Damiano, the chapel
where everything began and where Clare and her sisters lived. His sufferings would not let up. For fifty days, says the *Legend*, he was in a dark cell
and could not see the light of day nor the fire by night. The pain in his
eyes would not let him sleep or even rest. This was the setting–seemingly
the opposite of anything ecological–in which he broke into a hymn of the
purest holistic ecology.

The text reads:

> One night, as he was thinking of all the tribulations he was enduring,
> he felt sorry for himself and said interiorly: "Lord, help me in my
> infirmities so that I may have the strength to bear them patiently!"
> And suddenly he heard a voice in spirit: "Tell me, Brother: if, in
> compensation for your sufferings and tribulations you were given an
> immense and precious treasure: the whole mass of the earth changed
> into pure gold, pebbles into precious stones, and the water of the
> rivers into perfume, would you not regard the pebbles and the wa-
> ters as nothing compared to such a treasure? Would you not re-
> joice?" Blessed Francis answered: "Lord, it would be a very great,
> very precious, and inestimable treasure beyond all that one can love
> and desire!" "Well, Brother," the voice said, "be glad and joyful in
> the midst of your infirmities and tribulations: as of now, live in peace
> as if you were already sharing my kingdom."

At that moment the day broke into his dark night. He felt he was in the
Kingdom, the symbol of complete reconciliation of human beings with
their own heart, with others, with the cosmos, and with God. He got up
and began to meditate for a moment. And then he intoned the hymn to all
creatures. "Altissimu, omnipotente, buno Signore." He called the brothers and with them he sang the freshly composed hymn. Inner ecology met
outer ecology. The physical sun, which he had not seen for a long time,
being almost blind, continued to shine within him. The same was true of
the water, fire, wind, and earth. This is not just a poetic and religious
discourse on these things. The things are an instrument for a deeper discourse, that of the unconscious which touches his center and thereby the
Mystery permeating and setting all afire and making it converge. Through
sun, light, wind, air, plants, and human beings in their grandeur and tragedy, and hence outer ecology, he expresses his inner ecology.

An outstanding French Franciscan scholar, Eloi Leclerc, drew out the wealth of archetypes in the hymn to Brother and Lord Sun. In doing so he intelligently utilized the findings of Jung's depth psychology, Gaston Bachelard's analysis of poetry, and Paul Ricoeur's hermeneutical philosophy.[35] Leclerc draws attention to matters that are highly significant for an interior ecology. Let us consider a few.

The very structure of the canticle reveals the search for and the encounter with overall unity. The number seven in the verses shows the emergence of this deep structure; it is made up of 3 + 4, the greatest symbols of totality and unity.

Vertical and horizontal lines cross in the hymn. Together they form a well-known symbol of cosmic totality. The first moment goes upward toward God:

> Most high, all-powerful, all good, Lord!

That is the search for transcendence, the dream upward. But Francis then becomes aware that he is not succeeding in singing to God, for

> No mortal lips are worthy
> To pronounce your name.

He does not become bitter, nor does he withdraw into an apophatic posture. He then turns to the horizontal dimension where all creatures are, for they speak of God:

> All praise be yours, my Lord, through all that you
> have made.

He then opens to horizontal and universal kinship. He sings to creatures who bear the likeness of the Most High. If we cannot speak of God, we can speak of creatures, who are marked by God's presence and by uncovering the sacramentality of all beings.

There is another aspect of archetypes in the inner whole that shines through the hymn: the male and the female. According to Jung, this is one of the most universal archetypes in the human psyche. All elements are arranged in pairs, where female is combined with male: sun-moon, wind-water, fire-earth. All these couples are encompassed by the great couple, sun-earth, from whose cosmic marriage all other couples derive. He begins singing to the sun, which he calls, under the influence of the archetype, Lord. But since it is created by God, he also calls it brother. He says the same of Earth, which in terms of archetype is Mother, and theologically is sister. Then he speaks of "sister Earth, our mother."

The canticle has two other verses, added later by St. Francis. In them it is no longer the material cosmos that is being sung but the human cosmos that is also seeking reconciliation. One verse deals with the reconciliation between the bishop and mayor of Assisi effected by Francis. The other takes up the most basic complex of life, that having to do with death. Human beings are reconciled with one another. Life embraces Death, because she is his sister and bears a life that is fuller and immortal.

The dimension of light and shadow, Earth and heaven, inner and outer ecology finds a privileged interpreter in the Poverello and Fratello. He is like a fiber of the universe in which the least movement and the softest musical note can be felt. Hence his sensitivity has become a reference point for our own searching for an integration that proceeds by way of the cosmos and through a covenant of reverence and love for all the created. Paradoxically, our society lives between the ideal of Pietro Bernardone, Francis's father, a man of business and power, and Francis of Assisi, universal brother.

Arnold Toynbee humorously and correctly said,

> In order to keep the biosphere habitable for two thousand more years, we and our descendants will have to forget the example of Pietro Bernardone, the great thirteenth-century textile merchant, and his material welfare, and begin to follow the model of Francis his son, the greatest of all the men who have ever lived in the West. . . . The example given by St. Francis, is what we Westerners ought to imitate with all our heart, for he is the only Westerner in this glorious company who can save the earth.[36]

I LEAVE THE BODY AND HAND YOU MY HEART

There is no better way to conclude than by recalling a well-known goodbye of St. Francis that is conserved in a seventeenth-century manuscript in the venerable convent on Mount Alverno. In it Pathos and Eros speak, brought together in a *logique du coeur*, as Blaise Pascal might say. Outer ecology meets inner ecology in a heartfelt fusion.

Francis is leaving Mount Alverno on an ass after making a forty-day spiritual retreat there. Every morning a falcon would wake him up in the cave for the canonical hours (2 Celano, 168). When his spiritual retreat ends, he emotionally leaves his heartrending farewell:

> Farewell, farewell, farewell, Friar Masseo. Farewell, farewell, farewell, Friar Angelo! Farewell, farewell, farewell, Friar Silvester, Friar Iluminato! Peace be with you, beloved sons of mine, farewell! *I am*

leaving you in my person, but my heart remains here. I am now going away with Friar Little Lamb of God (Friar Leo) . . . and I will not be coming back. I am going away from here, and you, farewell, all of you! Farewell, dearly beloved brother falcon: I thank you for the love with which you were at my service! Farewell, great cavern, I will never see you again. Farewell, farewell, farewell, rock, you took me into your bowels and so left the devil confused! Farewell, Blessed Mary of the Angels, to you, Mother of the Eternal Word, I commend these my children.

The *Speculum* preserves this memory:

While our dear father said these words, our eyes were pouring out rivers of tears. And he also went away taking our hearts with him and leaving us orphans.

And at the bend in the road, where he saw Alverno for the last time, Francis got down off the ass, knelt down facing the mountain, and addressed his final farewell:

Farewell, mountain of God, beloved mountain, flowering mountain, fruitful mountain, mountain where God chose to dwell; farewell, Mount Alverno, God the Father, God the Son, God the Holy Spirit bless you; remain in peace for we shall never again see one another.

"Io mi parto da voi con la persona, ma vi lascio il mio cuore." Francis has left his heart in the heart of the world so as to be in the heart of all who seek a new covenant of the heart with all things.

NOTES

CHAPTER 1: THE ECOLOGICAL ERA

1. For data, see C. Allais, "O estado do planeta em alguns números," in M. Barrére, *Terra patrimônio comum* (São Paulo: Nobel, 1992), 243-51.

2. D. Meadows, et al., *The Limits to Growth: A Report for the Club of Rome Project on the Predicament of Mankind* (New York: Universe Books, 1972).

3. J. A. Lutzenberger, *Fim do Futuro?* (Porto Alegre: Movmiento, 1980).

4. Cf. *Allgemeine Entwicklungsgeschichte der Organismen* (Berlin, 1868).

5. J. A. Lutzenberger, *Revista Vozes* (January-February 1979), 64.

6. Ernst Haeckel, *Natürliche Entwicklungsgeschichte* (Berlin: 1879), 42.

7. See the entire issue of *Concilium* 5 (1995) on ecology and the poor.

8. See the excellent book by E. Turrini, *O Caminho do Sol* (Petrópolis: Vozes, 1993), 68-120.

9. H. Leis, et al., *Ecologia e Política Mundial* (Petrópolis: Vozes, 1991).

10. F. Guattari, *As Três Ecologias* (Campinas: Papirus, 1988).

11. G. Bateson, *Mind and Nature: A Necessary Unity* (New York: Dutton, 1979).

12. A. Auer, *Umwelt Ethik* (Düsseldorf: Patmos, 1985); H. Jonas, *Das Prinzip Verantwortung* (Frankfurt: Suhrkamp, 1984).

13. Cf. J. R. Regidor, "Etica ecologica," in *Metafora Verde* (Rome) no. 1 (July-August 1990), 61-75.

14. The main author is A. Naess, *Ecology, Community and Lifestyle* (Cambridge: Cambridge University Press, 1989).

15. René Descartes, *Discourse de la méthode*, vol. 6 (Paris: Seuil, 1965), 60ff.

16. Francis Bacon, quoted by J. Moltmann, *Doctrina ecológica da criação: Deus na criação* (Petrópolis: Vozes, 1993), 51.

17. Thomas Kuhn, *The Structure of Scientific Revolutions* (Chicago: University of Chicago Press, 1970), 175, 182, 187.

18. A. Koyré, *Études d'Histoire de la Penséee Scientifique* (Paris: Gallimard, 1973).

19. I. Prigogine, *La Nouvelle Alliance: La Métamorphose de la Science* (Paris: Gallimard, 1986).

20. Ibid., 31.

21. Cf. J. Moltmann, "Die Entdeckung der Anderen. Zur Theorie des kommunikativen Erkennes," in *Evangelische Theologie*, no. 5 (1990), 400-14.

22. See F. White, *The Overview Effect* (Boston: Houghton Mifflin Company, 1987).

23. Ibid., 38.

24. Isaac Asimov, *New York Times*, October 9, 1982.

25. Cf. F. Capra, D. Stendl-Rast, *Belonging to the Universe* (San Francisco: HarperCollins, 1992).

26. J. Gleick, *Chaos: Making a New Science* (New York: Penguin Books, 1988).

27. I. Prigogine, *Self-Organization in Non Equilibrium*, (New York: Wiley-Interscience, 1977); idem, *Order out of Chaos* (London: Heinemann, 1984); idem, *Structure, stabilité et fluctuations* (Paris: Masson, 1971).

28. Cf. J.-P. Dupuy, *Ordres et Désordres: Essai sur un nouveau paradigme* (Paris: Seuil, 1982).

29. P. Ehrlich, *The Machinery of Nature* (New York: Simon and Schuster, 1986).

30. E Neuman, K. Karény, *La Terra Madre e Dea: Sacralità della Natura che ci fa Vivere* (Como: Red Edizioni, 1989).

31. J. Lovelock, *Gaia: A New Look at Life on Earth* (Oxford: Oxford University Press, 1979); idem, *The Ages of Gaia: A Biography of Our Living Earth* (New York: Norton, 1988); E. Sahtouris, *Gaia: The Human Journey from Chaos to Cosmos* (New York: Pocket Books, 1989); J. A. Lutzenberger, *Gaia, o Planeta Vivo* (Porto Alegre: L&PM, 1990).

32. L. Margulis and D. Sagan, *Microcosmos: Four Billion Years of Evolution from Our Microbian Ancestors* (New York: Summit Books, 1987).

33. Lovelock, *Gaia,* 11.

34. Ibid. [Citation translated from the Portuguese.]

35. A. Gore, *Earth in the Balance: Ecology and the Human Spirit* (Boston: Houghton Mifflin, 1992).

36. S. Hawking, *A Brief History of Time: From the Big Bang to Black Holes* (New York: Bantam Books, 1988), 121-22.

37. Ibid, chap. 8.

38. Cf. data in B. Swimme and T. Berry, *The Universe Story: From the Primordial Flaring Forth to the Ecozoic Era: A Celebration of the Unfolding of the Cosmos* (San Francisco: Harper, 1992), 118-20. Cf. also Z. Massoud, *Terre vivante* (Paris: Odile Jacob, 1992), 27-30, 56.

39. Margulis and Sagan, *Microcosmos.*

40. E. O. Wilson, *The Diversity of Life* (Cambridge: Belnap Press of Harvard University, 1992).

41. Cf. the excellent observations of Swimme and Berry on this matter in *The Universe Story*, 51-61.

42. Nicolas Georgescu-Roegen, *The Promethean Destiny of Mankind's Technology* (Brighton: Wheatsheaf, 1987). [Citation translated from the Portuguese.]

43. Cf. R. R. Freitas Mourão, *Ecologia Cósmica: Uma Visão Cósmica da Ecologia* (Rio de Janeiro: Francisco Alves, 1992).

44. Ibid.

45. I. Prigogine and I. Stengers, *Entre o Tempo e a Eternidade* (São Paulo: Companhia das Letras, 1992), 147ff.

46. A. R. Peacocke, *Creation in the World of Science* (Oxford: Oxford University Press, 1979); W. Pannenberg, *Toward a Theology of Nature—Essays on Science and Faith* (John Knox Press, 1993), 29-49.

47. Formulated in 1974 by Brandon Carter. Cf. J. M. Alonso, *Introducción al principio andrópico* (Madrid: Encuentro Ediciones, 1989).

48. Cf. F. Fogelman-Soulié, ed., *Théories de la Complexité* (Paris: Seuil, 1991); E. Morin, *La Méthode 2: La vie de la vie* (Paris: Seuil, 1980), 355-93; idem, *Science avec Conscience* (Paris: Fayard, 1990), 165-315.

49. Cf. Wilson, *The Diversity of Life.*

50. See K. Wilber, ed., *The Holographic Paradigm and Other Paradoxes* (New York: Random, 1982).

51. Cited in Morin, *Science avec Conscience*, 167.

52. Niels Bohr, *Atomtheorie und Naturbeschreibung* (Berlin, 1931), 143.

53. See L. Boff, *Trinity and Society* (Maryknoll N.Y.: Orbis Books, 1988), 134-48.

54. Cf. C. F. von Weizächer, *Die Tragweite der Wissenschaft, Schopfung und Weltenstehung I* (Stuttgart, 1964), 179ff.; G. Picht, "Die Zeit und die Modalitatäten," in *Hier und Jetzt*, vol. 1 (Stuttgart, 1980), 362-74.

55. R. Ruether, *Gaia and God* (San Francisco: Harper & Row, 1992); idem, "Eco-feminism and Theology," in *Ecotheology: Voices from South and North*, ed. D. G. Hallman (Maryknoll, N.Y.: Orbis Books, 1994), 199-204; A. Primavesi, *From Apocalypse to Genesis: Ecology, Feminism and Christianity* (Tunbridge Wells: Burns & Oates, 1991).

56. C. Merchant. *The Death of Nature: Woman, Ecology, and the Scientific Revolution* (San Francisco: Harper & Row, 1980).

57. Cf. W. Souza, *O novo paradigma* (São Paulo: Cultrix, 1993), 47-70.; I. Hedström, *Somos Parte de un Gran Equilibrio* (San José: DEI, 1988), 7-14; C. Cummings, *Eco-spirituality* (Mahwah, N.J.: Paulist Press, 1991), 27-40.

58. See Swimme and Berry, *The Universe Story*, 75-76.

59. Cf. J.-P. Dupuy, ed., *L'Auto-organisation: de la Physique au Politique* (Paris: Seuil, 1983).

60. See the beautiful reflections along these lines by Daisaku Ikeda, in *La Vita, Mistero Prezioso* (Milan: Bompiani, 1991), 35ff.

CHAPTER 2: AN ECOLOGICAL VIEW OF THE COSMOS

1. Cf. the marvelous commentary by C. Westerman, *Genesis* (Grand Rapids: Eerdmans, 1987).

2. In this we follow the wonderful book by Carlos Mesters, *Eden: Golden Age or Goad* (Maryknoll, N.Y.: Orbis Books, 1971), 25-27.

3. Ibid., 28-29.

4. E. Durkheim, *The Elementary Forms of Religious Life* (New York: The Free Press, 1965), 462-96.

5. *Popul Vuh: The Mayan Book of the Dawn of Life*, trans. Dennis Tedlock (New York: Simon & Schuster, 1985), 72-73. [Boff uses *Popul Vuh Las Antiguas historias del Quiché*, ed. A. Recinos (Mexico: Fondo de Cultura Económica, 1986), 23-24, and M. D. Sodi, ed., *La Literatura de los Mayas* (Mexico City: Editorial Joaquin Mortiz, 1964), 97-98–*translator*.]

6. Robert Muller, from "Final Prayer and New Genesis," in *New Genesis: Shaping a Global Spirituality* (Garden City: Doubleday, 1982), 190-91.

7. Cf. B. Swimme and T. Berry, *The Universe Story: From the Primordial Flaring Forth to the Ecozoic Era: A Celebration of the Unfolding of the Cosmos* (San Francisco: Harper, 1992), 2.

8. S. Weinberg, *The First Three Minutes: A Modern View of the Origin of the Universe* (New York: Basic Books, 1977).

9. S. Hawking, *A Brief History of Time: From the Big Bang to Black Holes* (New York: Bantam Books, 1988).

10. Cf. C. Sagan, *Cosmos* (New York: Random House, 1980), 188.

11. Cf. James E. Lovelock, *Gaia: A New Look at Natural History* (Oxford: Oxford University Press, 1979); idem, *The Ages of Gaia: A Biography of Our Living Earth* (New York: Norton, 1988).

12. Jacques Monod, *Chance and Necessity: An Essay on the Natural History of Modern Biology* (New York: Knopf, 1971).

13. Cf. E. Morin, *Terre-Patrie* (Paris: Seuil, 1993), 53; E. Jantsch, *The Self-Organizing Universe: Scientific and Human Implications of the Emerging Paradigm of Evolution* (New York: Pergamon Press, 1980).

14. Cf. M. Longair, *The Origins of Our Universe* (Cambridge: Cambridge University Press, 1992).

15. Cf. E. Wilson, *The Diversity of Life* (Cambridge, Mass.: Harvard University Press, 1992).

16. *Order out of Chaos* is the title of one of Prigogine's major works.

17. Monod, *Chance and Necessity*.

18. Jean Guitton, *Deus e a Ciência* (Rio de Janeiro: Nova Fronteira, 1992), 58.

19. D. Zohar, *The Quantum Self: Human Nature and Consciousness Defined by the New Physics* (New York: Morrow, 1990).

20. Cf. V. Weidemann, "Das inflationäre Universum: Die Entstehung der Welt aus dem Nichts," in H. A. Müller, et al., eds., *Natuerwissenschaft und Glaube* (Berne: Scherz, 1988), 360.

CHAPTER 3: THE ECOLOGICAL CRISIS

1. *Cuidando DO Planeta Terra: Uma Estratégia para o Futuro da Vida* (São Paulo: Uniao Internacional para a Conservaçao da Naturaleza/Programa para Nacoes Unidas para Meio-Ambiente, 1991).

2. See the accusatory piece: E. Drewermann, *Der tödliche Fortschritt* (Regensburg: Pustet, 1986).

3. Cf. C. Amery, *Das Ende der Vorsehung: Die gnadenlosen Folgen des Christentums* (Reinbeck, 1972).

4. Cf. Ch. Link, *Schöpfung: Schöpfungstheologie angesichts der Herausforderungen des 20: Jahrhundets* (Gütersloh: Gerd Mohn, 1991), 40-46.

5. E. McGaa, *Eagle Man, Mother Earth Spirituality: Native American Paths to Healing Ourselves and Our World* (New York: Harper & Row, 1992); J. B. McDaniel, *With Roots and Wings: Christianity in an Age of Ecology and Dialogue* (Maryknoll, N.Y.: Orbis Books, 1995); M. Paciornik, *Aprenda a Viver com os Índios* (Rio de Janeiro: Espaço e Tempo, 1987).

6. See J. L. Phelan, *The Millennial Kingdom of the Franciscans in the New World* (Berkeley: University of California Press, 1956).

7. From a Latin American perspective, I. Hedström, *Volverán las Golondrinas?* (San José: DEI, 1988).

8. Cf. J. Huber, *Die verlorene Unschuld der Ökologie* (Frankfurt, 1982); J. Maddox, *Unsere Zukunft hat noch Jukunft: Der jügste Tag findet nicht statt* (Stuttgart, 1973).

9. Cf. B. McKibben, *The End of Nature* (New York: Random House, 1989).

10. Cf. D. Duclos, "La nature: principale contradiction culturelle du capitalisme?, in *L'Écologie, ce Matérialisme Historique* (Paris: PUF, 1992), 41-58.

11. Selene Carvalho, Herculano, "Como passar do insuportável ao sofrível," in *Tempo e Presença*, no. 261 (1992), 14.

12. Cf. T. Benton, "Marxisme et limites naturelles: critique et reconstruction écologiques," in *L' Écologie, ce Matérialisme Historique*, 59-95.

13. P. Schmitz, *Ist die Schöpfung noch zu retten?* (Würzburg: Echter Verlag, 1985), 21-30.

14. Cf. W. and D. Schwartz, *Ecologia; Alternativa para o Futuro* (Rio de Janeiro: Paz e Terra, 1990), 163-74.

15. F. Nietzsche, *Der Wille zur Macht: Versuch einer Umwertung aller Werte* (1887) (Stuttgart: Kröner Tb., 1964).

16. See the complete text in Paulo Suess, ed., *A Conquista espritual* (Petrópolis: Vozes, 1992), 227.

17. Ibid., 249.

18. Cf. F. Turner, *O Espírito Occidental contra a Natureza* (São Paulo: Capmus, 1991).

19. Fragment 1 in H. Diels, *Die Fragmente der Vorsokratiker* (Hamburg, 1957), 121.

20. Cf. G. Haussman, *L'Uomo Simbionte* (Florence: Vallecchi Editore, 1992), 31ff.

21. J. Plaskow, C. Christ, *Weaving the Visions: New Patterns in Feminist Spirituality* (New York: Harper & Row, 1989).

22. J. Haught, *The Promise of Nature: Ecology and Cosmic Purpose* (Mahwah, N.J.: Paulist Press, 1993), 39-55.

23. Cf. S. Moscovici, *Sociedade contra a Natureza* (Petrópolis: Vozes, 1975), 321-25.

24. Cf. J. Ladriére, *Les Enjeux de la Rationalité* (Paris, Aubier-Montaigne: UNESCO, 1977).

25. Cf. J. Habermas, *Der philosophische Diskurs der Moderne* (Frankfurt, 1988), 352ff.

26. Cf. L. White Jr., "The Historical Roots of our Ecological Crisis," *Science* 155 (1967), 1203-7.

27. T. Berry, *The Dream of the Earth* (San Francisco: Sierra Club, 1988), 202.

28. Turner, *O Espírito Occidental contra a Natureza.*

29. C. F. Weiszächer, *O Tempo Urge* (Petrópolis: Vozes, 1993).

30. See the five-volume collection *World Religions and Ecology* (London: Cassell, 1992).

31. I. Bradley, *Dios es "Verde": Cristianismo y Medio Ambiente* (Santander: Sal Terrae, 1993).

32. "The Historical Roots of Our Ecologic Crisis," *Science*, no. 3767 (1967), 1203-7.

33. Amery, *Das Ende der Vorsehung.*

34. Cf. E. D. Gray, *Green Paradise Lost* (Wellesley, Mass.: Roundtable Press, 1981).

35. Cf. D. Hervieu-Léger, ed., *Religion et écologie* (Paris: Cerf, 1993), 29-45.

36. G. Paris, *Meditações pagãs* (Petrópolis: Vozes, 1994), 8-14.

37. Cf. Y. Congar, "Political Monotheism in Antiquity and the God of the Trinity," *Concilium* no. 163 (1981), 38-45.

38. See the notable attempt by J. Moltmann, *God in Creation: A New Theology of Creation and the Spirit of God* (San Francisco: Harper & Row, 1985).

39. Cf. R. Garaudy, *Vers un guerre de religion? Le débat du siècle* (Paris: Desclée de Brower, 1995), 87-110.

40. Bradley, *Dios es "Verde,"* 70-107.

41. Cf. various interpretations by L. Boff, "Pecado original. Discussão antiga e moderna e pistas de equacionamento," *Grande Sinal* 29 (1975), 109-33.

42. G. F. McLeod, *The Whole Earth Shall Cry Glory: Iona Prayers* (Iona: Wild Goose Publications, 1985), 8. [Citation translated from the Portuguese.]

43. See Boff, "Pecado original"; Bradley, *Dios es "Verde,"* 93-107.

44. Cf. John Cobb and Charles Birch, *The Liberation of Life: From the Cell to Community* (Cambridge: Cambridge University Press, 1981).

45. See this matter further spelled out in L. Boff, *Teologia do Cativeiro e da Libertação* (São Paulo: Círculo do Livro, 1985), 123-40.

46. Cf. the relevant observations of W. Asmar, *Por que o Homem Destrói o Meio Ambiente: O instinto de more e a entropia* (Rio de Janeiro: Imago, 1991).

CHAPTER 4: ALL THE CAPITAL SINS AGAINST ECOLOGY

1. Cf. F. Mires, *El Discurso de la Naturaleza: Ecología y Política en América Latina* (San José: DEI, 1990), 119-23.

2. Cf. Núcleo Difusão Tecnológica do Instituto Nacional de e Pesquisas Amazônicas, *Ciência Hoje*, no. 26 (1986), 92.

3. Euclides da Cunha, *Um Paraíso Perdido: Reunião dos Ensaios Amazônicos* (Petrópolis: Vozes, 1976), 15.

4. H. Sioli, *Amazônia: Fundamentos da Ecologia da Maior Região de Florestas Tropicais* (Petrópolis: Vozes, 1985), 15-17.

5. E. Salati, *Amazônia: Desenvolvimento, Integração, Ecologia* (São Paulo: Brasiliense/CNPq, 1983); cf. J. P. Leroy, *Uma Chama na Amazônia* (Petrópolis: Vozes, 1991), 184-202; B. Ribeiro, *Amazônia Urgente: Cinco Séculos de História e Ecologia* (Belo Horizonte: Itatiana, 1990), 53.

6. Viveiros de Casto, "Sociedades indígenas e natureza na Amazônia," *Tempo e Presença*, no. 261 (1992), 26.

7. Ribeiro, *Amazônia Urgente*, 75.

8. James Redfield, *Celestine Prophecy* (New York: Warner, 1994).

9. Cf. V. Baum, "Das Ökosystem der tropischen Regenwälder," in P. Stüben, *Nach uns die Sinflut* (Giessen, 1986), 39.

10. Sioli, *Amazônia*, 60.

11. S. Davis, *Victims of the Miracle: Development and the Indians of Brazil* (New York: Cambridge University Press, 1977).

12. Cf. C. Benjamin, *Diálogo sobre Ecologia, Ciência, e Política* (Rio de Janeiro: Nova Fronteira, 1933), 177.

13. See Ph. Fearside, "Deforestation in the Brazilian Amazon: How Fast Is It Occurring?," *Interscientia*, no. 2 (March-April 1982); J. Lutzenberger, "Besidlungspolitik und Zerstörung des Regenwaldes Amazoniens," in *Yanomamis*, ed. J. Helbig, O. Iten, and J. Schiltknecht (Frankfurt: Piquin-Innsbruck, 1989), 18-23.

14. See E. Salati, in *The Geophysiology of Amazonia*, ed. R. E. Dickinson (New York: John Wiley & Sons, 1987).

15. Cf. E. Morel, *Amazônia Saqueada* (São Paulo: Global, 1984), 60-62.

16. See A. U. Oliveira, *Amazônia, Monopólio, Expropriação e Conflitos* (São Paulo: Papirus, 1980), 21-33.

17. See D. Ribeiro, *Os Índios e a Civilização: O Processo de Integração dos Índios no Brasil Moderno* (Petrópolis: Vozes, 1984).

18. Benjamin, *Diálogo sobre Ecologia, Ciência, e Política*, 110.

19. Cf. detail in A. Hall, *Amazônia para Quem? Desmatamento e Conflito Social no Programa Grande Carajás* (1980), 176-80.; Oliveira, *Amazônia, Monopólio, Expropriação e Conflitos*, 35ff.

20. Cf. M. Waldmann, *Ecologia e Lutas Sociais no Brasil* (São Paulo: Contexto, 1992), 83.

21. Cf. the data in Hall, *Amazônia para Quem?* 59ff.

22. C. O. Valverde, "Sacrifício Verde," in *Ecologia,* no. 33 (1993), 19.

23. Hall, *Amazônia para Quem?*, 195.

24. Valverde, "Sacrificio Verde," 16-19.

25. Ribeiro, *Amazôna Urgente,* 196.

26. Hall, *Amazônia,* 200ff.

27. Ibid., 273-74.

28. P. Birraux, "Die Yanomami Brasiliens vor dem Genozid," in Helbig, et al., *Yanomamis,* 82-86.

29. See an overall vision in M. P. Gomes, *Os Índios e o Brasil* (Petrópolis: Vozes, 1988), 65ff.; L. Beltrão, *O Índio, um Mito Brasileiro* (Petrópolis: Vozes, 1977), esp. 255ff.

30. See Davis, *Victims of the Miracle,* 106.

31. Ribeiro, *Amazônia Urgente,* 197.

32. For a wealth of details, see A. Zeidler, "Waimiri-Atroari: Dokumentation eines Völkermordes," in Helbig, et al., *Yanomamis,* 45-75; E. Scwade and J. P. F. Carvalho, *Waimiri-Atoari: A História que Ainda não Foi Contada* (Brasília, 1982).

33. Oliveira, *Amazônia, Monopólio, Expropriação e Conflitos,* 130.

34. Cf. C. Mesters and P. Suess, *Utopia Cativa: Catequese Indigenista e Libertação Indígena* (Petrópolis: Vozes, 1986).

35. See C. Grzybowski, ed., *O Testamento do Homem da Floresta: Chico Mendes por Ele Mesmo* (Rio de Janeiro: Fase, 1989), 24.

36. See *Jornal do Brasil* (December 24, 1988).

37. Cf. data in L. F. Pinto, "Depois q a Rio-92 passou," *Tempo e Presença,* no. 265 (1992), 17.

38. E. Moran, *A Economia Humana das Populações na Amazônia* (Petrópolis: Vozes, 1990), 293 and 404-5; H. Schubart, "Ecologia e Utilização das Florestas," in Salati, *Amazônia,* 101-43.

CHAPTER 5: LIBERATION THEOLOGY AND ECOLOGY

1. Cf. D. Hallmann, ed., *Ecotheology: Voices from South and North* (Maryknoll, N.Y.: Orbis Books, 1994); Th. S. Derr, *Ecology and Human Liberation* (Geneva: World Council of Churches, 1973).

2. F. Guattari, *As Três Ecologias* (Campinas: Papirus, 1988).

3. See further data in L. Boff, *Ecology and Liberation: A New Pardigm* (Maryknoll, N.Y.: Orbis Books, 1995), 15ff.

4. See the collection *L'Ecologie, ce Matérialisme Historique* (Pris: PUF, 1992); F. Herbert Bormann and Stephen R. Keller, eds., *Ecology, Economics, Ethics: The Broken Circle* (New Haven and London: Yale University Press, 1991).

5. See M. Longair, *The Origins of Our Universe* (Cambridge: Cambridge University Press, 1992); R. R. Frietas Mourão, *Ecologia Cósmica* (Rio de Janeiro: Francisco Alves, 1992); D. S. Toolan "Nature is an Heraclitean Fire: Reflections on Cosmology in an Ecological Age," *Studies in the Spirituality of Jesuits,* no. 25 (New York, 1991).

6. See F. White, *The Overview Effect* (Boston: Houghton Mifflin Company, 1987).

7. Isaac Asimov, *New York Times,* October 9, 1982.

8. J. Lovelock, *The Ages of Gaia: The Biography of Our Living Earth* (New York: Norton, 1988).

9. E. Jantsch, *The Self-Organizing Universe: Scientific and Human Implications of the Emerging Paradigm of Evolution* (New York: Pergamon Press, 1980).

10. T. Berry, *The Dream of the Earth* (San Francisco: Sierra Club, 1988).

11. H. Assmann, "Teologia da solidariedade e da ciudadania, ou seja, continuando a teologia da libertação," *Notas, Jornal de Ciências da Religião*, no. 2 (1994), 2-9.

12. See the classic book of Clodovis Boff, *Theology and Praxis: Epistemological Foundations* (Maryknoll, N.Y.: Orbis Books, 1987).

13. See F. J. Hinkelhammert, "La lógica de la expulsión del mercado capitalista mundial y el proyecto de liberación," in *Pasos* (San José, 1992).

14. R. Garaudy, *Le Debat du Siécle* (Paris: Desclée de Brower, 1995), 14.

15. Cf. UNDP, *Human Development Report* (Oxford and New York: Oxford University Press, 1990).

CHAPTER 6: RECLAIMING THE DIGNITY OF EARTH

1. "Outer Space to Inner Space: An Astronaut's Journey," in *Saturday Review* (February 22, 1975), 20.

2. R. Otto, *The Idea of the Holy* (London: Oxford University Press, 1950); M. Eliade, *The Sacred and the Profane* (New York: Harcourt Brace, 1959); G. Van der Leeuw, *Religion in Essence and Manifestation* (London: G. Allen and Unwin, 1938); R. Caillois, *Man and the Sacred* (Glencoe: Ill.: Free Press, 1959); M. Meslin, *A Experiência Humana do Divino* (Petrópolis: Vozes, 1992), 55-84. Studies summarizing discussion in recent years include E. Castelli, *Le Sacré, études et Recherches* (Paris: Aubier, 1974); H. Cazelles "Sacré (sainteté)" in *Supplément du Dictionnaire de la Bible*, vol. 10, fasc. 60, bibliography 1343-44; J. Splett, *Die Rede vom Heilegen* (Freiburg/Munique: Karl Alber, 1971).

3. L. Boff, *Sacraments of Life, Life of the Sacraments* (Washington, D.C.: Pastoral Press, 1987).

4. Cf. in this regard the thoughts of M. Dowd, *Earthspirit* (Mystic, Conn.: Twenty-Third Publications, 1991), 17-22.

5. Cf. Carl Sagan, *The Dragons of Eden: Speculations on the Evolution of Human Intelligence* (New York: Random House, 1977), 14-16.

6. Robert Muller, *O Nascimento de uma Civilização Global* (São Paulo: Aquariana, 1993), 7.

7. Cf. H. van der Berg, *La Tierra no Da Así no Más* (La Paz: Hisbol-UCB/ISET, 1989), 165.

8. E. Moran, *A Economia Humana das Populações da Amazônia* (Petrópolis: Vozes, 1990).

9. William Balée, "Cultural Forest of the Amazon," *Garden*, no. 11 (1987), 12.

10. Prince Charles, quoted in "Idéas e Fatos," *Jornal do Brasil* (June 16, 1991), 6.

11. S. Davis, *Victims of the Miracle: Development and the Indians of Brazil* (New York: Cambridge University Press, 1977). See also the testimonies gathered by J. Araújo, *Estamos desaparecendo da Terra* (São Paulo: Editora Bahá-i do Brasil, 1991), 3-35.

12. See H. Sioli, *Amazônia: Fundamentos da Ecologia da Maior Região de Florestas Tropicais* (Petrópolis: Vozes, 1985), 24-29.

13. Cf. M. A. Altieri, *Agroecologia* (Rio de Janeiro: Fase, 1989), 25-63.

14. See A. L. Hall, *Amazônia: Desenvolvimento para Quem?* (Rio de Janeiro: Zahar, 1991), 270; M. Waldmann, *Ecologia e Lutas Socais no Brasil* (São Paulo: Contexto, 1992), 69-78.

15. Chief Seattle, quoted in *Revista Vozes* (January-February 1979), 66-67; cf. other testimonies in J. D. Hughes, *American Indian Ecology* (El Paso, Tex.: Texas Western Press, 1983).

16. G. Archibold Pemasky, in "Kuna Yala: Protegiendo a la Madre Tierra . . . y a sus Hijos," in *Hacia una Centroamérica Verde* (San José: DEI, 1990), 37; see also E. Potiguara, *A Terra É a Mãe do Índio* (Rio de Janeiro: Grumin, 1989).

17. Pemasky, "Kuna Yala," 41. An overview of the ecological knowledge of indigenous peoples may be found in F. Mires, *El Discurso de la Naturaleza: Ecología y Política en América Latina* (San José: DEI, 1990), 83-91; for Brazil, see B. Ribeiro, *O Índio na Cultura Brasileira* (Rio de Janeiro: Unibrade, 1987), 15-94.

18. Cf. CIMI/CNBB, "Semana do Índio de 14-20 de 1986," *Revista Vozes* (April 1986), 71.

19. See Mires, *El Discurso de la Naturaleza*, 105-11.

20. See J. Quan, "Le Colture Agricole dei Maya: un Exempio di Creatività e di Respettodel Suolo," in *Educaziones al Volontarioato e ai Problema, Pace Ambiente, Sviluppe e Disagio, Atas do encontro de 1990/91*, 3.

21. Ailton Krenak, quoted in *Jornal do Brasil*, caderno Ecologia for July 8, 1991, 3.

22. See the well-documented book of J. Sangirardi, *O Índio e as Plantas Alucinógenas* (Rio de Janeiro: Technoprint, 1989).

23. P. Velasco Rivero, *Danzar o Morir* (Mexico: CRT, 1983), esp. 247-370.

24. Pedro Agostinho, *Kwaríp: Mito e Ritual no Alto Xingu* (São Paulo: Edusp, 1974), 89-157.

25. See E. Viveiros de Castro, *Arawaté, O Povo do Ipixuna* (São Paulo: CEDI, 1992), 76-85.

26. See one of the best works published on Latin America, Manuel M. Marzal, et al., *The Indian Face of God in Latin America* (Maryknoll, N.Y.: Orbis Books, 1996).

27. See R. Kaiser, *God shäft im Stein, Indianische und abandländische Weltansichten im Widerstreit* (München: Kösel, 1990), 86.

28. G. van der Leeuw, *Phänomenologie der Religion* (Tübingen: Mohr, 1956), §9, 3.

29. Cf. F. Hinkelhammert, "La lógica de la expulsión del mercado capitalista mundial y el proyecto de liberación," in *Pasos* 3/1992, 3-21; M. Beaud, "Risques planétaires, environnement et développement," *Economie et Humanisme*, no. 308 (1989), 6-15.

30. Cf. G. J. Brown, et al., "Global Sustainability: Toward Definition," *Environmental Management*, no. 11 (1987), 713-19.

31. Cf. E. Morel, *Amazônia Saqueada* (São Paulo: Global, 1984).

32. Cf. I. Sachs, *Stratégies de l'Éco-developpement: Economie et Humanisme* (Paris: Editions Ouvrières, 1980).

33. Lewis Mumford, *The Myth of the Machine*, 2 vols. (New York: Harcourt Brace, 1967).

34. Ivan Illich, *Tools for Conviviality* (New York: Harper & Row, 1973).

35. E. F. Schumacher, *Small Is Beautiful: Economics as if People Mattered* (New York: Harper & Row, 1975).

36. Cf. E. Drewermann, *Der Tödliche Fortschritt: Von der Zerstörung der Ende und des Menschen im Erbe des Christentums* (Regensberg: Pustet, 1981), 46-110.

37. World Commission on Environment and Development, *Our Common Future* (New York: Oxford University Press, 1987).

38. "Rio de Janeiro Declaration of the Global Forum" (Rio de Janeiro, 1992).

39. Cf. Muller, *O Nascimento de uma Civilização Global,* 80-83.

40. N. Bobbio, *Democrazia como Valore Universale* (Milan: Il Mulino, 1983); D. L. Rosenfeld, *O Que É Democracia* (São Paulo: Brasiliense, 1984).

41. See L. Boff, "Social Ecology: Poverty and Misery," in *Ecotheology, Voices from North and South,* ed. D. Hallman (Maryknoll, N.Y.: Orbis Books, 1994), 235-47.

42. C. G. Jung, *Entrevistas e Encontros* (São Paulo: Cultrix, 1984), 189. [Citation translated from the Portuguese.]

43. See M. Damien, *L'Animal, l'Homme et Dieu* (Paris: Du Cerf, 1978); T. Regan, *The Case for Animal Rights* (Berkeley: University of California Press, 1983).

44. Cf. L. Ferry, *a Nova Ordem Ecológica: a Árvore, o Animal, o Homem* (São Paulo: Ensaio, 1994), 167-188.

45. Cf. D. Worster, *Nature's Economy: The Roots of Ecology* (New York: Doubleday, 1977).

46. Cf. H. Henderson, *Paradigms in Progress: Life Beyond Economics* (Indianapolis: Knowledge Systems Incorporated, 1991).

47. Cf. H. Daly, *Economy, Ecology, Ethics: Essays toward a Steady-State Economy* (San Francisco: Freeman, 1980).

48. Cf. A. Alvater, *Ökologie und Ökonomie* (Berlin: Prokla 67, 1987); R. Costanza, "Economia ecológica: uma agenda de pesquisa," in P. H. May and R. Sorôa da Motta, *Valorando a Natureza: Análise Econômica para o Desenvolvimento Sustentável* (São Paulo: Campus, 1994); idem, "What Is Ecological Economics," *Ecological Economics,* no. 37 (1989), 1-7.

49. Cf. W. Jackson, "Nature as the Measure for Sustainable Agriculture," in *Ecology, Economics, Ethics,* ed. F. H. Bormann and S. R. Kellert (New Haven: Yale University Press, 1991), 43-58.

50. Cf. W. Hyams, *Soil and Civilization* (New York: State Mutual Books, 1980).

51. Cf. E. Götsch, *Homem e Natureza, Cultura e Agricultura* (mimeo) (Salvador, 1995).

52. Hans Jonas, *Das Prinzip Verantwortung* (Frankfurt: Shurkamp, 1984), 36.

53. Albert Schweitzer, *Kultur und Ethik* (München: Kösel, 1960), 332.

54. Cf. Hallman, *Ecotheology,* 227-311.

55. Cf. L. Boff and Frei Betto, *Mística e Espiritualidade* (Rio de Janeiro: Rocco, 1994).

56. Cf. B. Swimme and Thomas Berry, *The Universe Story: From the Primordial Flaring Forth to the Ecozoic Era: A Celebration of the Unfolding of the Cosmos* (San Francisco: Harper, 1992), 250.

57. Cf. V. Frankl, *The Unconscious God: Psychotherapy and Theology* (New York: Simon and Schuster, 1975).

58. Cf. Müller, *Geliebte Erde* (Bonn, 1972), 7-9.

59. See commentary, Drewermann, *Der Tödliche Fortschritt,* 160-65.

60. Cf. A. Naess, "Intuition, Intrinsic Value, and Deep Ecology," *The Ecologist* 14, no. 5-6 (1984); Bill Devall and George Sessions, *Deep Ecology* (Layton, Utah: Gibbs Smith, 1985).

61. Cf. M. Fernández Pérez, "La convergencia científico-mística como alternativa al 'orden' mundial vigente," in *Cristianismo, Justicia, y Ecología* (Madrid: Nueva Utopia, 1994), 103-27.

CHAPTER 7: ALL IN GOD, GOD IN ALL

1. Albert Einstein, *Ideas and Opinions* (New York: Crown Publishers, 1954), 11.
2. See the classic work of E. Jüngel, *God as the Mystery of the World,* trans. Darrell L. Guder (Grand Rapids, Mich.: Eerdmans, 1983).
3. For this whole question, see Ch. Link, *Schöpfung* (Gütersloh: Gerd Mohn, 1991), 400-54.
4. A. Gore, *Earth in the Balance* (Boston: Houghton Mifflin, 1992).
5. David Bohm, in interview with R. Weber, *Diálogos com Cientistas e Sábios* (São Paulo: Cultrix, 1988), 41.
6. Ibid., 26-27.
7. Ibid., 40, 63.
8. This is brilliantly shown by Stephen Hawking. See S. Hawking, *A Brief History of Time: From the Big Bang to Black Holes* (New York: Bantam Books, 1988).
9. Augustine, *Confessions* XI, 12, 14.
10. Cf. I. Prigogine and I. Stengers, *Entre o Tempo e a Eternidade* (São Paulo: Companhia das Letras, 1992), 23-36.
11. Cf. the explanation in Hawking, *A Brief History of Time.*
12. Fred Hoyle, "The Universe: Past and Present Reflections," *Annual Review of Astronomy and Astrophysics* 20 (1982); see also J. Guitton, and I. and G. Bogdanov, *Deus e a ciência* (Rio de Janeiro: Nova Fronteira, 1992).
13. Cf. the classic book of David Bohm, *Wholeness and the Implicate Order* (London: Routledge & Kegan Paul, 1980).
14. See the observations of J. F. Haught, *The Promise of Nature: Ecology and Cosmic Purpose* (Mahwah, N.J.: Paulist Press, 1993), 31-38.
15. Hawking, *A Brief History of Time,* 175.
16. For this whole section see, Swimme and Berry, *The Universe Story: From the Primordial Flaring Forth to the Ecozoic Era: A Celebration of the Unfolding of the Cosmos* (San Francisco: Harper, 1992), 19-29; Erich Jantsch, *The Self-Organizing Universe: Scientific and Human Implications of the Emerging Paradigm of Evolution* (New York: Pergamon Press, 1980); J. F. Haught, *The Cosmic Adventure* (Mahwah, N.J.: Paulist Press, 1984).
17. Cf. P. Evdokikmov, "Nature," *Scottish Journal of Theology* 1 (1965), 1-22; P. Gregorios, *The Human Presence: An Orthodox View of Nature* (Geneva, 1977), 54ff.
18. Swimme and Berry, *The Universe Story,* 73-79.
19. See L. Boff, *The Maternal Face of God: The Feminine and Its Religious Manifestations* (San Francisco: Harper & Row, 1987).
20. For further details on this category, see Leonardo Boff, *Trinity and Society* (Maryknoll, N.Y.: Orbis Books, 1988).
21. Cf. G. M. Teutsch, *Lexikon der Umweltethik* (Göttingen/ Düsseldorf: Vandenhoeck-Ruprecht/Patmos, 1985), 82-32; J. Moltmann, *God in Creation: A New Theology of Creation and the Spirit of God* (San Francisco: Harper & Row, 1985); J. B. McDaniel, *With Roots and Wings: Christianity in an Age of Ecology and Dialogue* (Maryknoll, N.Y.: Orbis Books, 1995), 97-112.

22. See how this category of transcendence is constructed in L. Boff, *Die Kirche als Sakrament* (Paderborn: Bonifatius Druckerei, 1971), 271-98.

23. Pierre Teilhard de Chardin, *The Divine Milieu: An Essay on the Interior Life* (New York: Harper & Row, 1965), 131.

24. Ibid., 127.

25. On this point see R. Panikkar, *The Trinity and the Religious Experience of Man* (Maryknoll, N.Y.: Orbis Books, 1973); idem, *The Silence of God: The Answer to the Buddha* (Maryknoll, N.Y.: Orbis Books, 1989); C. G. Jung, "Paralelos pré-cristãos da idéia da Trindade" in *Psicologia da religião ocidental e oriental,* Obras XI (Petrópolis: Vozes, 1980), 113-30.

26. John Paul II, quoted in John Eagleson and Philip Scharper, eds., *Puebla and Beyond* (Maryknoll, N.Y.: Orbis Books, 1979), 78.

27. For a basic introduction to this question see L. Scheffeczyk, "Formulação magisterial e história do dogma da trindade," in *Mysterium Salutis* II/1 (Petrópolis: Vozes, 1972), 131-92 (translation of German original); a classic is the study by Th. Régnon, *Études de théologie positive sur la Sainte Trinité,* 4 vols. (Paris, 1892-1898).

28. See the recent discussion on these formulas in W. van Remmen, *Die Dreifaltigkeit Gotes in Lebel des Christen* (Uedem: Editora do Autor, 1992), 65 ff.; Boff, *Trinity and Society.*

29. Augustine, *De Trintate* VI, 10, 12.

30. Cf. D. Edwards, *Jesus the Wisdom of God: An Ecological Theology* (Maryknoll, N.Y.: Orbis Books, 1995), 111-33.

31. See V. Lossky, *Théologie négative et connaissance de Dieu chez Maître Eckhart* (Paris, 1960), 102-3, 117-20, 366-67.

32. On this entire question see Panikkar, *The Silence of God;* idem, "Das erste Bild von Buddha: Einführung in den buddhistischen Apophatismus," *Humanitas* 21 (1966), 608-22.

CHAPTER 8: "THE SPIRIT IS SLEEPING IN THE ROCK"

1. E. B. Tylor, *Primitive Culture* (London, 1903).

2. G. van der Leeuw, *L'Homme Primitif et la Religion* (Paris, 1940), 25-162; idem, *Religion in Essence and Manifestation,* trans. J. E. Turner, 2d ed. (London: Allen & Unwin, 1964); D. Salado, *La Religiosidad Mágica* (Salamanca: Sal Terrae, 1980), 255-80.

3. See H. Cazelles, "Saint Esprit, Ancient Testament et judaisme," in *Supplément au Dictionnaire de la Bible* (Paris: Letouzey et Ane, 1926-), 9:129; J. Galot, "L'Espirt Saint, milieu de vie," *Gregorianum* 72 (1992), 671-88; A. Arnada, *Estudios de Pneumatología* (Pamplona: Ediciones Universidad de Navarra, 1983), 17-47.

4. Cazelles, "Saint Esprit," 132.

5. Cf. W. Wolf, *Antropologia do Antigo Testamento* (São Paulo: Loyola, 1975), 52ff.

6. Cf. F. R. Dumas, *L'Oeuf Cosmique: le Symbolisme de la Genèse Universelle* (St. Jean-de-Braye: Dangles, 1979).

7. Cf. F. Mayr, "Die Enseitigkeit der traditionelle Gotteslehre," in *Erfahrung und Theologie des Heiligen Geistes,* ed. C. Heitmann and H. Müllen (Munich: Kösel, 1974), 249.

8. Cf. E. Schweizer, *Heiliger Geist* (Stuttgart: Kreuz Verlag, 1978); L. Bouyer, *Le Consolateur: Esprit Saint et Vie de Grâce* (Paris: Cerf, 1980); J. Comblin, *The Holy Spirit and Liberation* (Maryknoll, N.Y.: Orbis Books, 1989).

9. Cf. H. W. Robinson, *The Christian Experience of the Holy Spirit* (London: William Collins, 1962), 62-78.

10. See the texts gathered by L. F. Ladaria, *El Espíritu Santo en San Hilario de Poitiers* (Madrid: Eapsa, 1977), 40-41.

11. Cf. J. Kovel, *History and Spirit* (Boston: Beacon Press, 1991), 22-39; K. Wilber, ed., *Quantum Questions: Mystical Writings of the World's Great Physicists* (Boston/ London: Shambhala, 1985), 115-22, 129ff.

12. See the monumental work of Y. Congar, *I Believe in the Holy Spirit*, 3 vols. (London: Geoffrey Chapman, 1981).

13. Cf. the classic work by R. A. Knox, *Enthusiasm: A Chapter in the History of Religion* (New York: Clarendon Press, 1950); C. A. Keller, "Enthusiastiches Tranzendenzerleben in den nichchristlichen Religionen," in Heitman and Müller, *Erfahrung und Theologie des Heiligen Geistes*, 49-63.

14. Cf. H. Brandt, *O Risco do Espírito* (São Leopoldo: Sinodal, 1977), 62-68.

15. See the systematic reflections of Paul Tillich on this matter, *Systematic Theology* (Chicago: University of Chicago Press, 1963), 3:162-282.

16. Called the Tomus Damasi (tome of Damasus). See *Denzinger-Schönmetzer*, no. 152-80. Hereafter referred to as *DS*.

17. Cf. L. Boff, *Trinity and Society* (Maryknoll, N.Y.: Orbis Books, 1988).

18. Cf. G. Schiwy, *Der Geist des Neuen Zeiltalters: New Age Spirituality und Christentum* (München: Kösel, 1987).

19. Cf. W. Siebel, *Der Heilige Geist als Relation: Eine Soziale Trinitätslehre* (Münster, 1986).

20. Cf. Y. Congar, *The Mystery of the Temple* (London, 1962); S. Verges, *Imagen del Espíritu de Jesus* (Salamanca: Secretariado Trinitario, 1977), 330ff.

21. Cf. the superb observations of J. Santa Ana, et al., *La Economía Política del Espíritu Santo* (Buenos Aires: Consejo Mundial de Iglesias, Ed. La Aurora, 1991), 13-25.

22. Cf. J. Moltmann, *God in Creation: A New Theology of Creation and the Spirit of God* (San Francisco: Harper & Row, 1985).

23. Cf. R. Kaiser, *Gott Schäft im Stein* (Munich: Kösel, 1990), 86, with relevant comments and references to other texts from various spiritual traditions along the same line.

24. Cf. Congar, *I Believe in the Holy Spirit*, 3:155-64.

25. Cf. this and other texts in J. Moltmann, *Dieu, homme et femme* (Paris: Cerf, 1984), 120.

26. L. Boff, *The Maternal Face of God: The Feminine and Its Religious Manifestations* (San Francisco: Harper & Row, 1987); idem, *A Ave-Maria: O Feminino e o Espírito Santo* (Petrópolis: Vozes, 1980), 91-95.

27. Boff, *The Maternal Face of God*, 93.

28. Cf. Acts 6:8; 10:38. For exegesis of these texts, see S. Lyonnet, "Chaire, kechairitoméne," *Biblica* 20 (1939), 131-39; E. R. Cole, "What Did St. Luke Mean by kecharitoméne?," *American Ecclesiastical Review* 139 (1958), 228-39.

29. Cf. L. Boff, "A Era do Espírito Santo," in *O Espírito Santo: Pessoa, Presença, Atuação* (Petrópolis: Vozes, 1973), 145-57.

30. Cf. J. Mambrino, "Les Deux Mains du Père dans l'Oeuvre de S. Irenée," *Nouvelle Revue Théologique* 79 (1957), 355-70.

31. Cf. H. Berkhof, *Lo Spirito Santo e la Chiesa: la Dottrina dello Spirito Santo* (Milan: 1971), 128-29; J. Moltmann, *The Future of Creation* (Philadelphia: Fortress Press, 1979).

CHAPTER 9: "SPLIT A PIECE OF WOOD . . . AND I AM THERE"

1. Cf. M. Schmaus, *Dogma*, vol. 4: *God and His Church* (Kansas City: Sheed and Ward, 1971); H. Küng, *The Church* (New York: Sheed and Ward, 1967).

2. Cf. L. Boff, *A Resurreição de Cristo e a Nossa na Morte* (Petrópolis: Vozes, 1976), 41-55.

3. For this whole set of questions, see L. Boff, *Jesus Christ Liberator* (Maryknoll, N.Y.: Orbis Books, 1978); idem, *Ecclesiogenesis: The Base Communities Reinvent the Church* (Maryknoll, N.Y.: Orbis Books, 1986).

4. See the explanations provided by M. Fox, "Is the 'Cosmic Christ' a Term That Is Anti-Ecumenical?" in *The Coming of the Cosmic Christ* (San Francisco: Harper & Row, 1988), 241-44.

5. Cf. C. G. Jung, *Psychology and Alchemy* (Princeton: Princeton University Press, 1968).

6. See Pierre Teilhard de Chardin, *Christ and Science* (New York: Harper & Ros, 1965); L. Boff, *O Evangelho do Cristo Cósmico* (Petrópolis: Vozes, 1971), 17-40; C. F. Mooney, *Teilhard de Chardin and the Mystery of Christ* (London: Collins, 1966), 22ff.; G. Schiwy, *Der Kosmische Christus* (München: Kösel, 1990), 71ff.

7. Pierre Teilhard de Chardin, *Human Energy* (London: Collins, 1969), 104, 105.

8. Pierre Teilhard de Chardin, *Letters from a Traveller* (New York: Harper and Brothers, 1962), 300.

9. Pierre Teilhard de Chardin, *How I Believe* (New York: Harper & Row, 1969), 3.

10. See the many passages of Teilhard in E. Martinazzo, *Teilhard de Chardin: Ensaio de Leitura Crítica* (Petrópolis: Vozes, 1968), 115-20.

11. Cf. J. B. Lightfoot, *St. Paul's Epistles to the Colossians and to Philemon* (London, 1875), 155.

12. Pierre Teilhard de Chardin, *The Phenomenon of Man* (New York: Harper & Brothers, 1959), 294.

13. Cf. D. Edwards, *Jesus and the Cosmos* (Mahwah, N.J.: Paulist Press, 1991), 64-77; idem, *Jesus the Wisdom of God: An Ecological Theology* (Maryknoll, N.Y.: Orbis Books, 1995), 69-87.

14. Cf. C. G. Jung, "Jesus Archetypisch Gesehen," in *Ges. Werke 11* (Olten: Walter Verlag, 1971).

15. See the carefully elaborated work of J. Moltman, in *The Way of Jesus* (Minneapolis: Fortress Press, 1993); Edwards, *Jesus the Wisdom of God*, 77-83.

16. See texts in Y. Congar, *La Parole et le Souffle* (Paris: Desclée, 1984), 195.

17. Cf. L. Boff, "For What May We Hope Beyond the Skies?" in *Faith on the Edge: Religion and Marginalized Existence* (Maryknoll, N.Y.: Orbis Books, 1991), chap. 9.

18. Julian of Norwich, *Revelations of Divine Love* (London: Methuen, 1945), 40.

19. William Bowling, cited by I. Bradley, "El Cristo Cósmico," in *Dios es "Verde":
Cristianismo y Medio Ambiente* (Santander: Sal Terrae, 1993), 116.

20. Teilhard de Chardin, *Christ and Science,* 63-64.

21. J. Moltmann, cited by Bradley, "El Cristo Cósmico."

22. Cf. A. Feuillet, *Le Christ: Sagesse de Dieu d'après les Epîtres Pauliniennes* (Paris:
Bauchesne, 1966), 80-81; 203-04.

23. Cf. N. Kehl, *Der Christushymnus im Kolosserbrief* (Stuttgart: Verlag Katholisches
Bibelwerk, 1967), 99-137.

24. Cf. J. Ernst, *Pleroma und Pleroma Christi* (Regensburg: Pustet, 1979), 66-148.

25. Cf. H. J. Gabathuler, *Jesus Christus Haupt der Kirch–Haupt der Welt* (Zurich-
Stuttgart, 1965), 125-91.

26. Cf. H. Schlier, *Der Brief an die Epheser* (Düsseldorf: Patmos, 1957), 65.

27. Robert J. Miller, ed., *The Complete Gospels: Annotated Scholars Version* (San
Francisco: HarperSanFrancisco, 1994), 317. [Boff cites from J. Jeremias, *Unbekannte
Jesuworte* (Gutersloh, 1963), 100–*translator.*]

28. Leibniz. The texts may be found in M. Blondel, *Un Énigme Historique: le
Vinculum Substantiale d'aupres Leibniz et le Débauche d'un Réalisme Supérieur* (Paris,
1930).

29. Cf. J. Wolinski, "Le Pancristisme de Maurice Blondel," *Teoresi* 17 (1962),
97-120.

30. Pierre Teilhard de Chardin and Maurice Blondel, *Correspondence* (New York:
Herder and Herder, 1967).

31. Duns Scotus, *Opus Oxoniense,* III, d. 7, q. 3, n. 5; C. Koser, "Cristo homem,
razão de ser da criação," in *O Pensamento Franciscano* (Petrópolis: Vozes, 1960),
37-45; the main Scotist texts have been translated and published in *Revista Vozes*
60 (1966), 34-39; Ae. Caggiano, "De mente Joannis Duns Scoti cerca rationem
Incarnationis, *Antonianum* 32 (1957), 311-34; R. Nooth, "The Scotist Cosmic
Christ," in *De Doctrina Johannis Duns Scoti,* vol. 3 (Rome, 1968), 169-217.

32. Cf. A. Orbe, "La unción del Verbo," *Analecta Gregoriana* 113 (1961), 67-72.

33. Cf. J. B. Carol, *The Absolute Primacy and Predestination of Jesus and His Mother*
(Chicago: Franciscan Herald Press, 1981).

34. Cf. W. Beinert, *Christus und der Kosmos* (Freiburg: Herder, 1974), 89-97.

35. Cf. R. Rosini, *Il Cristocentrismo di Giovanni Duns Scotus e la Docttrina del
Vaticano II* (Rome, 1967); Carol, *The Absolute Primacy and Predestination of Jesus and
His Mother,* which brings together an impressive bibliography, esp. 145-56; ex-
amples of this are K. Rahner, "The Theology of the Symbol," *Theological Investiga-
tions,* vol. 4 (New York: Seabury, 1974), 221-52, and, in the same volume, "On
the Theology of the Incarnation," 105-20; Fox, *The Coming of the Cosmic Christ;*
Edwards, *Jesus and the Cosmos,* 84-89, and his more recent work, *Jesus the Wisdom of
God,* 153-73, among others.

CHAPTER 10: ECO-SPIRITUALITY

1. Werner Heisenberg, *Physics and Beyond: Encounters and Conversations* (New
York: Harper & Row, 1971).

2. Ibid.

3. Ibid.

4. Thomas Aquinas, *Summa Contra Gentiles* 1, 2, c.3.

5. Cf. the observations of J. Moltmann in *God in Creation: A New Theology of Creation and the Spirit of God* (San Francisco: Harper & Row, 1985).

6. Cf. K Wilber, ed., *Quantum Questions: Mystical Writings of the World's Great Physicists* (Boston/London Shambhala, 1985), especially the contributions of de Broglie, 115-22, and Jeans, 129ff.

7. Cf. G. Gutierrez, *The God of Life* (Maryknoll, N.Y.: Orbis Books, 1991); J. Sobrino, *Spirituality of Liberation: Toward Political Holiness* (Maryknoll, N.Y.: Orbis Books, 1988).

8. See some of the more significant titles: P. Casaldaliga and J. M. Vigil, *Political Holiness* (Maryknoll, N.Y.: Orbis Books, 1994); G. Gutierrez, *We Drink from Our Own Wells* (Maryknoll, N.Y.: Orbis Books, 1984); P. Richard, *La Fuerza Espiritual de la Iglesia de los Pobres* (San José: DEI, 1987); E. Bonnin, *Espiritualidad y Liberación en América Latina* (San José: DEI, 1982); L. Boff, *Vida Segundo o Espíritu* (Petrópolis: Vozes, 1982).

9. P. Tillich, *La Dimensión Perdida* (Bilbao: Descleé, 1970).

10. E. Durkheim, *The Elementary Forms of the Religious Life* (New York: The Free Press, 1965).

11. For one of the best of books popularizing the new cosmology, see F. Weber, *A Dança do Cosmos* (São Paulo: Pensamento, 1990).

12. R. Garaudy, *Vers un guerre de religion? Le débat du siècle* (Paris: Desclée de Brower, 1995), 126; idem, *Danser sa Vie* (Paris: Seuil, 1973).

13. Cf. H. Rahner, *Man at Play* (New York: Harper & Row, 1972), 89.

14. For one of the best writings on ecological spirituality, see *Aufbruch von Ihnen*, published by the Beaulieu group (Frankfurt: Fischer Taschehbuch Verlag, 1991), 63-102.

15. Cf. J. J. ver der Leeuw, *The Fire of Creation* (Wheaton, IL: Theosophical Publishing House, 1976).

16. Cf. M. Fox, *Creation Spirituality* (San Francisco: HarperCollins, 1991), 43-55; idem, *Original Blessing* (Santa Fe: Bear & Company, 1983), 66-81, 227-86; J. B. McDaniel, *With Roots and Wings: Christianity in an Age of Ecology and Dialogue* (Maryknoll, N.Y.: Orbis Books, 1995), 42-58.

17. Henry David Thoreau, *Walden and Civil Disobedience* (New York: Harper & Row, 1965), 67.

18. Ibid., 52.

19. See the main testimonies in F. White, *The Overview Effect* (Boston: Houghton Mifflin Company, 1987).

20. James Irwin, cited by M. Dowd, *Earthspirit: A Handbook for Nurturing an Ecological Christianity* (Mystic, Conn.: Twenty-Third Publications, 1990), 94.

21. Gene Cernan, quoted in White, *Overview Effect*, 39.

22. Joseph P. Allen, ibid., 123.

23. Gene Cernan and Salman al-Saud, ibid., 95.

24. For exercises for being initiated into such eco-spirituality, see: K. Keyes, Jr., *Handbook to Higher Consciousness* (Coos Bay: Living Love Publications, 1975); A. LaChance, *Greenspirit: The Twelve Steps of Green Spirituality* (New York: Element Books, 1991); J. B. McDaniel, *Earth, Sky, Gods and Mortals: Developing an Ecological Spirituality* (Mystic, Conn.: Twenty-Third Publications, 1990); M. Dowd, *Earthspirit*, 79-101; J. B. McDaniel, *With Roots and Wings*, 131-231.

CHAPTER 11: ALL THE CARDINAL ECOLOGICAL VIRTUES

1. Lynn White, Jr., *Science* 155 (1967), 1203-7.

2. Ibid., 1207.

3. Text in H. Baggio, *São Francisco: Vida e Ideal* (Petrópolis: Vozes, 1991), 41.

4. O. Englebert, *Saint Francis of Assisi: A Biography* (Chicago: Franciscan Herald Press, 1965).

5. See D. L. Miller, "Polytheism and Archetypical Theology," *Journal of the American Academy of Religion* 40 (1972), 513-27; idem, *The New Polytheism* (New York: Harper & Row, 1974).

6. Cf. J. Hillmann, *Psicologia Arquetípica* (São Paulo: Cultrix, 1985), 62-69.

7. Titles along these lines, in addition to those already cited, include A. H. Armstrong, "Some Advantages of Polytheism," *Dionysius* 5 (1981), 181-88; G. Paris, *Meditações Pagãs* (Petrópolis: Vozes, 1994); J. B. Wolger, *A Deusa Interior* (São Paulo: Cultrix, 1994); E. C. Whitmont, *Return of the Goddess* (New York: Crossroad, 1982).

8. G. K. Chesterton, *Saint Francis of Assisi* (New York: George H. Doran Co., 1924), chap. 1.

9. A. Fortini, *Nuova Vita di S. Francesco*, vol. 2 (Assisi, 1959), 115-16.

10. I. Magli, *Gli Uomini della Penitenza* (San Casciano: Capelli Editore, 1967), 66-79.

11. *São Francisco de Assis: Escritos e Biografias* (Petrópolis: Vozes, 1981), 727ff. [This is Boff's source for the classic texts. Where quoted, translations are from Marion A. Habig, ed., *St. Francis of Assisi–Writings and Early Biographies: English Omnibus of the Sources for the Life of St. Francis* (Chicago: Franciscan Herald Press, 1973). What Boff calls 2 Celano is the first life of Celano in Habig–*translator*.]

12. *Et dixit mini Dominus quod volebat, quod ego essem novellus passus in mundo,* n. 114. English translation from Habig, 1088-89.

13. *Escritos*, 168.

14. Ibid., 131-32.

15. Cf. R. May, *Power and Innocence: A Search for the Sources of Violence* (New York: Norton, 1972).

16. Louis Lavelle, *Quatre Saints* (Paris: Seuil, 1951), 89.

17. Bonaventure, *Itinerarium Mentis in Deum*, prologue, n. 2 and 3 (Petrópolis: Vozes, 1965); cf. C. Surian, *Elementi di una Teologia del Desiderio e la Spiritualità di San Francesco d'Assisi* (Rome, 1973), 188-91.

18. Max Scheler, *The Nature of Sympathy* (New Haven: Yale University Press, 1954); cf. V. Mazzuco, *Francisco de Assis e o Modelo de Amor Cortês-Cavaleiresco* (Petrópolis: Vozes, 1994), 111-27.

19. See the biography of Clare by A. Rotzetter, *Clara de Assis: A primeira Mulher Franciscana* (Petrópolis: Vozes, 1994).

20. C. L. Boff, "Francisco, homem pós-modern: o triunfo da compaixão e da ternura," in *Francisco: Ternura e Vigor* (Petrópolis: Vozes, 1981), 32-61; idem, "Questionamento da cultural atual e fundamentação franciscana à ecologia, in *Francisco e a Ecologia* (Petrópolis: Sinfrajupe, 1991), 47-58; "Franciscanismo e reverência pela criação," in *Cadernos Franciscanos* 3 (Petrópolis: Vozes, 1994); J. A. Merino, *Manifesto Franciscano para un Futuro Mejor* (Madrid: Paulinas, 1985); M. Dennis, et al., *St. Francis and the Foolishness of God* (Maryknoll, N.Y.: Orbis Books, 1993); R. Sorrel, *St. Francis of Assisi and Nature* (New York: Oxford University

Press, 1986); K. Warner, "Was St. Francis a Deep Ecologist?" in *Embracing Earth*, ed. A. J. LaChance and John E. Carroll (Maryknoll, N.Y.: Orbis Books, 1994), 225-40.

21. Cf. E. A. Armstrong, *Saint Francis, Nature Mystic: The Derivation and Significance of the Nature Stories in the Franciscan Legend* (Berkeley: University of California Press, 1973).

22. Francis always called them brothers and sisters. See the beautiful commentaries of E. Balducci, *Francesco d'Assisi* (Florence: Edizioni Cultura della Pace, 1989), 145-50.

23. Cf. H. Schneider, *Brüderlich Solidarität durch Franziskus von Assisi* (Mönschengladbach: B. ühlen Verlag, 1981), 44-52.

24. See "S. Francisco, admirável homem novo?" in I. Silveira, *São Francisco de Assis d "nossa Irmã e mãe Terra* (1994), 63-72.

25. See *Major Life*, XII, 8.

26. J. Lortz, *Francisco de Assis: O Santo Incomparável* (Petrópolis: Vozes, 1982).

27. Adolf Holl, *Der Letzte Christ* (Stuttgart: Deutsche Verlags-Anstalt, 1971).

28. Cf. Th. Matura, "Franz von Assisi und seine Erbe heute," in *Franz von Assisi: En Anfang un was davon Bleibt* (Zürich: Benziger, 1988), 278ff.

29. Ibid., 284.

30. See Armstrong, *Saint Francis, Nature Mystic*, 18-43. Armstrong has shown these influences and the positive stance of the Irish monks and pilgrims toward nature.

31. Cf. *Speculum*, n. 85.

32. A. Rotzetter, *Clara de Assis, a Primeira Mulher Franciscana* (Petrópolis: Vozes, 1944), 59.

33. See L. Boff, "Mestre Eckhart: A mística da disponiblidade e da libertação," in *Mestre Eckhart: a Mística de Ser e Não Ter* (Petrópolis: Vozes, 1989), 11-89.

34. See the classic book of Th. Desbonnets, *De l'Intuition à l'Institution: Les Franciscains* (Paris: Editions Franciscaines, 1983).

35. See Eloi Leclerc, *Le Cantique des Créatures ou les Symboles de l'Union* (Paris: Artème Fayard, 1970).

36. Arnold Toynbee, in Spanish newspaper *ABC*, December 19, 1972, 10-11.

Index

Also in the Ecology and Justice Series

DATE DUE

OCT 3 0 1998			
GAYLORD			PRINTED IN U.S.A.